The Seasoning Of A Soul

When Comprehension Comes through Trial and Experience

Athena Demetrios

Outskirts Press, Inc.
Denver, Colorado

For my sister Judy, my brightest light in my darkest night.
And,
For my beautiful daughter Tina, whose journey began in
the shadow of my searching for self. Your loving nature,
resilience and innate wisdom are a testimony to the
brilliance of your own spirit.

I dedicate this book to the heart of every man, woman, and child who has suffered the pain and agony of becoming, whose every breath for life felt labored but who would not quit.

"Life is a pure flame and we live
by an invisible sun within us."
—Sir Thomas Browne

Acknowledgments

It was in my darkest hour that the Beloved Ascended Master Saint Germain awakened me to the higher laws of the universe and to my own individualized God Presence within.

To Dr. Peebles, my spirit guides, masters and teachers, my gratitude is beyond words.

For my family members on the spirit side and, for my siblings still living and full of spirit. We surmounted the odds despite ourselves! It must have been the pack mentality, all for one and one for all. Our laughter formed a bond unbreakable. You are magnificent beings of light, teachers in your own unique way. You have always accepted that I walk to the beat of my own drum. For that my heart is full.

Dr. Daniel Slavin, you are a healer of heart and soul, in a category all your own. My gratitude is endless. Your brilliance, willingness, and collaboration with my higher self helped to put Humpty Dumpty together again.

In the early eighties, my life crossed paths with Dr. Peebles, my spirit guide. He encouraged me to write about my journey in life. "Let it be raw," he said. No easy task; the thought alone paralyzed me with fear. I could barely face my own flaws, let alone strip myself naked for others to see. I wanted to protect myself from the giant eye peering through the magnifying glass. I began writing in a spiral notebook, which progressed, several years down the road, to typing classes. With little progress made, I tucked the manuscript in a metal filing cabinet. Fear was getting the upper hand. Insight was excruciating. My mystical experiences were accelerating at warp speed, and the thought of documenting my odyssey exhausted me to the bone.

But I knew in my heart this was something I had contracted with spirit to accomplish in this lifetime. One day while in a shopping mall, a complete stranger approached me, shaking a finger in my face: "You need to be writing; you could be helping millions of women." Unbeknownst to me, she was a well-known clairvoyant. Those words shot through me like a lightning bolt. I threw caution to the wind and blew the dust off the manuscript. Thank you Sheri Sidebotham!

When I was given the gift of a computer, I didn't even know how to operate it. Spirit placed in my path angels of patience, resources, and generosity who gave selflessly of their time, instruction, and gifts. They all saw value in the telling of my story, and their encouragement grew larger than my fear of public ridicule and vulnerability.

Susan Dobra, Ph.D, God could not have placed a more perfect person in my path. Your editorial skills, insight, and great expertise helped to shape an overwhelming amount of life experience into something I can be proud of. You helped me find my voice without hesitation and encouraged me to speak my truth with clarity. Your editorial sidebar notes, often written with great humor, are worthy of framing.

Thank you, Brian Gardner, Andrea Morgan, Ken White, HeathCliff Rothman, Debbra Cooper, Dottie

Galliano, Val Deveraux, Steffny Wallace, Michelle Davis, Ann Taylor, Leigh Taylor Young, Lisa Kaz, Janet Price, Patti Smith and Lynne Handy.

A special thanks to Michael Hoppe, David Guerrero, Ivan Allen, Sabra Petersmann, Michael Bates, Gloria D. Benish, Shawn Randall, Jan and William Gregory, Thomas Jacobson, Fred Bader, Dee Hart, Sally Snow and Anne Preciado-Rich.

Thank you, Linda Pendleton, gifted author and friend, whose constant prodding ("How's the book coming?") finally paid off.

Thanks to my grandson Noah, a shaman in the making, and last but not least, Ali, my grandchild, who at age seven presented me with a book at Christmas that she had written, illustrated, and published within three weeks. I must admit I was green with envy. Mine has been a twenty-five year journey. There's nothing like a little healthy competition from a young "whippersnapper." Thanks for motivating me to finish!

Table of Contents

Introduction

I walk between worlds and I love it. I see spirits as if they were in the physical realm, and I talk to them as friends. I have encountered aliens, and I have found them of great fascination and not sources of fear. I am a telepath, clairvoyant, a medium and channel, a voice for others who dwell in states of consciousness other than our own. I see the auras of plants and trees, and at times, those who are guardians of them, and if I have embraced any philosophy in life, it would be, "To believe is to see." Pull on the thread, I always say, and see where it leads.

I see nothing abnormal about piercing the veil between dimensions, looking through windows into other worlds; to me, it's the natural evolution of my most silent and sacred prayer: to *feel connected* to life.

I want to know God. I was born a soul searcher, and trying to understand who I am, why I am here, and what's it all about is the keynote to my soul. I can't remember ever feeling another way. It's my passion; it's my rhythm. Knock and the door shall be opened. I haven't knocked; I've used a battering ram. I've screamed at God, I've pleaded and I've threatened, I've cursed, I've begged, and I've bargained, and in the end I've fallen to my knees in a broken heap and I have agonized over the relentless pull inside my heart to connect with what I didn't know.

It was a hard childhood: alcohol, poverty, and chaos, terror and rape, but perhaps the most acidic and corrosive of all, *feeling* as if I was never enough. Most of my adult life I fought fragmentation and envisioned my splintered soul floating aimlessly in a black universe.

The human spirit is a wondrous thing, and so is our ability to heal. It has been a difficult path, and I have felt forged by fire—and have found myself resurrecting from ash. As a result, my life has taken on a new color and a different vibration. My universe speaks to me through symbols and I have learned to interpret and embrace those signposts.

My life, full of psychic phenomena and mystical visions, has been called by most weird and mysterious, strange and bizarre; it has also been called inspirational and fascinating. I call it all of the above. It is at the prodding of the many—and of the silent voice inside my heart—that I begin at the beginning.

Prologue

To suffer one's own death and be reborn is not easy.
—Fritz Perls

Dr. Slavin: In a moment, I am going to count down from ten to zero and with each number back, I'd like you to feel more and more relaxed, comfortable, and to slowly move back in time to the time period that we were talking about last week, or any time period that comes up, to slowly layer with each number, each step, each regression back. Ten . . . nine . . . eight . . . seven . . . six . . . five . . . four . . . three . . . two . . . one . . . zero. Start to get a sense of where you are, how you feel . . . how old you are . . . When you feel ready to start, tell me what it is that you see . . . what you feel. Where are you?

Athena: *I'm not born yet . . . I'm with people that I feel really safe with . . . that I love a lot . . . some of them are masters and teachers, and they are showing me . . .*

Dr. Slavin: What are they showing you?

Athena: *They are showing me where I'm going to be going and what some of my opportunities are . . . I don't think I'm going to like being down there.*

Dr. Slavin: What kind of things are they showing you?

Athena: *They are showing me that there's going to be a family, and I'm going to be part of this family, and there are going to be some situations that are going to be really hard and trying.*

Dr. Slavin: How do you feel about that? *Athena: Well . . . I know . . . oh, boy . . . I know it's going to be pretty hard, and they're showing me . . . almost like on this big film strip, and I'm seeing my life, and it starts to take shape and form, and I'm seeing what can be, and I'm seeing what might be, but it is going to depend on how I perceive to learn from it—and it's just . . .oh, boy, there's a feeling coming into my body.*

Dr. Slavin: How does it feel?

Athena: *I feel kind of like this pull and I think it's getting time to go.*

Dr. Slavin: Go where?

Athena: *Into the body . . . inside my mother and . . . it feels so different here. . . . Oh . . . I don't think I want to do this. . . . I don't want to do this.*

PART ONE

LOST

Beginnings

1
God . . . What *Were* You Thinking?

We are not human beings on a spiritual journey. We are spiritual beings on a human journey.
—Pierre Teilhard de Chardin

"You were born angry. You came out screaming, with your fists clenched." That's what Mother told me, and I believed it. I did not want to be here. When I looked at the stars at night, I was filled with a longing to return to the heavens, for everything told me that's where I belonged, and I desperately wanted to go back. Somehow, I knew I had been hurled from a far larger womb than the one from which I had just emerged. I can't remember ever feeling any other way, not for many years at least, nor could I help but feel that this place called Earth was the worst form of punishment that could ever be inflicted on my soul.

I am one of seven children born into a dysfunctional alcoholic environment. Mother fired us out of her womb in rapid succession. I am the middle child, and with two babies still in diapers left under the supervision of my sister Judy, I made my entrance into the world. For the record, I was born Anita James, a name I always hated and since then have changed.

My father, Dimitrious V. Dimitrious, a Greek immigrant with almost no command of the English language, had wanted to name me Athena. I have heard that the soul chooses the name and the parents simply become receptive to the request and honor it in the physical dimension. Either my mother was deaf, or I had a lot of growing to do until I became the *vibration* of who I am. I knew Athena was my name from the moment I heard it; it felt to me like an old slipper that held the indentation of every toe, worn to absolute comfort through the ages.

I never knew my father, for he was to become an elusive stranger who would show up at times without warning, a suitcase in hand, a box of Hershey Bars packed snugly amongst the stack of neatly folded shirts. Funny the things one remembers, like the way his clothes always smelled of cigar smoke, and how his attempt to settle into a situation would eventually overwhelm him, and that it was only a short time until the lack of order and the chaos sent him packing. To Mother, his parting words were always, "You'll see me when you see me." She never knew when that would be. Neither did he.

Once, I pushed the screen door open and followed him outside. He was unaware of my presence. I stood on the ledge of our porch and watched as my father walked towards some unknown destination. He never did look back and I never looked away. It was in those moments of silent observation that I could *feel* how lost he was. His demeanor flooded my senses with a knowing of who he was, who he *wished* he was, but the most telling of all, who he *felt* like he *never* was.

His head wasn't held with purpose or pride but rather cast downward towards the sidewalk. The weight of his suitcase caused him to walk slightly off kilter and his footsteps seemed slow and labored. He knew this journey would be long, arduous, and without direction.

So did I. I could feel his spirit was broken and that his heart felt as heavy as the luggage that contained his worldly belongings. That made me feel sad. I watched my father disappear from sight.

Money was scarce, and it would constantly thrust our family into one crisis after another. I felt overshadowed by a feeling of hopelessness and the lack of power to change the conditions in which we lived. Those emotions were as familiar to me as breathing, and the scars that deprivation brought were the only thing, it seemed, in abundance. I hated the way they made me feel; shame and embarrassment, the lack of "normalcy" in any sense of the word, only fed my young psyche with resentment. I felt trapped inside a body I didn't want to be in, for it kept me bound to a situation from which there didn't seem to be any way out.

My mother, a beautiful woman of Norwegian descent, born on a homestead in the plains of the Dakotas, sought to escape through her imagination the harshness of my grandmother's depression and her constant threats of suicide. Grandmother, it seemed, would take the shotgun, tell her children she was going to kill herself, and disappear into the night. Huddled together inside their weather-beaten shack, they waited for the echo of her demise to reverberate through their souls. I never knew much about my grandmother, only stories that were relayed to me, and those stories were invariably always followed with a heavy sigh.

When I was little, I had two treasures. I guarded those possessions fiercely. One was a tiny black Bible no bigger than my hand, and the other, a naked doll with no name. I pushed them both around in my baby buggy. I never knew the origin of that tiny Bible or of the *"ominous presence"* that filled its contents, and if anything, felt it was I who was being pushed around by some force I couldn't see. I felt a thousand years old, trapped in a little kid's body, and I knew that life was serious business.

My mother, a product of fire and brimstone, hell and damnation, had her own internal feud about what God *was* or *wasn't*. Her statements were always more like questions, as if trying to convince herself of His existence and of His moral character. "God wouldn't do that, now would He?" she would say with a puzzled look on her face, as if I had the answer. Her questioning was always based around "feeling" as if *this presence* were sitting in judgment of her or of the larger world. She commented often, "How can I be happy if the rest of the world is miserable?"

Her world was miserable, and she succumbed, tired and defeated.

Mom was a great storyteller, and words that flowed like water would paint vivid pictures in great depth and detail, and became etched within the listener's mind as if a scene on canvas suddenly came to life. You could almost smell the fragrance, feel the texture, and through imagination, become at one with the surroundings like a silent spectator of a memory that once held life but had been carefully tucked away and preserved in some remote corner of her mind.

The fireplace in our house served as the perfect stage, as did the beat-up wooden picnic bench that would creak and wobble with the weight of our bodies perched like crows, warming our backs against the flickering flames. Somehow, the furniture didn't look so disgusting, the walls not quite so dirty or in need of paint when Mother told her tales. I loved the patterns of golden color that danced in the darkness casting shadows on the ceiling and floor. During those times, I didn't feel so afraid.

I have asked myself over and over again, "Why in the hell, with conditions as they were, did she continue to get pregnant?" I resented that ignorance, and the times were many when I wanted to shout at her through frustration, "Jesus Christ, Mother! Why did you make it so damned tough on yourself by bringing more kids into this world when your life was such a fucking mess? Why did you make it so hard for me? What the hell was going on in your mind?"

It was that type of ignorance in Mom I always resented, for if I were to ask her that very question, she'd make excuses, none of which would make any sense at all. Mother was far from ignorant though, and it would be unfair to paint a picture of her in that light. She was intelligent, sensitive, and seemed to have a *"sixth sense,"* as she would say, a *"feeling"* about things.

Born into a sick environment, she sought to free herself through books, poetry and her love of nature. As a child she invented three imaginary playmates, Free-Free, Froy-Froy and Sim-a-dee-dee. Each little character had a very distinct personality. Free-Free was frivolous, carefree and happy, while Froy-Froy, was the sinister and evil of the lot, the instigator of evil thought. Sim-a-dee-dee was passive, non-emotional, and as Mom puts it, the "regular you."

In the autumn of the year, she would lay on her stomach amongst the crumbling leaves, enveloped in their pungent spicy odor. Beaming through the branches of the tree, a hazy shaft of light spotlighted a toadstool on which her fairy friends frolicked. Mother played with them for hours to escape reality.

I remembered my mother moving about in the kitchen, taking two cups from the drain board upon which were piled in disarray chipped, unmatched dishes, stained and cracked like the veins in a leaf. I observed the yellowish wet dishtowel soaking up the water beneath the battered pots and pans. Everything was dented or broken, even the prongs on the forks. I hated those dishes.

"Someday, Mom, I'm going to buy you some new dishes! I mean it, Mom, someday I am!" I said with conviction.

She replied, "Well, God bless you honey. God willing, someday, maybe I'll be able to buy them myself."

She smiled as if she was touched by my gesture, but her eyes gave away the feeling of despair she tried so hard to hide. She poured the steaming, dark, muddy liquid out of the old tin coffee pot into the cups. I watched the coffee grounds sink to the bottom of my cup. A few dark flecks continued to swirl into the center of the whirlpool.

"Ahh . . . Nectar of the Gods," she said as she raised the cup to her lips while in transit to the front room.

"Panther piss!" I mimicked as I trotted behind, "This shit is strong!"

I loved these times with Mom, for it wasn't often I could have her attention. When I could, I took full advantage of it, prodding her relentlessly for one story after another.

She set the coffee cup on the fireplace mantel and stooped over to grab a large piece of wood that was stacked in the corner of the hearth. She shoved the wood into the dying embers with a force that scattered grey ashes with pieces of half-burnt newspaper in a frenzied movement of explosive color. The pitch began to sizzle and, in a few moments, the wood burst into flame.

Mother settled herself on the bench, crossing her legs, leaning forward to rest an elbow on her knee. I watched her squirm back and forth as if trying to root herself into a firm foundation, like a hen preparing to sit on a nest of unhatched eggs, a ritual in its own right I kept quiet. I did not want to disturb the memories being brought into focus for voice. In a strange way, I felt something almost sacred about these moments, for her face reflected emotions she was totally unaware of.

With her coffee cup in one hand, she turned towards the fire and her face was bathed in a saffron glow. I listened to her sigh as she struck the wooden match across a blackened brick to light a cigarette. Lifting her hand to push a limp strand of hair back into place, she tilted her head slightly as if to arm herself with a sense of dignity in a situation that had none. She inhaled deeply on the Pall Mall, holding the smoke in her lungs. I watched as it escaped from her lips.

After quiet deliberation, she began, "Well, let's see now. I can remember one time when I was three years old; Mother was giving me a bath in an old galvanized tub. The house was toasty and warm, and I could see the red hot coals peeking out of the old pot-bellied stove. It was winter then, and we were having a blizzard." She paused and stared off into space. For a moment her eyes grew vacant as if she were suspended in another time and place.

Realizing that she had drifted off, she shook her head. "Good God! Was Mother Nature merciless! All of a sudden a gust of wind blew the front door open and I was hit by this icy blast of powdery fine snow that stung my skin. I looked up and saw this tall figure hesitating in the doorway. He was dressed in black, his face was gaunt, and his skin was ashen grey. His beard and moustache were covered with ice, and I'll never forget the sound of the wind howling as it was whipping his coat frantically around his legs. He looked like the 'Grim Reaper.' Mother stopped washing me, and I remember him saying with exhaustion in his voice, 'Hello, Baby.' He came home to die. That's all I remember of my father," she said, as she wiped a tear from the corner of her eye.

Grandmother

If anyone could see a rose in a pile of shit, it was Mom. She had a way of glamorizing the most deplorable of situations, seeing the best in people to the point of ignoring discernment crucial to one's innate sense of knowing. Red flags were seen more as pretty red lights, and that constant state of invalidation left gaping holes in my ability to trust myself.

What I felt in my gut was never validated as truth. When I had a feeling that something was wrong or a person was evil, her response was, "Oh, you're just getting it mixed up with something else." Her unwillingness, denial, or inability to confront what was real continued to spiral our family into great distress.

Mother's parenting skills, or lack thereof, created the perfect environment for several a misfit, including any flea-bitten dog or scroungy cat, looking for a safe haven to lick their wounds.

Mom referred to us as her "seven little stair steps." We referred to ourselves as "the seven mistakes." My brother Bill, once described us to a therapist as a "pack of fuckin' wild dingoes." Personally, Bill's description gets my vote.

Talk to any number of kids who found shelter in our home and they would sing her praises. Her exhaustion left us to fend for ourselves, with no rules to follow; we were simply told, "Let your conscience be your guide." No structure—what the hell, one more mouth to feed won't make any difference. But it did make a difference.

It was a rare occurrence when we were afforded the luxury of running water and power at the same time. It was always a race between pennies counted, payday, and cut off dates. Sometimes we made it, and if not, Mom would cook dinner in the fireplace, stirring the beans in an old dented pot, charred and blackened from the soot of the flames. Tilting her chin upward, she would say with a heavy sigh, "Well, children, looks like we will dine by candlelight tonight."

I always felt flawed, different, and disconnected. It would be years before I could identify what lived within my psyche as a constant state of discomfort.

I remember the moment I became aware of the shame associated with poverty. I had a playmate, Kathy, who came from a wealthy family. Her mother was slender, pretty, and kind. Her father wore starched white shirts and striped ties, and his neatly cut "Vitalis" hair had teeth marks from the comb where his pink scalp showed through.

They waited, parked in our driveway with the motor running in their shiny new car while mother hurried to get me dressed. That afternoon, Kathy said, "Let's take off our dresses and dance in our panties like ballerinas."

I made up an excuse. I didn't want her to see my panties that were full of holes, bunched together by an oversized safety pin, hooked to the stretched out elastic. I wanted to feel the freedom I always did when I danced.

Instead, I felt the shame of poverty.

It was the awareness of *feeling* so flawed and less than—not one and equal like the other kids who wore pretty dresses for school pictures, white lace collars and freshly pressed skirts, with sweaters and bows to match. *At that moment,* I became aware of the strange sensation that I was viewing life as an observer—feeling a barrier of glass, a pane of window that separated me from everything and everybody.

I knew we were different, I knew I was different. I wanted to be like kids who got called in for lunch, who had to take naps or even got spanked. I was so excited once when my mother called me in for lunch. "I have to go now!" I said. "I can't play; I have to eat lunch!"

For a brief moment, I was not different. I was like the other kids.

In my soul I have dreamt of freedom, to feel whole and to feel loved. I have fought fragmentation, and have felt as disjointed as an amputee trying to find a limb that fit properly, but the end result was that I still felt like a stride out of rhythm. No matter how hard I tried, I could never shake the feeling of something missing.

There have been those angels, a select few, who have been placed in my path, and I have learned now the import of their divinity *sparked within my consciousness, a protection and a fanning of my own internal flame.* My sister was one of those angels, and if ever there was a soul whose very existence shone as a jewel in the crown of God, *Judy shone the brightest.*

I have often wondered where I would be had it not been for Judy, for I believe with all my heart I would have succumbed through exhaustion. The attraction toward suicide was a constant struggle, although I kept it hidden from others, I so desperately wanted relief. The problem was, what I struggled with was elusive; the memory of my childhood was marred and riddled with gaping holes. My family seemed surprised by this.

"Don't you remember?" they asked.

"No," I'd reply.

I'd look at their faces and try to recall what produced such a puzzled look.

"Come on! You remember!"

"No, I really don't," I'd reply. And I didn't.

Judy and I often spoke in the later years of our maturity, how our bond, deep and ancient, reached far beyond this incarnation. We must have made a pact while on the spirit side to be born into the same troubled household, for we knew it was going to be a difficult life, and our love and sisterhood left us with a connection telepathic of heart and spirit that is difficult to describe.

Judy came into this life as a caretaker; although she was our half-sister, a child from Mom's previous marriage, she became the mother, the matriarch of our family, and tried her best to provide whatever support and consistency we were to know. She was but a child herself, quitting school at fourteen to take care of six brothers and sisters. It must have felt to her like trying to stand erect on a lake bed of half frozen ice with no sure footing for the weight of her own body, let alone those who desperately clung to her hem for support.

It was a crazy time. Alcoholism was rampant, and my mother, who married a wealthy Greek as a source of security, soon found that gambling, booze, lack of literacy, and crooked employees ate away at the family fortune as well as my father's sense of pride. His presence became as sporadic as his ability to provide for his family, and mother's drinking and inability to cope thrust us into greater depths of deprivation from which there didn't seem any way out.

With Father's absence, Mother's boyfriend—in the guise of a boarder—lived in the root cellar of our basement like a troll. He terrorized our family. He terrorized me.

It would be years before the festering wounds would create such chaos in my life that it would demand of me, as a rite of passage, the decision to explore and retrieve my battered spirit.

2

Blame It On The Jukebox

*I looked up my family tree and
found three dogs using it.*
—Rodney Dangerfield

She plucked the chickens bare, glued the feathers to card-board wings, and jumped off the barn in hopes she would take flight like an eagle in the sky. I think Mom was in as much shock as the naked chickens when she hit the dirt.

It seemed to me, no matter how hard she "flapped her wings" in life, there was part of her held back by underlying currents of undeservingness. It was the way she would speak of things, how her shoulders would slump, a wistful sadness one couldn't help but feel that let you know she, on some level, had resigned herself to the fact that things could never change.

They say we inherit traits from our relatives, but I swear the most dangerous of all are those *we learn to accept as real* in the emotional part of our nature. No doubt *that* has been my greatest challenge: chipping away at the cement of "false acceptance" to free the light inside my heart that wants to sing, "Yes! There is another way to live. You don't have to buy into the despair of poverty and limitation."

In her heart, Mother dreamt of an ideal world, with equality for all races, all God's creatures, big and small. As a young girl, she cleaned houses for board and keep, and would, at any given opportunity, release mouse traps from springing on their unsuspecting prey, leaving behind the cheese as a token snack for the grateful critter. That was one of mother's most beautiful qualities. My daughter once said, "Nani adopted everything." Indeed, she did.

She dreamed of a prince in shining armor, someone to charge in on a white horse to save her. He didn't ride in on a horse. He rode in on a boat from Greece to Ellis Island, seeking his fortune in the land of opportunity. Both seekers of new beginnings, dreamers in their own rights, it was the promise of something more that forged their spirits and spurred them west.

Mom and Judy

My mother, Ruth Larson, stepped off the bus in Klamath Falls, Oregon, with plans for an overnight stay.

With five-year-old daughter Judy in hand, they entered the Arcade Hotel. If she could have gazed into a crystal ball and seen what lay hidden behind the mist, she would have sprinted out of Klamath Basin, vaporizing like an apparition in the night.

Beautiful Mom

He noticed her from where he stood behind the counter. A beautiful woman of Scandinavian descent, her ash blonde hair, green eyes and red lips were accented by exceptionally white teeth. She turned and smiled at him as she dropped the nickel in the jukebox. It stuck.

He seized the opportunity and charged out from behind the counter, dressed in his chef's hat, starched white jacket and black checkered pants. In his "bigger than life" style, he slammed his fist on the jukebox and gave it a good shake. It worked.

He was charming and charismatic. A Greek

immigrant, one of fourteen children, he had voyaged alone to the United States as a young teenager to join an elder brother in an attempt to avoid the ravages of war that had taken the lives of several of his brothers. His elder brother being single and already a successful businessman, he stood to inherit a significant fortune. It was at Ellis Island where authorities changed his name, Dimitrious to the English translation James. He soon became known as Jimmie James, AKA Diamond Jim.

My Father with Connie

His build was short and stocky, and he was meticulous in his personal hygiene and dress: tailored suits, shined shoes, black hair neatly trimmed and combed in place. His golden olive skin, close-shaven, smelled of

Old Spice, and the constant gnawing on a cigar caused one eye to squint in an attempt to avoid the sting of swirling smoke.

Although he found humor in his own jokes that would make his dark eyes sparkle, he often was the only one laughing.

The Arcade Hotel

Mother took a room in the hotel above the restaurant and began to work for my father as a waitress, leaving Judy to play alone in their room or with the companion-ship of a playmate, whose mother was a prostitute.

Mother was dating another man at that time, one she obviously felt chemistry with, and Judy remembers the way Mother's eyes would light up and how her voice would change when she spoke of him, for their shared love of poetry and literature created a bond of mutual interest.

Five-year-old Judy was given the deciding vote. "Who do you want for a daddy? This one has this," she remarked, enumerating the meager holdings of the poet, "and this one has that," recounting for the child all the bounty of the immigrant heir.

Mother and "Diamond Jim" married in 1943.

For the first four years of their marriage, Mother was content. She loved the quiet of pre-dawn hours, and with coffee in hand, would head outside to enjoy the morning sunrise. There, while digging in good ol' Mother Earth, she would contemplate God and the larger mysteries of the universe.

The children came as fast as the social invitations, one after another, and their status quickly elevated to new heights among the "who's who."

Aristotle Onassis came to the United States to purchase several ships from Uncle Gus, who lived in Portland, Oregon. Mom remembers dancing with Onassis when she was pregnant with me.

"Yousa watch my father said in his thick accent, "that man eesa gonna be reechest man in the world."

Mother once told me, "That was one of the most profound things your father ever said."

Upon Gus's death, Dad inherited an amount that would be worth millions today. Most of the estate was tied up in the form of stocks, bonds, and real estate. My father, a man with little education, had to struggle like a child in kindergarten to sign his name, and had no concept of wealth or what he was worth. Stocks and bonds were nothing more than worthless pieces of paper, so worthless in fact, Mother caught him once burning them in the fireplace.

Dad was interested only in what he could feel in his hands as cold cash, so he hired a lawyer, "Sell out, and get what you can for it," he instructed, and the lawyer did, and took for himself whatever he was able to embezzle.

Diamond Jim was an alcoholic and compulsive gambler, a "big shot," and a real showman. Sitting at the head of a table, surrounded by his Greek cronies and fellow gamblers, it was not unlike him to tip outrageous amounts of money or to light a cigar with a hundred dollar bill.

Family, "Bookies" and Friends

"I was so damned mad at him one night!" Mother's face was animated and alive. "He used to invite his Greek friends over for dinner after we closed the restaurant, so I had to cook at the spur of the moment after putting in a long day myself. They'd all drink too much and your father would usually pass out at the head of the table. I'd be left with a god-awful mess to clean up and a bunch of Greeks I couldn't communicate with just sitting there staring at me!"

"Well, . . . one night I got even with him." Her face looked sly and mischievous, and a self-righteous smirk began to emerge. "Everyone had finally left and I just stood there looking at him. I was infuriated! I spotted a poor unsuspecting spider hanging right above his mouth, so I plucked him from his thread and let him drop! Your dad made some muffled, gurgling sounds and swallowed him. By God, he deserved it!"

The bets got larger, the losses greater. Mother began to panic about the finances. Judy often states that she would lie in bed crying and feeling guilty that she had chosen Dad as the one she wanted Mom to marry. She remembered a lot of fighting between them, and it was always about money.

Dad lost it all and, with $16.00 in his pocket, leaving Mom with strict instructions to sell the house, he took off to "Happy Camp" in Josephine, the old family Oldsmobile.

I believe it was the shame, fear, and bill collectors that drove Dad out of town. And it was the anxiety and financial crisis that drove Mother further into the bottle. She never sold the house.

TELEGRAM

CLASS OF SERVICE DESIRED

| TELEGRAM | | DAY LETTER | | NIGHT LETTER | |

PATRONS SHOULD CHECK KIND OF SERVICE DESIRED, OTHERWISE THE MESSAGE WILL BE SENT AS A TELEGRAM

| RECORDER'S NUMBER | | TIME FILED | M. | CHECK |

Tacoma, Washington   August 17 1949

Jimmie James

Happy Camp, California

Must have at least 500 dollars guarantee 60 % of it goes to the winner & 40 % goes
to loser. Let me know if the terms are satisfactory and I will wire you the name of
opponent

Frank

A few months passed and Dad sent for us. He had opened up another restaurant. Three months later, and $9,000 in debt, Dad took off. Two days later, the electricity was shut off and the creditors locked the door to the restaurant, repossessed our car, and off they drove with our Christmas dolls as backseat passengers.

The only money Mother had was the loose change she was able to scrape from the cash register.

That night, she raided a potato field to feed us.

Two days later, Mom hocked her wedding rings to get us back to Klamath Falls.

I remember nothing of that time, and my memories of childhood are select and few. I don't know if that is normal. Strange as it is, I remember certain conversations and events with great clarity. People often comment, "You've got a great memory." *That* I find fascinating.

What to leave in, what to leave out?

And why?

The following memory etched deep within my consciousness has remained throughout the years, and I could never think of this event without my insides quivering with repulsion.

Some time after we returned home, Mother's drinking accelerated, and she took in a boarder who slept in the root cellar of our basement. He scared me. Ed would sit at the kitchen table, slumped over a bottle of whiskey, in a drunken stupor, with his hand clutched around an empty glass.

He stunk. I didn't like him.

I was asleep on my stomach. I felt a hand on my back. I opened my eyes and, raising myself up on my elbows, I turned my head to see who was scratching my back.

"Get up. Come into the front room."

I followed the slurred command, walked down the dark hallway into the dimly lit front room, and stood by the corner of the couch. I felt myself being lifted and positioned on his right leg. He was drunk. I didn't like him. He scared me. He fumbled with the zipper of his brown trousers, as I began to squirm in an effort to free myself.

With his right arm across my back, he tightened his hold. I was trapped. He took my arm and placed it on the top of his shoulder like trying to position it in a romantic pose, as if I was a willing partner who wanted to engage in a long and passionate kiss. He was going to show me how "the big people did it."

Filled with terror, I instantly pulled my hand away and pushed against his chest struggling to get free.

A grip like an iron vice clamped down on my wrist, and he began to moan as he forced my hand in his pants on his penis in a circular motion. His skin felt hot and sweaty there, and I wanted to scream, "Help me! Help me! Someone please help me!"

But I couldn't scream. He forced his tongue down my throat. I felt myself gag.

I couldn't fight the weight of his body. I felt powerless and small. The stubble of his beard felt like nails on my skin and his breath stunk from alcohol and decayed teeth.

That's all I remembered for many years. Like I said, *what to leave in, what to leave out.*

I never did know what happened after that, nor did I have any recall of how I got away. It was like watching a television show when the program goes off air and the screen suddenly turns to snow.

I do remember, however, praying every night, "Please God, let me tell someone, please God."

I didn't know *what* I was praying to or *who* God was. I just wanted *Him* to make it go away.

He never did.

3
How I Spent My Summer Vacation

You can turn painful situations around through laughter. If you can find humor in anything—even poverty—you can survive it.
—Bill Cosby

I stood on the porch and stared through the screen door at my mother, who was lying on the floor in a crumpled heap. Her shoulders heaved from the uncontrollable sobs that wracked her body. I watched our neighbor stoop over, grabbing her by the arm. "Come on, Ruthie," she said in a compassionate whisper, "let me help you up."

She just lay there, sobbing.

There was no furniture in the house, just an old silver bucket filled with dirty mop water. Nothing looked familiar. Not the house, not mother, nothing. I looked at the wooden scrub brush lying on its back in a puddle of grey water. It had scrubbed its final plank of the hardwood floor that held the battle scars and scratches from the feet of seven children.

It looked as worn out and lifeless as my mother.

Connie, our neighbor, must have sensed my presence; her dark eyes shot me a look giving me strict instructions not to enter or speak. I didn't.

I felt the sounds of her grief reverberate through me. I wanted to shout at her, "Mom, tell me what's wrong! Why are you crying? Stop it! Get up, Mom! I'm afraid!"

I wanted to do whatever I had to do to make Mom feel better, and I couldn't. I wanted to make her hurt go away, and I couldn't. I felt helpless. So I did the next best thing. As a nine-year-old, I took it in. I felt her grief enter me. I experienced, in my body and soul, her hopelessness, despair, and sorrow.

Mom had lost the house with only a few mortgage payments left.

Who knew where Dad was? Somehow, we got moved into another house, and it wasn't long before our pervert of a landlord poisoned our dog and set our house on fire while we had gone off to work in the bean fields. Most of our belongings were destroyed. When we arrived back home, we were farmed out to different houses temporarily.

Mother took off to California—felt the need, as she put it, "to get the hell out of Dodge." I remember how she would pace, driven by anxiety, saying tensely, "Something will come through, something will come through."

And it did.

California, here we come! Just like the Beverly Hillbillies, we piled our pitiful shit in the back of a few pickup trucks driven by two compassionate souls and were dropped off in front of a dilapidated old house with no yard—just hard compact dirt, a fallen foundation, plumbing that didn't work, and a bedroom full of windows and ripped screens. When we opened the door to the bedroom, there was a mass exodus of flies that had been breeding in there for God only knows how long.

The two men who drove us to "our summer home"

in Anderson, California, cried as they said goodbye to Mom. They gave her a hundred dollars and then headed back up to Oregon.

Smokey, our Australian shepherd, had survived the poisoning, and I have a vague recollection of a family "pow wow" about the cost of the vet bills and the decision to ship him down to be with us, as opposed to using the money for necessities like . . . food. He damned near peed on himself when he saw us.

My sister Connie had one outfit that she wore to school everyday: a black skirt, white blouse, and a lapel pin in the shape of a 45 record. Paul remembers having to curl his toes under in his shoes because they were too small, and taking them to the cobbler, who kept telling him, "Jesus Christ! Tell your mother to buy you some new shoes." Susie sported a six-inch sliver from our front porch that never received medical attention, and Johnny, dressed in ragged hand-me-downs, used to hang like a monkey in the tree in front of our house. My brother Bill, a sophomore in high school, walked by the house and up the alley to come home through the back door, so no one would see where he lived.

Mom continued to pass out, and me . . . I got better at tuning out.

The plumbing seldom worked. I remember the sink would be filled with dirty, grey, cold water and pieces of soggy cornbread floating in circles, and the house smelled like shit.

Poverty has its own stench.

We would gather around our only source of heat, an old potbelly stove in the front room, burning anything that was available: shoes, magazines, old furniture. It got so hot it almost glowed. I recall no furniture, or very little of it, in the room; I am told, however, there were pee-stained mattresses on the floor.

"Oh, there's no place like home for the holidays!"

Judy, now twenty, had not been home since her move to San Francisco before Mother lost the house. Now she was home for Christmas!

Judy had thought it strange that Mom insisted her friend drop her off at the restaurant where she worked rather than drive her directly to the house. Mom needed time to prepare Judy for what she was about to walk into.

Some years later, Judy told me how she lay in bed and cried when she saw the deplorable conditions in which we lived; how excited she had been at going home for Christmas, thinking about each one of us, what we would like; how deep in debt she had gone buying gifts for the family; and how long it took to pay off her bills.

I still remember to this day how guilty and ashamed of myself I felt because I wanted a skirt to go with the robin's egg blue sweater she bought for me.

I don't know how long we stayed in the town of Anderson—perhaps a year. I will *never* forget the day my father found us and moved us to Chico, California. My God, it was as if the heavens parted and the cavalry came riding in on the clouds. Maybe Mom had been right after all. Perhaps knights in shining armor do exist. If ever there was a time my father redeemed himself in the eyes of Mother, it was then—as short-lived as it was.

As we pulled into town and drove down the tree-lined boulevard, it was as if we had come upon a green, lush oasis. It was the most beautiful place I had ever seen. It felt as if we had been delivered from the clutches of some black force and all of a sudden hope was alive in our hearts.

We moved into the house on Broadway—not one we had to be ashamed of. There was a green lawn and side-walks, cement steps that led to a big porch with stone pillars, ledges to sit on, flowering bushes, hydrangeas in colors of bluish violet and pink.

Although school had started three weeks earlier, my sister and I lagged a little longer, waiting to get our first welfare check, so we could buy shoes.

I asked my sister Judy once, "When we were little, were things as bad as I remember?"

"Worse," she said flatly.

Recently, I found myself recounting vague memories of Anderson, the *hellhole* as I call it, and as spirit would have it, simultaneously as I questioned, I was led to the answer. My niece gave me a paper bag in which was a crumbled letter written by Mom around those events. Mom was writing a letter to Judy who was still living in San Francisco at the time.

Dearest Judy,

Thought I'd write you a real cheerful letter for a change! So many good things have happened in the past week I just thought it might make you feel good to know . . . I had 3 jobs offered me last week and so I took one (naturally). I'm working at the "Silver Dragon" Chinese joint. In fact I just got through work about an hour ago . . . it is now 2 am.

Mr. James is still working and seems to be in real good with his boss so I guess he will be working steady as business has picked up since he started cooking there, and that makes the boss real happy. And to top everything else off, I finally got those back checks from Klamath Falls which amounted to about $450.00 and that was a boost to this household!

The little girls about went wild when I gave them $25.00 a piece to get new shoes and stuff last Friday (when I got my job and also the back checks). It seems when everything starts going wrong, everything, but everything follows suit and does like-wise, and then all of a sudden when things change for the better, we hit the jackpot. They get so good we don't know how to act! Ha! And to add to our good luck, it all happened last week.

Mr. James received notice from the Veterans administration that he will be getting a small disability pension each month. Not much, but $66.00 a month, and dating back since August of '59 which will amount to over $400.00, which he will receive in a lump sum, so he was told. That money will be given to me, and I'm going to invest it as a down payment on a home as Mr. James can get one on a G.I. deal.

We lost the one we had, and I'm going to see that these kids have a home of their own again! Not only that, but new and decent furniture as well! We made a start already on that. Mr. James brought home a good used Maytag automatic to-day-it works just grand and for only $75. ($5.00 per mo.) Someone gave him a used gas range just like the one you had on Rose. It works fine, too. Our refrig died and to me, spending $100.00 to put in a new unit doesn't make sense so I'm going to get a new one with a larger freezing capacity than the one we had, as we need it if one wants to buy wisely. So now I'm convinced our luck is changing for the better . . . and it never fails to amaze me how things can change so suddenly!

A month ago we were living like rats in Anderson! We practically lived on beans and potatoes! It was so bitterly cold with no heat except old "Pot Belly" and it got to the point too, where I didn't have money to buy wood, and I had to burn leaves! Also old shoes, clothes and even old love letters (what a heat that created!)

How we managed to live like we did is beyond

me now. No washing machine, no hot water, a sink plugged up for 2 months, a bathroom too cold to use even if we had hot water, which we didn't . . .no refrig . . . (not that we had anything to put in it) and no money! The kids went without lunch, or sneaked off through the alley to come home to a big batch of French fries or "lotsa" potatoes! potatoes! Yet we managed to make fun of our situation and we'd hole up for the night in the dining room, mattresses on the floor, and watch T.V. with no light, save the light from the old "Pot Belly." We all got attached to it!

We'd sit around it at night and talk about life and what was happening to us . . . try to figure out "why" and keep hoping there was a reason for it and that some day we'd laugh about it, and be the stronger and better for going through it. It got to the point finally though, where the poor darlings I felt, had reached the breaking point. They were just forcing themselves to be hopeful and funny.

Athena for instance, and the "cornmeal pancake" episode! Remember when I wrote you shortly after Thanksgiving when I had "cracked up?" Neighbors came to help, and help came from every direction and people were so good? We received oodles and oodles of canned goods, but were bombarded with potatoes, corn meal and flour. The kids referred to it as "charity chow." Well, when I left the 49Club Dec 3rd, and there was no more work . . . no money . . . we lived on what we had . . . we had to! We ate the best first, naturally, and left the worst . . . potatoes, beans, and cornmeal. We finally got down to cornmeal pancakes!

Poor little Athena was trying to clean up that

dump one day, and the corn meal pancakes were floating on top of the cold dirty dishwater in the sink . . . she started bailing out the water and throwing it on the porch. It looked like Niagara Falls (the steps). The pancakes kept getting in her way and everything was so impossible she went berserk and started throwing those wet pancakes all over, and I joined her, too. We even hit outer space, and they're still there I guess, but we had a good laugh over it. Better yet we're laughing now!

It seems so wonderful to see the kids so happy in nice new clothes . . . well adjusted and happy in a new school, making friends, and hope in their eyes instead of doubt and despair. They just love this town and I do, too. I haven't met my next-door neighbor yet. We have met indirectly through our common vices, cigs. We run out and send our kids over to borrow cigarettes from each other. Now I don't have to, thank goodness. I can buy them by the carton!

Connie and Athena, missed 3 weeks of school as they didn't have shoes. They "holed up" in their room, watched T.V., got on each other's nerves and picked fleas from "Chow Chow" to pass the time away. Prisoners of Poverty, I called them. When I took them downtown last Friday to buy their new "do–dads," we laughed all the way as they acted sort of dazed, they actually hadn't been out of the house in 3 weeks and everything seemed so new and wonderful to them . . . It was lots of fun, but they acted like "little hermits" emerging from the hills. They hadn't been downtown, so I showed them the little places of interest. We stopped at the pet shop where they had this darling little monkey and a myna bird that kept saying, "Hi ya kid . . . wanna play ball?"

Then we walked through this lovely little park right in town, where there were orange trees laden, roses blooming and all kinds of birds and doves flying around. College students were sitting in the sun reading and watching the girls go by.

We did our shopping, splurged on milk shakes, then I had to rush home and go work at 5 PM. It seems so nice to smell good cooking smells like pork chops, lamb and turkey in this house! "Essence of Beans" has been our standby for so long.

So when I sum it all up, I feel our misfortunes must have helped us all grow in some way. It amazes me how very popular and much in demand the kids are. Everyone seems to think they're different and outstanding. God! If they only knew what they went through . . . maybe that's why they are what they are.

Now about your time off . . . when do you plan on taking it? Soon I hope. Maybe you and I can have a ball fixing this place up. Mr. James is in good with a lot of people here in town, some Greek people too, and they want to help him get started again with credit references, etc. I'm going to take advantage of it and get new things for a change.

I figure with both of us working as we are now, and with his monthly check, we will be making $565.00 a month, and we sure as heck can stick our necks out and afford new things to make our youngsters proud and happy. Such are our hopes. Like I said before, he is doing his best. The damage is done as far as he and I are concerned . . . he doesn't exactly know it . . . but I keep letting him know he is doing the most wonderful thing any man can do, and that is to make his children happy by doing for them and building something for them again.

I see I must quit . . . my paper is all used up and there is no more. I'm tired too, as I have put in a long day . . . (also drank 6 beers) Ha! I'm hoping I'll hear from you soon, and that you're well and happy and will soon have some time to spend at home. Let me know!

Love from all, but mostly me . . . Mom

Judy and Mom

4

When It Hurts Too Much To Love

Anger ventilated often hurries towards forgiveness;
and concealed, often hardens into revenge.
—Edward G. Bulwer-Lytton

Somehow, we redeemed ourselves in the eyes of God. He must have said, "All right, the poor bastards have had enough." For it seemed as if things, although still difficult, never reached the depth of what *felt* as such insurmountable odds, where our living conditions were concerned.

Dad was around for a short period. Mother, relieved he had found us, was just as relieved when he left, and us "chillens," well, we were just happy we had plumbing that worked and a nice house to live in.

Our house filled up quickly with newfound friends and our screen door constantly banged, announcing the arrival of more kids after school. We became the local hangout. Music blared and could be heard from the street; voices were loud, competing with the volume of the records playing on the phonograph. Mother arrived home from work exhausted, fixed us dinner, and retreated to her room to read her *Fate* and *UFO* magazines, sneak a few beers, and find some peace and quiet.

School was a blur. I excelled, strangely enough, at public speaking, turning boys' heads, and I was shunned by the senior girls as I entered high school. My grades were pitiful. I didn't care about them, didn't study, didn't give a shit. Who knew what study habits were. I don't think I can ever remember anyone saying to me, "Did you get your homework done?" I could bring home a report card full of Cs, Ds, and Fs. Mother would sigh and say, "Well, . . . if you did your best." I didn't know what my best was, but I knew and she knew that her best and my best weren't good enough. I didn't care, and I think she was too tired to care, because it took too much effort.

I cut school a lot. We'd hang out by the garage until Mom would go to work, wrote our own excuses, and got pretty good at it, too. "Athena was absent on Mon. the sixth as she was working out in the yard this weekend and got soaked by a leaky hose and caught a bad cold."

I had a natural ability to style hair. Word soon got out, and girls would arrive at my house on the weekend, their hair set in orange juice cans and their bangs taped flat against their forehead with scotch tape. Piled on the bed, they would await their appointed slot, discussing the cool senior men and what they were going to wear to the dance that night, oohing and ahhing as they watched me. Armed with Aqua Net hair spray, with bobby pins sticking out of the corner of my mouth, I backcombed their hair, styling it into these god-awful 'dos that resembled drum majorettes' hats. What the hell, we thought we looked hot, cruisin' up and down the Esplanade on a dollar's worth of gas, listening to the Beatles on the radio, stopping at the local hangout for hamburgers, French fries, and vanilla Cokes.

Judy

Judy, living in San Francisco at that time, had become the epitome of sophistication. She thrived in the cosmopolitan environment, and it showed. Six foot in stocking feet, 6'3" in heels, her tall, statuesque frame, with perfect posture, dressed impeccably in black with her Grace Kelly blond hair pulled into a French twist and eyeliner skillfully applied to her green eyes, she was beautiful, and I adored her.

In her exploration of knowledge, Judy was completely self-taught, and whether it be classical music, jazz, literature, poetry, or art, she was passionate about her endeavors and gave herself fully over to any current fascination. The Catholic religion had become her point of focus (short-lived though as it was); while home for a visit, she got on her bandwagon, and I, her only captive audience, sat next to her on the old picnic bench in front of the fireplace, warming the palms of my hands while she tried to convert me. None of it made any sense, but I didn't care. I wasn't listening. When she really wanted to drive a point home, she'd lean forward, resting her elbows on her knees, her hands positioned securely on the Bible. Listen to this she would say, reading the passage slowly. "Did you get it?"

I'd just nod and smile. I was more fascinated with her iridescent blue eye shadow and how she applied her makeup.

That fascination stuck with me, and makeup became a life-long career.

With high school came my first love. Although he was older, had already graduated, and lived four hours away, still we managed to see each other every few weeks. Full of anticipation and excitement, I stood on the ledge of our front porch straining to spot his red Corvette as he drove through town up the one-way street that led to our house. We had plans to marry when I graduated; however, my life was about to take a drastic turn, at the tender age of 17.

Food was tasting weird, my period was late, and I began to feel a growing sense of anxiety. . . . "What if I am pregnant?" With my heart racing, I would try to convince myself that it was only my imagination. To be single and pregnant was to be a social outcast, the talk of the town, and all poor souls who found themselves in such a predicament suddenly without warning became "sick with mononucleosis," or went "to live with a distant aunt" for five or six months.

It was okay, though, we were going to get married, he said; he would drive down from Oregon where he lived and we would tell my parents. That's what he said, and I believed him. My father liked him, my mother liked him, and I loved him. The weekend he said he was coming, I stood on the ledge of the porch and waited for him. He never came.

When I finally got him on the phone, his voice was dead and monotone. "Oh hi, Sunshine," he said flatly. "How are you?"

"Well," I stammered, "I'm pregnant."

"Well," he said in a dry lifeless tone, "here's what ya do. You walk into a drugstore and you get some quinine tablets and drink some turpentine, and if that doesn't work, we'll see about getting you an abortion."

"What about getting married?" I said.

"I never said I'd marry you."

Mother came into my bedroom wanting to know what in the world was the matter.

"He can't come down this weekend," I told her.

"Good God!" she said completely irritated. "It's not the end of the world!"

That's what you think, I thought to myself.

I couldn't concentrate in school and I couldn't stop crying. We were poor. I couldn't go away and have it. No one knew, I couldn't tell anyone, and I didn't know what to do.

I was sitting on the old picnic bench in front of the fireplace staring at the flames. I could *feel* mother's presence behind me. I didn't acknowledge her; I just stared at the fire. She stood there for the longest time before she spoke. "Honey," she said quietly, "are you pregnant?"

I didn't look at her or answer, but I could feel the tears streaming down my cheeks.

"Well," she said, "don't worry, we'll work something out." Mother called Judy who was living in Sacramento at that time. I still remember the relief I felt when Judy came home to see me that weekend. She just held me and let me cry, saying "poor baby." Both Judy and Mother argued about what was in my best interest. Mother wanted me to have the baby; Judy said she could find a way for me to have an abortion. I felt removed from all decision-making and began to tune out.

I was caught in a vortex that was pulling me into a whirlpool, and all I could think of were ways to make the pain go away. I pleaded with God: I'd be good; I'd do anything he wanted—just make it go away. "Help me, I need help," I cried, but it all seemed to fall on deaf ears.

I took baths as hot as I could stand; still, I couldn't scrub away *feeling* dirty and soiled. I thought about killing myself a lot.

I felt completely rejected, abandoned, alone, and totally without hope. Once, while in the bathtub, I held a razor blade in my hand. If I could just do it, I could be free, I could be free and I wouldn't have to feel anymore. Mother began knocking on the door, "Athena? What are you doing in there? Are you okay?"

Judy got pissed and hired a lawyer, and so did he. Still to this day, I remember word for word his lawyer's words: "It's a shame to have a girl such as this that has committed violations so many times that she finally finds herself pregnant, and looks for the most likely person to live with."

Dad had come home for a brief visit, and I holed up, hiding out in the bedroom, afraid of facing the inevitable. I listened to the boys pounding on the bathroom door, yelling at the girls to hurry up, that they were making them late for school. I didn't want the noise and early morning chaos to end. Suddenly, the house became still and quiet. I could hear Dad's footsteps getting louder as he approached the bedroom.

I lay in bed with the covers pulled up around me and watched the doorknob turn. There, standing in the doorway, stood my father with breakfast on a tray for me.

"Whot hoppened?" He asked in his thick accent. "I thot youse two loves each othor. No damned German isa gonna to walk over Greek's daughtor," he muttered.

I don't know what Mom said to him, but I was relieved beyond words. I didn't know what to expect, as I had never had a confrontation with my Dad. I don't think I could have survived a tongue-lashing; I was so full of shame and fear. I don't think anybody could have said anything to me I hadn't already said to myself.

Part of me, on some level, knew I was about to begin a journey into a dark underground world. Events had taken a crazy twist and I didn't know what the next moment would bring, what was going to happen to me, or how to prevent myself from swirling into the vortex.

I wanted someone to tell me, "Don't worry, everything is going to be all right; you don't have to be afraid, it will be fine. Go to sleep and get a good night's rest and when you wake in the morning, you'll see, he really does love you and it was all a bad dream and the sun will be shining and life will return to normal. It's just a bad dream. . . . Go to sleep. . . . Go to sleep."

I dreamt it was night. I was walking down a dirt path, unsure of its direction. A grey mist hung in the air, making my skin feel cold and clammy. It was pitch black and the fog made it impossible to see. I was terrified. I was lost. The sides of the road were lined with haunting shapes and outlines, menacing and eerie. I saw a church far off in the distance. . . . It seemed so far away. A shaft of light illuminated the dirt beneath the wooden doors. I pushed the doors open and stood at the entrance.

A few people sitting in the pews with their heads down cried softly. A black casket lined with white satin was open for viewing. I walked down the aisle, curious as to who it was that died. I stood at the coffin's edge and looked at the hands crossed at the chest by the heart. There against the white gown, in stark contrast, lay a single red rose. I looked at the face. The skin was grey, the lips blue, the hair black and shiny.

It was me.

I ceased standing outside observing myself and

went inside my corpse. My daughter's father, Ben, was standing at the side of the coffin. He looked at me and threw his head back, laughing. My eyes and mouth flew open and with a vengeance, I snarled and hissed, exposing vampire fangs, ready for the kill.

I quit school in my junior year and went on welfare. Full of shame, feeling like white trash, I sat in the lobby with fat women and screaming kids waiting for my name to be called. I was showing now, and I recall how difficult it was to go out in public and let the world see me in all my swollen glory.

I replayed Mom's words a lot. "Hold your head up high. If you run from this, you'll be running from other things the rest of your life." I felt like I was walking into a lion's den.

Although I was the talk of the town, the center of gossip, I found myself utterly confused and bewildered at what transpired in the later months of my pregnancy. I had four proposals from high school boys to "marry me" to give the baby a name. A few of them even went up to Oregon to find him to "beat him up," I guess to save my honor in their eyes.

People threw a shower for me, and there were faces there I didn't recognize. I was embarrassed but grateful, and that whole scenario would down the road become something I learned to view as an incredible lesson in letting myself be vulnerable. They accepted me, with all my flaws, and embraced me.

I, on the other hand, was filled with a hurt I didn't know how to escape from. It was if something on the inside of me was stoking some embers, stirring it up. I replayed his words over in my head. I could feel the anger and vindictiveness grow, and *I wanted it to.*

God, I had determined, was out to get me and had me

singled out on his hit list. I bargained, and begged for Him to make it better, make things like they were, just make him love me again, fix it. I couldn't understand what was happening to me or why. I wondered what made me such a bad person that I would have to suffer the type of rejection I did. I figured I must have been a really rotten person, or somehow inherently within my soul had done some horrible deed that was beyond redemption, and was now firmly planted in the reality of what my life was to be. I felt old, completely exhausted, and so sad.

To me, God was an absolute undeniable and bona fide asshole, and furthermore, I was going to banish the remote possibility in any form in my consciousness whatsoever that He even existed. *Fuck you and the horse you rode in on! I'd become an atheist! I'll punish you, you creep! I will never give you the satisfaction of my belief or faith!*

It was raining the day I gave birth to my daughter. She was a beautiful baby with a perfectly shaped head full of black hair, and I wondered how I would take care of the two of us. That night, I lay in the hospital bed with my head close to the window. I didn't want the nurses to see me crying. It was the one-year anniversary of John Kennedy's death. I thought of Jackie; as I watched the sheets of rain trickle down the window, I cried for her, I cried for me, and it was as if Mother Nature was crying for the both of us. I thought of Ben. "Here you are, running around, you bastard, and here I am with a baby to support." I thought of him telling me to drink turpentine, and I began to vow over and over again, I will never love anyone again, and I will *never* let any man *ever* hurt me like that again. *Never.*

I paid dearly for that vow, and so did others.

I had a child to support. I used the welfare checks to pay for the doctor and hospital, bought a beat-up old

Volkswagen bug, and after my daughter's birth, paid for a babysitter and put myself through beauty school.

Tina was a sickly baby; she'd cry, I'd cry. I'd cry, she'd cry. Nothing seemed to console her, but on the other hand, nothing consoled me either, and I'm sure she was responding to my ever-growing depression and melancholy.

The day I received my license from the state as a cosmetologist, I also received a check from the state. The thought of living on welfare the rest of my life was simply not an option. I wrote them, thanked them for their assistance, and sent the check back, for I had already received two job offers. I will, to this day, be forever grateful to them.

Raising Tina was a joint effort of my whole family, for it became apparent I had in many ways begun to detach myself from reality. Deeply melancholy and depressed, I went to great extremes to "put on another face" where people were concerned. I was outgoing to the public eye, but in my private thoughts I harbored deep feelings of hurt and anger, fantasized a lot about revenge and being anywhere other than where I was. I wanted off the planet, but something in my gut always told me that if I killed myself, I would have to come back and do it again. This I innately knew.

"Athena! Do you realize that you get up with a scowl on your face like you are mad at the whole world?"

Early in the morning, Mother would take Tina out of her crib, place her in her highchair, and together they would have their "morning coffee." Mother drank hers black, and poured coffee with lots of milk and sugar into Tina's Tommy tippy cup. An hour later, "revved up" on caffeine, she'd be tearing around the house like a bat out of hell in her little walker, slowing down only long enough to gain traction as she rounded the corner on the slippery linoleum. God help you if your feet were in the way. And we wondered why she was hyper.

It didn't matter if it was a warm afternoon or not. If Mother could, she packed an old charred frying pan in the back of Tina's stroller and off they would head to Chico Creek to fry pork chops, make hobo coffee, hunt for fairies, and contemplate God.

I am sure it was the aromatic smells filling the air that enticed a hippie, floating down the creek high on marijuana, to respond to mother's invitation to join her for a cup of coffee and a bite to eat. I have no doubt the topic of discussion was the government's cover-up of UFOs, Martin Luther King, and the Viet Nam War.

Hours later, she would come home and say, "I met the nicest young man. The youth of this world have so much on the ball." If I made a comment like, "Jesus, Mother, he had hair down to his ass," I was always reprimanded with a "Shame on you! You can't judge a book by its cover."

When I returned home late one afternoon, Mom met me at the door, her face completely animated and full of life. She began to tell me excitedly how earlier that day, she spotted a little mouse that was "scampering" across the kitchen counter. It took a nosedive off the edge of the tile and fell in the dog's bowl of water. Of course, in her unique story-telling manner, the scene came alive: "I was walking out of the kitchen, when all of a sudden I heard this splashing. I looked down and there, paddling for his life, was this tiny little mouse who had fallen in the dog's bowl of water. He was gasping for his breath. The poor little darling looked up at me, and it was clear he was almost a goner, so I picked him up, grabbed a washcloth, laid him on his back and pumped his little arms up and down and gave him mouse to mouse resuscitation. [I swear it's the truth.] He was about to take his last gulp of air. I named him 'Humphrey!'" she said happily.

"What's that?" I inquired.

"Oh, here, come take a peek inside and see for yourself! I built him a home," she said proudly. I bent down and peered inside a gourd where she had created a "condo" fairyland for her new-found friend. There he was, no bigger than a minute, scurrying around, busily exploring his new environment. A ladder made from twigs and twine led to the loft and a fluffy piece of cotton shaped like a bed. There was a mound of green velvet moss and snippets of foliage, creating a magical Beatrice Potter forest. Nestled in the corner was a half a walnut shell filled with water, a hunk of Swiss cheese and piece of bread—the little sucker had hit the Mouse Lotto! Here, bar none, was my all-time favorite: a thimble full of red wine—I kid you not. No alcoholic likes to drink alone.

Mom caught our tomcat named "Dinner Bucket" trying to eat the mouse, so she choked the cat till he dropped the mouse. My brother Bill came home one night "three sheets to the wind" and threw out the mouse. Mom was so damned mad she wouldn't speak to him for three weeks. Dinner Bucket, our "mouser," as we called him, eventually died, but like all our pets, he received a last farewell. On a small scrap of paper secured to Popsicle sticks shaped in a cross, Mother wrote a tribute to grace the mound of his freshly dug grave. It was a proper and fitting memorial for our tomcat.

> Here lies Dinner Bucket
> So mean and so lean—
> May the land that he's in,
> Abound with the fin . . .
> And may he get fat off
> Drinking all jersey cream.

With help from my family and the babysitter, I settled into a routine, began work, and met a man that I was soon to marry. Everybody thought he would be a good father for my daughter, but I felt ambivalent, didn't much care one way or the other. Maybe they knew something I didn't.

My Dad had come home for one of his short sporadic visits, and I remember the distinct feeling, as I watched him walk away, that I wasn't going to see him again. Dad died of cancer a few months later.

Sad Dad

5

A Visitation

Every time I close the door on reality,
it comes in through the windows.
—Jennifer Yane

Mother was finally asleep. It had been one of those rare times when she couldn't stuff her feelings down for another second. We listened outside the bedroom while her sobs echoed through the walls. Smokey, our dog, had been acting strangely all day. Shivering and cowering, he had followed close behind Mother's legs as she walked from room to room. A strange tapping on the window had caught my attention, and I opened the curtain. Perhaps a bird had flown into the pane. Something in the air felt strange and unsettling. I dropped the curtain back into place.

I flipped on the switch to the bathroom light as I did every night before going to bed. Tina's crib was next to the door, and the soft glow illuminated the room, enabling me to get up quickly to tend to her and not stumble around in the dark. I loved the way she slept on her stomach with her arms tucked under her chest with her tiny butt hiked in the air. I tucked the blanket closer to her little body. Going to my own bed, I threw back the covers and climbed in. I was tired.

What a day. I hated it when Mom cried. I was 19, yet those outbursts, rare as they were, never failed to reduce me to a mere child myself. That is how I felt: helpless and scared. I wasn't the only one who felt like that. I could feel the unspoken panic in my siblings as our eyes connected with each other. We were all at a loss.

All was quiet now. Mother was asleep, spent and exhausted. I felt like a limp rag that had been rung out. I lay in bed and thought about death, what it was like to be dead. No soul, nothing. A no-thing. What was the point to life? In life I felt dead. None of it made sense to me. Eventually I fell asleep.

Tina's piercing wail brought me to consciousness. "Jesus, not now," I thought to myself. It seemed as if I had just fallen asleep. I lay there listening, hoping she would go back to sleep, but her cry became angry and insistent, like when she wanted a bottle *and* to have her diaper changed. I kicked off the covers, swung my legs around the side of the mattress and sat on the edge of the bed. I looked up. Adrenaline shot through my body. My heart began to pound hard and fast.

He stood in the doorway, slowly turning his head from left to right, his body completely lit by the bathroom light. I threw the covers over my head full of fear as my daughter continued to wail. My breathing was rapid and fast. "Wake up!" I repeated the command. "Wake up!" But I wasn't asleep. I was wide awake. I finally mustered the courage and pulled the covers down enough to peek out of the corner of my eyes. He stood there, staring back at me. I was paralyzed with fear.

It was Dad. We had buried him that day.

The following morning, I told Mom something really strange had happened that night, but because she was so emotionally drained from the day before, I made no further comment about the event. A year later, on the anniversary of Dad's death, Mother was sitting on the couch with her coffee cup in one hand. Suddenly, she turned and said to me, "You know, something weird happened the night we buried your father. Do you remember how I cracked up that day?" *How could I forget,* I thought to myself. *It was horrible.*

"I'm sure it was the guilt and the failures, thinking about what could have been and the god-awful waste of his life because of the gambling." She squirmed for a moment and I could tell by her expression she was feeling uncomfortable. She brushed it off in an attempt to rid herself of the feeling, and said quickly, "Oh well, I guess we can't cry about spilled milk. Anyway," she continued, "I had fallen asleep and all of a sudden I felt a hand on my shoulder, shaking me awake. 'Ruth! Are you okay? Are you okay? Wake up, Ruth!' I shot up instantly, and there, standing next to my bed, was your father. I was dumbfounded. He said, 'Are you sure you're going to be okay?' 'Yes,' I stammered, 'yes, Jim, I'll be okay.' 'Well,' he said, 'I have to go now but I'll be back to get you soon.' The room smelled of cigar smoke. There was such compassion in his voice," she said quietly, "like how I always wished he would be."

"I saw him the same night, Mom."

"You're kidding! You did? You saw him too?"

"Yeah, I did."

"Tell me!" Mom instantly became more animated, as phenomena of any kind never failed to breathe more life into her body.

I saw my father. He was dead, yet he was alive. So there has to be some form of life after death. Where did he go? I had seen him in his coffin. Why did he appear?

That singular experience left me contemplating life and death and opened a portal through which gifts from other lives would come forward in their own time.

6
Is There An Elephant In The Room?

To not communicate is to be in walking death.
—James Martin Peebles

Two weeks after my father's death, I married. I cried at my ceremony, for I knew I was making a mistake. I wasn't in love with him; everyone knew that, including him. I married on the rebound. I had made specific vows of my own, not to feel or to let anyone close. I was determined to push them away. I thought I was creating a world that was safe and untouchable. As far as I was concerned, it hurt too much to love.

Like mother, like daughter. I settled into the daily routine of going through the motions where my "wifely duties" were concerned. It was rhythmically boring and oh, so predictable. Mother's philosophy, "Man is king of the castle," rubbed me the wrong way. But despite the growing resentment I felt at following in her footsteps, I waited on him hand and foot. It left me with the unspoken feeling that women were second-class citizens and we didn't matter. A woman's wants and desires were of little importance compared to what his needs were. I learned to be quiet.

I didn't want to rock the boat, as he would use any

excuse to belittle me in public with his macho "I-am-going-to-show-you-who-is-man-of-the-house" attitude. Funny, though, when we were alone in the house, he was more affectionate. Not that I reciprocated, except with what I *thought* I should be doing or how I should respond, but there was no heart in it at all. I know he felt tremendous frustration at my lack of response. Hell, *I* was frustrated at my lack of response. But it was my job as a woman (I thought) to make him *feel* like a man, to be the perfect housewife. How do you make someone feel like a man if you are unresponsive? Those were "Mom tapes" playing in my head. I cooked, cleaned house, and did my wifely duties as mother would put it, but beneath the façade, I still felt like a second-class citizen.

I was still occupied with the experience of seeing my father the night of his funeral. There must be some form of life after death. There had to be. I *saw* him. I felt instinctively that meditating would lead me closer to understanding, so I asked Judy, my sister, what was meditation and how do you do it? "Concentrate on a blue dot between your eyebrows in your third eye." What the hell is a third eye? The only thing I could relate it to was Cyclops, and he gave me the willies.

One day while trying to make contact with my father, I heard three knocks on the bedroom window. Although it jolted me back to reality, I instantly thought back to the same rapping I heard the day of his funeral. I had a feeling it was him.

I held the image of the blue dot between my eyes as instructed, and after about three weeks, the strangest thing happened. I felt a tingling sensation at the base of my spine. It shot straight up my spine, and I saw an explosion of white light. That scared the hell out of me, and I slammed the door shut to any further experiences for a number of years. Much later, I would find out that this meant I had awakened the *kundalini,* the spiritual energy coiled at the base of my spine.

My marriage lasted less than five years. I think. To this day, everything about that time period, the day to day of married life feels vague and undefined. Maybe because I felt that way. Things were just plain foggy. What I remember the most is coming home from work one night to a warm bath filled with Mr. Bubbles drawn by Tina, then four years old. It was as if some part of her knew that I needed that. I did. Bless her little heart.

God has a way of placing people in our path that become stabilizers in ways they are not aware of. If anyone stabilized me in an "off the wall way," it was a friend who became my saving grace. She had one of those slow Southern drawls and one of the most likeable personalities ever, and she babysat my daughter when I worked. The cul-de-sac she lived on along with another friend became our morning hangout after the kids were dropped off at school. You could always tell when her husband had been out drinking the night before, as she would call me with "That son of a bitch did it again! Let's meet at our favorite restaurant for lunch, but see if you can fit me in to do my hair first." I'd get all the details while I would lacquer the hell out of her hair with hair spray, giving strict instructions to hang her head over the side of the bed if they were going to get romantic and be sure to wrap it in toilet paper before she went to sleep. Dot had a sure-fire method of making sure that her volume curls didn't move. When I dropped my daughter off at her house in the morning, she greeted me wearing her husband's dingy white terrycloth robe cinched tight at the waist, hiding mismatched flannel pajamas. She polarized her ensemble with hot pink fluffy slippers that made her feet look like gunboats and silk underwear turned upside down on her head to preserve my creative hairdo. Invariably, two tufts of hair sprouted out of each pant leg. She was a vision.

Eventually I quit work, and it was then I began to feel myself detaching more, although I don't know where it was that I went. It was a void where I didn't have to feel or interact with anyone. I know my husband felt great frustration at my lack of response and my ever-growing sense of detachment. I wanted out of the marriage, I wanted out of my body, I wanted out of life. I wanted to be anywhere but where I was, and as I went through my wifely routine, I began to slip myself into neutral. It was an easy place to stay in. I didn't have to feel, I didn't have to think, it wasn't hard to get to—and that alone was the most frightening aspect of all.

"Athena . . . Athena!! . . . Athena!!!! JESUS! Are you deaf?!!! Can't you hear Tina? She's been trying to get your attention! Where the hell did you go?"

"Oh," I replied, "uh . . . I didn't hear her."

"God! She's been screaming 'Mommie' at you for the last five minutes!" I know my detachment and lack of parenting at times was a concern for my mother and other members of the family. I just wasn't present mentally.

My marriage was short lived. I simply went through the motions, and I know it had to feel that way to him. I had set my course into motion, and I was bound and determined it would remain that way.

The depression was deep, and it felt like I was pulled into a black hole that began to encase me in a straight-jacket. I felt like I was living in a snake's skin I couldn't shed. Everything felt constricted and uncomfortable, and I couldn't get a full breath of air into my lungs.

I began driving at great speeds, pushing the gas pedal to the floor. "DO IT! DO IT! DO IT!" The voices in my head were relentless. I was heading for a cement wall supporting the overpass. . . . "DO IT!" I pushed the pedal to the floor. . . . "DO IT!" Just then, my daughter's face flashed in my mind and I turned the wheel at the last moment. Years later, I was told by my spirit guide, through his channel, that I would have checked out of this incarnation through the form of an accident; however, my guides intervened and counseled me, and I decided to stay in the body and confront my issues. I knew instantly which event they were talking about.

I intuitively knew, as much as I longed for release from the human experience, that if I killed myself, I would be giving up, and ultimately, I would have to come back and do it again. I didn't know how I knew this; I just did.

This was the kind of innate and deep knowing I hated, because I couldn't see any way out. I knew my daughter would have enough to deal with herself without me leaving her saddled with a mother who committed suicide. *I couldn't see how change was possible.* One day I stared at myself in the mirror for the longest time. Who *was* she? I didn't know her at all, and I didn't like her.

I was 23 when I wrote the following:

> If I had the power to change the things I see,
> I'd change the girl inside the mirror, who's staring back at me.

I didn't know what I was looking for, and I hated what felt like a completely miserable form of existence. I hated not knowing why I was made to have life. I asked myself, Why does feeling hurt so much? Why does life exist, anyway? Why does it hurt to be alive? Why?

After my divorce, it was a whirlwind of relationships, short-lived, punishing, and cruel. My lack of emotional availability and my decision to make them pay for my hurt became a way of expression, a source of sick satisfaction that enabled me to say "Fuck you, God!"

I was terrified of letting anyone close, terrified of the place I was moving into, and in the silence of my private moments and thoughts, terrified I couldn't find my way out.

I threw myself into my work in retail. It was the only place I could find any level of success in my life. I became a workaholic. I put vacations off to work. I popped diet pills left and right, could sell anything on them, and quickly built a great clientele. I got the acknowledgment I had wanted and my career in cosmetics began.

The faces of the men I dated became blurs of one man after another; if they were married, even better—they couldn't ask for a commitment. To me it was a game. Set them up and slam down the hammer after they were hooked. "Jesus! You are really cruel when you break up with someone," a friend once commented. In my youth it was hard for me to walk into a room without being stared or gawked at. I hated it. But I never lacked for the attention from men.

Finally, one got through. He was an account manager for a cosmetic line whose territory included the retail store in which I worked. For two years I gave him a hard time, but beneath the surface I was secretly attracted to him. One afternoon, while writing an order, he nonchalantly said, "So what time is dinner?"

"Oh, about eight o'clock" I replied. He got so nervous he dropped his pencil. It had been six years since the birth of my daughter and six years since I had really felt anything for a man. We went to dinner and many dinners after, but of course I couldn't let it last. One night, he brought me face to face with a bitter truth. I had pulled my usual "we-are-seeing-too-much-of-each-other" three-month routine, and he got out of the car, slammed the car door with a force that damned near broke the windows, and yelled, "You've got a fuckin' wall built up around you that no one can get through!" Ed was certainly passionate, I'll give him that. And he was right. I did have a wall around me. I felt it, my family knew it, and my short-lived encounters with men proved it. Don't let them touch your heart, keep them at arm's length. My succession of relationships were all surface, a defense, a strategy to protect myself from pain. I was cold, detached, and calculating.

The problem was, this man had touched me and left me emotionally on the edge of knowing I had a choice to make. I did love him, but I was scared to death. The only thing that occupied my mind was, what if I get hurt again? I sought professional help.

"If you don't learn to let yourself go, you will never be capable of loving anybody." I sat across from the psychologist and cried. I knew it was pure unadulterated truth. I replayed in my mind the time I spent lying in the hospital bed, hearing his words echo, "Drink turpentine, take quinine tablets." I will never let anyone hurt me like that again, I'd repeat to myself. I will never let anyone close, never . . . never . . . never.

Whatever the psychologist said must have gotten through. I decided to jump in with both feet, and when I let go, I let go. It felt good to feel. Ed and I became engaged and I gave up my job and moved to Sacramento. His best friend, a psychologist, asked me once, "How did you get through his defenses?"

"He got through mine."

I never forgot that observation. Once we began living together, however, I saw things that I couldn't ignore, although I tried to. When he drank he went from Dr. Jekyll to Mr. Hyde and that's what I began to do: hide. I knew he drank too much, and when he did, a mean-spirited side of him emerged.

I, on the other hand, was feeling totally out of my element and in a situation in which I had no control. I began to withdraw again to a place that felt safe. I wouldn't go out of the house, unless I had to drive to the store. I began having horrible panic attacks, breaking out in a sweat at the thought of having to get behind the wheel. The relationship continued to deteriorate, along with any self-esteem I had left. What was self-esteem, anyway?

I was walking on eggshells, in denial that the inevitable was waiting in the wings. I was in a town I didn't want to be in, completely dependent on a man financially, hating that feeling, hating myself, and scared to death because I could feel him pulling away, getting distant and cold. He had been promoted to district manager, which meant a move to Texas, and he began making up excuses, putting the wedding off. I withdrew more and never left the house. He was social; I had become a full-blown agoraphobic. He began staying away for longer periods of time. Finally, he moved out. I was pathetic: afraid and panicked. School was starting, and I had no job—and even if I did, I would need a babysitter. The thought of getting behind the wheel and being among people made my heart pound, and I would break out in a sweat. I wanted to curl up in a ball and go to sleep.

Everything he had been attracted to in me was no longer apparent: my independence, my self-reliance, and the ability to take care of myself and my daughter. My daughter never really liked him. Tina said he piled too much peanut butter on her sandwich.

I ate once in three weeks, took tranquilizers and drank beer to go to sleep. I sent my daughter to live with a friend back in Chico. I knew it wasn't good for her to be with me. Thank God for that wisdom. I thought constantly about killing myself, and one day, I decided to go in the garage, start the car, and shut the door. It was at that exact moment I heard a key in the lock of the front door. He walked past me, ignoring me as he went into the closet to take the tail end of his belongings. I was pathetic. I followed him from room to room like a whipped puppy, begging for him to talk to me. *Begging sucks!* He stared straight ahead, ignoring me. I could see his teeth clenched together and the tightening of his jaw in an attempt to hold back from blurting out, "I want out! I don't love you anymore. . . . I can't stand the sight of you! It's over! Now stop following me around so I can get my shit and get the hell out of here!"

Everything in my world had been kicked upside down. I felt emotionally as weak as a paraplegic trying to stand with atrophied muscles.

Something in me snapped. The anxiety began to manifest as shaking, and I could feel an energy, angry and vile, beginning to rise. The rage came out; I let him have it with both barrels. It shocked him, caught him off guard, and his eyes grew wide as he stared at me.

"You son of a bitch! Why don't you have the balls to tell me what is going on with you that you want out! Damn you, be honest! You walk in here ignoring the hell out of me and you don't have the guts to tell me the truth that you don't want to get married. . . . Get your shit and get out of here! I hate you!

"You damned men are all alike. . . . Split! . . . Leave! That's what your good at: leaving! Leave, you rotten son of a bitch! Get out! Get out of my life. . . . I hate you!"

I slammed the bedroom door so hard the force broke a window. To this day, I believe with all my heart that anger saved my life.

The universe, I have learned, has its own way of making you face what you don't want to look at. Can't drive in public, eh? Okay, try this on for size: Let's get you a job for a major cosmetic firm—Revlon—and give you half of California to cover. I shook like a dog shitting razor blades, but I did the driving and covered the territory.

Eventually, in the world of cosmetics, I found myself feeling more in control. I knew this terrain. I started focusing on where I could go within the company, and how to reach that objective. Some six months had passed since Ed and I had seen each other. He tracked me down while I was on the road and in bed with another man.

Joe was a pharmaceutical salesman and our territories put us in the same stores on a regular basis. Our conversations began between the aisles of toiletries and aspirin, and I knew he was genuinely attracted to me. At times I would glance up from my inventory book to catch him watching me. Joe was a handsome man with black hair, green eyes and thick eyelashes. He was tall and well dressed, and he seemed like a kind person. He was divorced, with two boys and proud of his sons, and although I revealed little about myself, he knew that I had just come out of a relationship. I am sure he could feel there were volumes behind what wasn't expressed or said.

Sometimes we would have dinner in the hotel restaurant or we would have dinner with some of his friends at his house. I welcomed the diversion from my thoughts of Ed, and although I would never allow any kind of relationship to develop with Joe, it was a pair of arms that could hold me when the ache became too great. I could shut my eyes and try to pretend briefly there was some form of intimacy. Ed somehow tracked me down. "Hello?"

"Honey . . . ," the voice cracked on the other end of the telephone, "I love you." I could tell that he was having a hard time controlling his emotions. I was elated. Joe sat up in bed and silently listened to the conversation. An awkward moment indeed.

Ed and I set the date again, and I put in for a transfer and flew to Texas to begin house hunting. That night he drank too much, got mean, and slurred, "You fucking pig. . . . So you had to come to Texas for a good fuck?"

Those words cut into my heart like a knife. He couldn't believe in the morning that he could have ever been capable of saying anything like that to me. He flew to California one more time. When I put him on the plane, he said, "I love you, and I'll see you next month." I never heard from him again.

I fought to stay sane and focused—God knows how, but somehow. My work was my salvation, but only until I got back in my car to drive home. My mind, no longer occupied by nail enamel and lipsticks, returned to statements Ed made, and waves of hurt would flood through my body. Tina had been back with me for some time, and I had arranged for a babysitter to keep her on the nights that I had to travel out of town.

I worked hard and was promoted into a job that few women held at that time. I was scared to death. The job involved a lot of math, my worst subject (thanks to a teacher who slapped the palms of my hands with a ruler in front of the class when I didn't know the answer). It meant a move from Sacramento to Los Angeles. I wanted to go back home to Chico, to family and to everything that was familiar. I was already panicking about the freeways and driving, for I was still white knuckling it to my accounts in Sacramento. I took the plunge and rented an apartment sight unseen in Brentwood; it was close to a school, and I would get settled and send for Tina. I looked through the window of the plane as I left Sacramento.

Everything felt so unsettled. I took a breath and cut off the feeling of fear. It seemed as if the universe was hell bent on pushing me forward.

7
Howdy Neighbor, Can You Spell Screwed Up?

Weather forecast for tonight: DARK
—George Carlin

The apartment was dark . . . literally no sunlight except for a one-inch patch that would illuminate the dark brown carpet at 2:00 every afternoon. This symbolism could not have been more appropriate or reflective of my state of mind. I had been dropped into maze of freeways, with accounts in all the surrounding suburbs of Los Angeles. My heart would race trying to merge onto the freeway. To find my way back home when nothing was familiar was awful. I was lost. I pulled over to the side of the road. With both hands gripped around the steering wheel, I said between clenched teeth, "Alright, get a grip! If you go far enough east, you'll wind up in New York, north . . . Alaska, south . . . Mexico, and west . . . the ocean. FUCK IT! I can't get lost!"

I began hearing voices constantly telling me to kill myself. The more I tried to push them away, the louder they became. "Kill yourself—you know you want to . . . go on, kill yourself." They were relentless. Predators baying in pursuit of their prey.

I held pillows over my head to drown them out as I

tossed and turned at night. I shouted at them to leave me alone, kept the light on all night and would climb out of bed exhausted, grateful that it was morning, that I had survived another night.

Work was my saving grace, and although it was becoming harder for me to focus, I was thankful for the diversion. But the harder I fought to maintain control, the more elusive and slippery everything became—the fake smile harder to plaster on, the laughter too loud, too forced.

I had a dream I was towing a car up a steep hill on my bicycle. The hill was almost vertical. My thighs were on fire from the pressure of trying to force the wheels of the bicycle to move. The tires of the bike flattened from the weight of the car, and it seemed as if any movement was no more than an inch at a time. "Can we help you?" I looked up and saw two men at the top of the hill staring down at me. "Can we help you?" one of the men repeated.

"NO!!! I can do it myself!" I snapped back with anger.

My despair must have been felt by my neighbor, for one night there was a soft rap on my door. Cautiously, I cracked opened the door. A full-bodied woman with two small dogs on a leash extended a hand towards me. "Hello, my name is Phyllis. I live upstairs from you," she said in a quiet voice. "I want you to have my card. . . . I know you're a single woman with a child." A few months later, as our friendship progressed, she confessed she felt such sadness and sorrow as she walked by our apartment that she had to make a connection to see if she could help. Phyllis, I learned, was a private person, and not one to mingle with neighbors. To me, she was an angel, sent by higher forces not yet understood. Swinging a lantern in the black of the night, she illuminated my path with her care and concern. There was something about her that reminded me of my sister Judy. Something that made me feel safe.

One morning, I poured her a cup of coffee and sat down at the kitchen table with mine in hand. I stared at the coffee in my cup, purposely avoiding eye contact with her. Silently I mustered up the courage. "I need help." I whispered. "I'm having strange dreams. I know I need help." I could feel my chest tighten.

I glanced up at her kind brown eyes and the large port wine birthmark that stained the left side of her face. Instantly, she reached for a piece of paper and wrote down the number of a gestalt therapist. She thrust it forward, directly in front of me. She tried to be matter of fact, but no amount of pancake makeup, no matter how heavily masked or skillfully applied, could have camouflaged the feeling of relief that shone through her spirit.

I dreamt I was stranded on an island. I was alone. The sky was heavy and black. The storm clouds hung low, full and menacing. I could not see light anywhere. I had to get off of this island or I was going to die. It was only a matter of time before the nature of my psyche would unleash a hurricane in which nothing could survive. I could feel it.

8

The Sky Is Falling! The Sky Is Falling!

What I am looking for is not out there; it is in me.
—Helen Keller

"Look at how you are breathing."

"What do you mean?"

"You're hyperventilating," the therapist replied.

I squirmed in the chair. I didn't know how to breathe another way. I had become accustomed to never being able to get a full breath of air into my lungs. The invisible cords tightened around my chest.

I didn't know how to respond. I sat there looking at my hands and the Kleenex I was shredding into strips. I felt her eyes watching me, waiting for my response.

Hildegard was a small woman, with chiseled features framed by short wavy brown hair. Her clothing was loose fitting, unstructured—a throw-back to the sixties. Mine was tight and restrictive. She walked with a stride and confidence that echoed her comfort in her own skin. I couldn't stand being in mine. Nothing about her demeanor reflected conformity. I envied that.

She probed about my history, made notes on a yellow legal pad, and at the end of the hour said quietly, "I would like to put you in the hospital tonight."

"NO! I can't do that! I can't do that! I have to take care of my daughter. . . . I have to work! NO! I'll lose my job. . . . I have to go to New York. . . . I'll get fired!" My head was spinning. My heart pounded harder and images of straightjackets and metal doors with small peep holes flashed in my mind's eye.

"Athena," she said compassionately, "You are completely out of touch with your feelings."

I agreed to see her three times a week after work. Week after week. Upon the encouragement of Hildegard, I told my boss I was seeing a therapist. "Don't worry, you are not going to lose your job. If you ever have a session you can't drive yourself home from, call me. I will take you home." To this day, I am grateful to Bill Kaufman.

But if any progress was made, it was very little. I anticipated what a response should be, and gave it to her. I could not understand her continually used phrase "living in the now." What does that mean? "Only in the now."

It sounded like horseshit: Be in the now. I lived in the future through daydreaming, or through my work— both forms of escape. My mind was always occupied by fragmented thoughts of doom and gloom, waiting for the next catastrophe to happen. I was chained to past events that played like a broken record.

"How many more men are you going to punish?" she asked one session. I looked her dead in the eye and replied in a cold, steely voice, "I am going to punish every one of the fuckers till the day I die." I enjoyed watching the look on her face. I could see her shake her head.

I left with homework. One, I was to listen to the song "Desperado," by the Eagles, and the other was write down words describing 'woman.' Old, tired, haggard, used, brow-beaten, workhorse, belittled, weak, second-class. I was to do the same exercise with the word 'lady.' That one was a no-brainer. Strong, independent, self-assured, respected, compassionate. I am not exactly sure why I associated the specific words I did with 'woman.' I know it had to be from observing my mother and listening to those heavy sighs that seemed to rise from the soles of her feet. Pure exhaustion. When I was working, however, and more in control—or so I thought-I associated myself with all of the adjectives that described my perception of 'lady.' At times it felt as if I were two different people.

Hildegard placed two empty director's chairs facing each other. I sat on the couch, growing more anxious. "I'd like you to sit in one of the chairs as Athena the adult, with teenage Athena in the other." I did not like this exercise. "Go on, talk to her," she instructed. "She's just told you she's pregnant." I sat in awkward silence.

After some prodding, I followed her cue and began speaking to the teenager sitting in the chair across from me. What began as a quiet dialogue began to gather emotional momentum. I was pissed. I began shaking a finger at her. "You stupid girl! You're pathetic. Look what you did! Getting pregnant! What makes you think anybody would want to marry you? You believed all that crap that he loved you? You're stupid! Now look at the mess you're in!"

I could hear Hildegard gasp and say under her breath quietly, "Good Lord, you are all parent!" I never understood about the so-called components of the personality, the adult, parent, and the child. All I was able to discern was that to be all of one was not healthy or emotionally balanced. The parent, I learned, was the one who normally said, the "should" word. "You should do this and you should do that." In my perpetual judgment of myself, I had become completely unbalanced.

Several months passed while I continued to see her three times a week. I could see the frustration in her face. I had told her about being molested by Mother's boyfriend; I recounted my memory of the troll waking me, scratching my back, forcing his tongue down my throat, and pushing me backwards. I recalled trying to free myself. That was all I remembered. There were huge gaps of memory loss. Things were simply foggy and sketchy.

"I had a strange dream this week."

"Tell me," she responded.

"I dreamt I was trying to rescue a little girl who was trapped in the basement of our house in Klamath Falls, Oregon, the house I grew up in. She was hiding in the dark behind a chair. I tried to get her out. I wanted to take her into the light. She wouldn't come to me, so I finally picked her up. I was scared because she went limp. 'Oh no! she's dead! She's not moving.' Finally there was a little movement, and I cried out of relief. I wanted to give her a bottle, but I didn't have one, so I began nursing her. There were two dark figures at the top of the stairs, blocking the doorway. I screamed at my mother, 'If you hurt her, I will kill you!' I had to leave her in the basement, but I gave her a little blanket to keep her warm."

Hildegard's face lit up with excitement and she jumped up from her chair and placed the two chairs in front of each other. A plastic bat leaned against the chair she sat in. She had been unsuccessful in getting me to release anger against my mother or Ed the troll. "I'm not really mad at her," I would say. My voice was barely above a whisper. "Times were hard. She worked hard. I'm not mad at Mom. Really, I'm not." I was afraid of my anger and Hildegard knew it. I could see her almost roll her eyes with a "Yeah right, you're not mad" kind of look.

"Okay, let's put Ed in the chair."

"I want out of here," I thought to myself. I could feel my heart begin to race.

"Go on," she said quietly. She pulled her chair closer and leaned forward. "Tell him what you think of him, what he did to you. Tell him."

I felt self-conscious as I gave the chair a little whack. "That's good," she said. "Hit him again." Whap! I hit it again and I hit it again. The rage was loose. I raised the bat over my head with both hands and came down with a force and power that made me shake inside and out. WHAP! Hildegard jumped from the force WHAP! "YOU FUCKING SICK SON OF A BITCH!" WHAP! WHAP! "YOU ROTTEN COCKSUCKER! YOU SICK FUCKING DRUNK! . . . YOU SICK FUCK!"

I broke the chair. A milestone had been reached.

From time to time, Hildegard tried unsuccessfully to get me to walk down the stairs into the basement of our house through guided imagery. I flat out refused. I felt nauseous at the idea and completely panicked at the thought. My defenses, I later learned, kept something hidden from my conscious mind. Tucked in a darkened crevice for future exploration, it would come forward in due time, as my oversoul knew.

There was light at the end of the tunnel. Early one morning, Tina came out of her bedroom rubbing her eyes. "Mom, there's grass growing out of my carpet."

"What?" "What are you talking about?"

"There's grass growing out of my carpet." I followed her into her bedroom and sure enough, her parakeet had been tossing birdseed out of the cage, and there were tender green sprouts shooting up from within the brown shag forest. *Everything was trying to find the light.* That same night, the toilet overflowed and there was shit and sewage everywhere.

"Alright . . . that does it. We're out of here!" I told Tina, and we moved out the next weekend.

9
She's Come Undone

You need chaos in your soul
to give birth to a dancing star.
—Friedrich Wilhelm Nietzsche

I loved our new apartment. I began painting the walls, bought new furniture. God knows where any sense of style and taste came from in me, being raised in such poverty, but it was as if there was an innate part of me that had to create beauty. It was flooded with light, and despite having to carry bags of groceries up a flight of stairs, I somehow felt as if this new environment was symbolic of dues paid in a world of darkness. Little did I know.

To me, we had moved up to another level. I settled into my routine of bi-weekly visits to Hildegard, and that one day less a week felt like a big stride forward. Although it had been almost six years since I last saw Ed, I still thought about him a lot. I buried myself in work and very seldom dated. Weekends were spent doing mounds of paperwork, writing orders, and, once in a while, smoking a joint and getting lost in scrubbing the grout between the tiles with a toothbrush while listening to George Benson's song titled "Masquerade." What a mess.

I had no idea of what was around the corner or of the life-changing events that must have had my soul waiting in a state of higher evaluation. On one level, I wanted to check out permanently, but if ever there was an exit, what was about to happen was it. Funny what goes on in the inner realms that we are so damned oblivious to in our outer world.

It started with physical pain. I wound up in the hospital with a bowel blockage and, through exploratory surgery, the doctors discovered that my intestines had grown onto my liver. A cyst had ruptured, creating a condition called peritonitis, and I was literally hours away from dying.

I begged the doctor to give me a hysterectomy. I wanted all of my reproductive organs cut out. I felt as if everything that was ever punishing or hurtful seemed to stem from this one source of absolute vulnerability. I thought if I could have it all cut out, then I wouldn't hurt so much. Once I found out that the dye they used to trace the blockage could still get through my Fallopian tubes, I insisted, despite my doctor's concern about my age, that he cut my tubes. It was an angry, defiant act, and it was my way of saying, "Fuck you! If I can't have kids, it will be by my own choice, not because of some disease!"

I made it through the peritonitis and subsequent surgery, but now work was becoming unbearable. I'd take home stacks of inventory books to write up orders on the weekends, and wanted to shoot the mailman for delivering what seemed like a five-pound stack of memos from New York every week, most of which was useless information but had to be gone through. But then my life took another unusual twist. It was as if a tree with roots in another dimension dropped a leaf that floated into my world, carrying with it the promise of change.

A friend and fellow coworker went to a psychic and

called me with a message. "It was strange," she said. "The psychic started reading you. She said to me, 'You work with a woman with short, dark hair who hates her job. She should be doing makeup. I see a lot of movie stars and celebrities, and a salon is where she will get her start.'"

I immediately made an appointment with the psychic. Her son, a young black man in his late teens, opened the door. He was muttering something about the Lord, like a chant that he repeated to himself. I quickly surveyed the room and sat down on a white couch that was covered in plastic. He sat on the chair, rubbing his hands together nervously and rocking back and forth while his black eyes darted from me to the wall to his hands and back to me, all the while chanting, "The Lord has given me a gift. Do you see my gift? He's blessed me. That's right, he's blessed me. Do you see that for me? Yes, sir, the Lord has given me a gift. . . . You see that for me?"

"Ah, . . . yeah, sure," I said.

Just then his mother walked into the room, a pretty woman with a pleasing manner, as meticulously dressed and manicured as her plastic decorated living room. "You almost died," she said matter-of-factly. "Don't borrow trouble. Your intestines have healed beautifully. I see you've met Jerome." I stood up. "Ah, . . . yes," I stammered. "He's . . . gifted."

I followed her down the hall and into a room filled with religious icons, then sat in a chair and listened as she began to recite the Lord's Prayer.

I listened intently to what she said to me after that and made notes, although a lot of what she said didn't make sense to me at the time. She said, "I see a man who loves you, but he is afraid for you to find something out; he's afraid he's going to lose you. He can go both ways," she continued, "and there is a woman wearing a red dress and she chases him; she doesn't stop. . . . A red dress, I see a red dress. She wants him. This makes it hard for him. She is relentless; she won't leave him alone," she continued. She spoke more about my desire to be a makeup artist and how, although it would be up and down at first, it would be the right move.

That encounter changed the direction of my life, and after great contemplation and despite tremendous fear, I took the leap off the cliff. I was letting go of all the trappings—the financial security, the company car, the bonus—and turned down a job offer to work in marketing in New York. There was no financial security in what I was about to do, and I was starting at the bottom. And it wasn't just me; there was my daughter to consider. Getting up everyday going to my current job felt exhausting; sitting writing order after order was beyond boring. I longed to create beauty, and I loved the art of makeup; the face to me was like a blank canvas. Even so, a move to New York was too fear-based for me, and I guess something in me knew on some level my life would have changed drastically in a direction that would have left me tuned out and cold, successful at my job but miserable in my heart. I was terribly afraid of the poverty if I couldn't succeed. I had been saturated with that feeling as a child and a teenager. The bottom line was, it became too painful not to take the risk. "Just do it." I was scared beyond the promises of change. When was change ever easy anyway?

I was still seeing Hildegard, even though I had cut the sessions down to twice a week, and just as Virginia the psychic had stated, I went to work in a salon and took a financial dive into the dumpster.

If I would have known then the ride I was about to take, I would have buried myself in like a sand flea. My life was about to change drastically; I call it "getting hit on top of the head with the cosmic hammer." "Did she get it yet? No? Okay, let's whack her again!"

Me

This is how it transpired: In 1979, I met the man who would change the course of my life. I was thirty-two; he was forty-one, and he electrified my whole being. He was a plastic surgeon, and I had met with him to discuss teaching his post-operative patients how to apply make-up. We laughed a lot, and I could tell that he was attracted to me. He called me three weeks later and asked me to dinner. He kept asking me very personal questions, ones I felt were hard to answer, and I remember that the underside of the tablecloth was looking like the only place to hide. I was thankful for the dimly lit room, the ambience of which help to conceal my cheeks, which were becoming heated and flushed. I couldn't remember any man affecting me that way.

He leaned over the table, put his hand on top of mine, and said quietly, "You are most gorgeous when you are vulnerable." I fought silently to regain control, for I was feeling completely exposed and naked. I don't know what it was about him that made me so shy in his presence; it felt as if this man could look at me in such a way that he could touch me beyond my defenses. When he walked me back to my door, he said. "I'll call you when I get back from New York."

"Call me when it feels right," I said.

He stopped at the landing of the stairs, turned around, and grinned at me, "I'll call you in a week."

"There is something so fragile and vulnerable about you," he said one night while we were in his living room. "You will have to ask me to make love to you. . . . You will have to make that decision."

In my life, I don't think I have ever felt so shy. It was as if there was nothing around to shield or protect me. I didn't want to go home; I wanted to lie with him, I wanted to feel close to him, but I didn't want to have to ask him. I got up from the couch, walked into the kitchen, and stood by the stove, dunking a tea bag for what seemed like forever, and mustered up the courage to say, "Stephen, I want to spend the night with you." I don't think that it was above a whisper.

"Outstanding!" he said, as walked into the kitchen and put his arms around me.

I felt alive with Stephen; he was everything that I had ever wanted in a man. He was kind and sensitive, gentle, with a wonderful laugh, and he took tremendous care and pride in his work. He seemed content in the life that he had created, and he thrived on ritual and routine. It was his meticulous manner and attention to detail that made him such an excellent surgeon.

Sunday mornings were always my favorite. I would sit on a stool, wrapped in his robe in the kitchen next to the counter, not saying a word, watching him go through his ritual of grinding the coffee beans, measuring the exact amount of grounds in the filter, and wiping the water off the outside of the glass carafe before he poured the water into the container. He'd always stop and look at me, and then would walk over and pull me close to his chest. If I could have melted into him I would have.

If ever I felt a sense of well being, it was then.

There are those fleeting moments of grace when the aching and the longing are filled, and contentment takes its place.

But a sequence of events that was less than mysterious was about to take place, and it would be months before I was able to see with any type of clarity that they had, indeed, been divinely orchestrated.

I seldom went to Stephen's office during the week, simply because of my personal views concerning his work; I just felt that it was wrong to interrupt someone that you were involved with, or, at least, wrong to make it a habit. I had to have minor surgery on my eye, and Stephen had set up the appointment for me with a doctor in the same complex. He told me to make sure and stop by the office so we could have dinner before returning to his home. The only time I went in his office was on Sunday mornings after breakfast when he did dictation for an hour or so. It was close to the time when he would be finishing up, so I took a seat in the waiting room instead of going back to his office as I normally would.

I sat down next to two very beautiful black girls, models I was sure. One was wearing a red dress, which I didn't even think twice about. Stephen spotted me and waved me into the other room with "I'm almost finished, Sweetheart, go into my office." I went into the bathroom, and one of the models and I started talking. When Nita learned that I was a make-up artist, she wanted to introduce me to her friend, the other model, Sherry— the one wearing the red dress. They were stunning. I found myself thinking, "God, it must be so hard for Stephen not to cross that line of temptation when he is confronted with women who are so beautiful." Sherry was primping and fussing with her appearance to the point that I thought it odd, as she had not yet seen

Stephen for her post-operative checkup because he was still with another patient. "Hey Sherry, I want you to meet Athena. She's a makeup artist."

Sherry barely looked up from the lipstick she was applying. Her dark eyes glanced quickly in my direction and back to the mirror for more primping. "Yeah, great," she said. "We should get your card."

Nita seemed embarrassed by Sherry's lack of enthusiasm at the meeting and asked for one of my cards. "I have a photo shoot coming up in a few weeks. Would you be interested in doing my makeup?"

"Yes, I'd love to, Nita. Here's my card. Give me a call with the details."

I was waiting in Stephen's office, thumbing through a magazine, when he walked in. He gave me a big hug and laughed when I said, "Good God! Those women were drop dead gorgeous! Makes me feel like a can of Alpo dog food!"

A few weeks passed and Nita called inquiring about my availability for a job she had been booked on. I liked Nita. She seemed laid back and real, and it was easy to have a conversation with her. I was in the process of applying makeup for her photo shoot and curiosity killed the cat. I wanted to know why they were there to see Stephen in the first place. I inquired in a way that wouldn't seem too obvious. She didn't know that I was dating him, nor was there any reason to bring it up. "Both of you are so beautiful," I said. "Surely you couldn't have needed any plastic surgery."

"Oh no, not me," Nita replied. "I just went with Sherry; he did her nose. She's dating him and is crazy about him. I told her that she's nuts, that it's not cool for her to date her doctor."

I was stunned. Inside, I was shaking like a leaf, in a total state of confusion. A friend of mine who was a nurse had told me a few weeks earlier that she had heard through the grapevine at the hospital that Dr. Madsen said that he was dating a thirty-two year old that he was thinking about marrying. At the time, I assumed it was me. He used to love to tease me, and delighted in making me blush. "God! You are so gorgeous that I could marry you just to look at you!"

"Stop teasing me!" I'd reply back. I could feel the heat rise in my face, and he would just laugh, watch my reaction and then pull me close to him.

Now I was confused, in love, and afraid. He had told me on more than one occasion how fragile and vulnerable I was, and I guess with him I was. All I knew was that I had never felt so alive in my life, nor had I ever met a man that could take my breath away like he did.

I didn't want him to feel pressured, because I felt we never "own" anyone, but I needed now to know, and I was afraid that everything was about to come undone. The ground beneath my feet felt as shaky as my insides.

I finally mustered up the courage to call and confront him. I told him that I had heard something that was confusing to me, without telling him what it was that I had heard. I also said that, if it were true, that it was okay, I just needed to know how to gear myself emotionally.

"You did the right thing," he said, with a little apprehension in his voice. "Now, what did you hear?" When I told him, he got instantly defensive and said, "I have to go." I had the distinct, intuitive feeling that he had to have time to get his story straight. I felt sick. He was right—I had allowed myself to become vulnerable. I felt as if my world, which had of late been one of elation, was, within seconds, turned upside down.

He called me a week later, and as soon as I said, "Hello," he told me that "there is no one else." I had been in the process of writing him a letter at the time that he called, in which I told him that he was worth every mile of the drive, and that, yes, I was too vulnerable but that was okay, because what he gave me was worth the risk. I wrote that I felt as if he had misjudged my capacity for understanding; he was not mine to own—and I meant that. I told him this on the phone, and he seemed relieved.

Still, something was not right, and I couldn't put my finger on it, but I could feel it. He had had a life-long friendship with a man who lived in Europe and would visit him a few times a year. I had met him once, and looking back, thought he was a bit feminine, but on the other hand, who was I to judge?

I felt myself going into a total state of anxiety. Where does it come from? I couldn't understand why this so-called "God" would tease me with everything I had ever wanted in a man, only to take him away within what seemed only seconds. I was angry and frightened. I didn't understand what was happening, but I knew there was more that I didn't know. I thought back to one night when we were in bed. Stephen was troubled about something, and he was lying on his side. It was very late, but I knew that he wasn't asleep, as he had continued to toss and turn. I propped myself up on my elbow, touched him lightly on the shoulder, and said, "Whatever it is, honey, the darkest hour is just before the dawn." He turned over and reached for me, took my face in his hands and kissed every part of my face over and over again, at first with intensity, and then with such tenderness. . . . I'll never forget that beautiful outburst of emotion. I loved him so much, and when he did that, I knew that he loved me, too, and I couldn't talk, nor could I have stopped the tears from rolling down my cheeks; it was one of those golden, silent moments where words were just not needed. The feelings said it all.

What is it about things coming in threes? People die in threes, events take place in threes. Is it like the straw that breaks the camel's back, that it takes just one more thing, the weight of an additional feather, to bring us to our knees?

In the end, it all transpired within 24 hours.

I had suffered a very acute attack of arthritis, and the pain was excruciating, beyond words. I've always shoved pain down. Emotional, physical—it made no difference. When I gave birth to my daughter, I stuffed a washcloth in my mouth to keep from screaming; for 48 hours before I went into the hospital for my exploratory surgery, I held my hand over my mouth and rocked back and forth to keep from crying. But from this I sobbed. The closest analogy would be to imagine having sprained ankles and being forced to jump off of a ten-story building, landing with full force on your feet. Both my hands were clubbed under, and it was pure agony.

I felt like a cat that somebody had tossed in a dryer, dizzy from the ride. Nothing but *nothing* felt familiar to me anymore, and I was so dammed afraid that I wouldn't make it this time. Stephen had made arrangements for me to see a specialist, and the diagnosis was rheumatoid arthritis, one of the top five cripplers.

I drove home, God knows how—angry wasn't even the word for it. I had left my appointment book at home, and as I entered my apartment, I found that Tina, my daughter, had cut school. She was sitting there, doing her nails. I just exploded. I ranted and raved like a lunatic, and none of it was justified. None of it. "Go ahead," I shouted, "grow up to be like these damned Beverly Hills bimbos and marry some rich sucker to take care of you! Sell out and don't make *anything* out of yourself! Don't worry about it! Your mother is strong! She'll always take care of you!! I am *always* the fucking strong one! I don't *give* a shit!" I walked out of the room and slammed the door behind me.

Several hours passed. I unlocked the door and instantly spotted a note on the dining room table. I felt a rush of fear that pumped adrenaline through every vein in my body. My heart began to race in unison with a trembling over which I had no control. Fear has its important uses, such as releasing an outflow of adrenaline that helps one "run away faster." The problem was, I had nowhere to run.

The wrath of God, the belly of the beast, the brunt of the storm—none of these were descriptive enough. Stephen had turned into someone I didn't know, my body was in excruciating pain, and now, Tina was gone and I had driven her away. I had entered into the dark night of the soul, the shadow, the underworld. Nothing in my life would remain the same.

PART TWO

TO WAKE A SLEEPING GOD

10
Initiation-The Cosmic Hammer

If you have a point to make, don't try to be subtle or clever.
Hit the point once. Then come back and hit it again.
Then hit it again, a third time—
a tremendous whack.
—Winston Churchill

I swung open the door and was hit by a deadly silence. My heart began to pound fast and hard. It was too quiet. Something was wrong. I glanced around the room trying to find something that would tell me things were okay. But I didn't feel that way, and the gut always knows. I spotted a scrap of paper on the dining room table. You leave notes when you are going somewhere; you leave notes when you commit suicide. "Mom, you have never loved me and you have never wanted me. I don't want to live with you anymore." Strewn about were notes of telephone numbers and quotes of air and bus fares.

I opened the door to her room. Relief flooded through my body. She was alive and breathing. I looked at her fourteen year-old body sprawled across the bed. Her blonde hair was sticking to her face in wet strands, and the area around her eyes was red and blotchy. Exhaustion had overtaken her body as she had cried herself to sleep. I didn't know how to make things right; I didn't know how. A split-second realization hit me full throttle. In the back of my mind, I had known this exact moment would arrive. There was no ignoring it, there was no place to hide, there was no place to turn away. It was here. The ugly moment of truth. Retribution. It had begun with its own momentum. It had now materialized into chaos.

The thoughts were whirling through my mind in a vortex of fear. I knew beyond a shadow of a doubt that if I wasn't strong enough to tell her the truth about me, the real truth, she would wind up just like me: cold, detached, angry, and bitter. I knew this with every fiber of my body. I fell to my knees in my bedroom. Fear and remorse shaped a prayer with such deep sincerity, a cry for help—not for me but for my daughter: "I don't know who you are, I don't even know if you exist, but if you do, God, you have to be every word that comes out of my mouth and help me reach my daughter. I am begging for forgiveness; if life hurts this bad, then the *cause* lies within me. I am so sorry for all of the people I have ever hurt. If you are real, help me reach her," I sobbed.

"Tina, wake up. Come into the front room, I need to talk to you," I said as I shook her awake. She was disoriented and groggy. She followed me into the front room and sat next to me on the couch. I sat there, shaking inside, and I could feel my lips begin to quiver as I tried to speak, and I felt the tears stream down my cheeks.

There is a type of terror that is so masked with confusion; it is a time when everything that is familiar is blown to hell. I felt like I was free falling in space, and I didn't know where I was going to land.

I looked at my daughter and thought to myself, *She never asked to be born . . . she didn't deserve the type of emotional neglect that I had inflicted upon her for fourteen years.* I spilled my guts out to her. I told her things I never told another human being—things even that I could never face about myself. "Tina, all of my life, I have never wanted to live. I have been so unhappy inside of myself. I thought I had to be strong and hard to survive. I have been so afraid of loving, because it just seemed anytime I really loved somebody, I would always get hurt. Do you remember the time that we were driving somewhere in the car and you asked me, 'My father really hurt you, didn't he, Mom?' I told you, 'Yes, he did,' and that's all I said about it. Do you remember that?"

"Yes," she replied.

"Well, there is more to the story than that. There are certain things I left unsaid. I loved your father so much, and although he lived in another state, he would make the four-hour drive every few weeks, and this went on for a few years. I remember a time when I was late with my period and he actually got mad when it started. He really did love me, Tina. He broke up with me for three months once; this was right before I got pregnant with you. He thought he had to go into the service and felt it unfair to tie me down, so he broke the engagement, and I returned his ring. A few months later, a friend of mine set me up with this guy; we double-dated and had a good time, and we started dating and I slept with him two weeks before your father and I got back together. I didn't know how to say no.

"Your father never did go into the service; he didn't pass the physical. That same weekend that we went back together, and we began making plans to get married. He wanted to get married that summer, but I had one more year of school left, and I wanted to graduate. I got pregnant that weekend. Things began to taste funny, and I felt panicked at the thought that I might be pregnant. I saw your father a month or so later and he guessed by the way that I was acting that I might be pregnant. He said, 'Don't worry, I'll come down this weekend and we'll tell your parents and get married.' I was so relieved."

I reflected back to the weekend, beginning late morning, standing on the cement ledge of our front porch, full of anticipation, peering off into the distance, my hand cupped over my eyebrow, shading the glare of the noonday sun, hoping to spot his red Corvette as it headed down the one-way street to our house. It never came.

"I was terrified when I found out I was pregnant; I didn't know who the father was. I couldn't tell Mom; she always told us that it was important for us to be virgins when we got married. I was afraid she'd find out. I was a junior in high school, and I did not want to be pregnant. It wasn't as if we were having unprotected sex because we weren't and I was on birth control when I became pregnant with you. I remember the moment I gave birth, and they laid you on my stomach before they cut the cord. Oh my God, she has his mouth. In one sense, I was relieved to know that you were indeed your father's child, and in another, I felt as if you would be a constant reminder to me. I didn't want to be a mother, not like this. Adoption was out. . . . Mother wouldn't hear of it. 'Every time you would walk down a street and see a child, you would wonder if it was yours.' Abortions were illegal, and highly dangerous, and it was a complete social taboo to be an unwed mother. I just felt numb. I remember, Tina, lying in the hospital bed crying and making a very conscious decision to turn off emotionally.

"I never told anyone about not knowing until I gave birth. It made it easy for me to play the victim, and my deception filled me with a hate that has damned near destroyed me, not to mention the damage it has caused you.

"The friend who set me up with the guy that I dated before your dad and I got back together had called him at a later time and told him, 'It's not yours; don't marry her." I only found this out about seven years ago, when your father came down to see me, and wanted to try again. I never could tell him the truth even then; I would have had to give up my game, and I didn't know how to change. Deep inside, I knew what I had been doing was destructive, but it was easier not to face it. I simply took the easier way out. It allowed me to stay in a state of self-justification that fed my inner turmoil and anger, which I projected on everyone, including you."

I told her how I felt growing up, the molestation, all of it; feeling suicidal, feeling things but afraid to let them out, feeling emotions for her deep inside, but not knowing how to express or release them. I didn't love myself; how could I love others? I sobbed, and so did she. "You know what, Mom? That must have been hard for you. This makes up for all of those years," she said. We sat and cried, holding each other, going through a mound of Kleenex. Where in God's name do all of the tears come from? Talk about a monkey on your back. I was riddled with guilt and self-hatred.

My head was throbbing; my nose felt raw from the Kleenex. We were silent. We had both exhausted our-selves. Me, from releasing years of feelings, and Tina from taking it in. I felt weak, and I know she did too. I sat there emotionally drained—staring, almost trance-like—and then the strangest thing happened. I felt a veil being lifted from my consciousness, and I found myself looking clearly into a pool of reflection.

Within a fraction of a second, this filthy murky pool of brown mud like water became clear; I was being shown with crystalline clarity that life had no choice but to return to me *exactly* what I had been doing to others. This I not only saw, because it was being shown to me, but I *saw it,* with a new level of comprehension. "Oh my God," I said aloud. "I understand." The exact moment I uttered those words, *a golden ray* came flooding into the room and *dusted everything with gold.* I understood karma, without ever having studied it. Hell, I hadn't even known what the word meant, but I did now. I saw that I had spent my whole life pushing people away, pushing love away. And now that there was something I loved and wanted, life was pushing me away. It was the only way I could understand what I had created and the effect it had on the rest of life. I understood fully, "What you sow, so ye shall reap," and "Do unto others as you would have others do unto you." I was reaping the harvest of what I had planted.

I felt, within my heart, almost a bursting, feelings of motherly instincts, things I had always wanted to feel for my child but never could or would allow myself; it all came flooding out. I wanted so desperately the chance to make it up to her, although I knew in my heart I never could. What was done was done. I couldn't stop crying, and this new comprehension felt like a curse.

The next morning, Tina told me that she had a dream in which I had died. How profound. She had cut the cord from me. My mind instantly flashed to a prediction a clairvoyant had told me about three months earlier. At the time, none of it made sense. He said, "Your mother is going to die, and you need to make amends with her, and if you are strong enough to do this, where your karma with her is concerned, it will elevate you, plateau after plateau, in this lifetime."

I felt with every fiber of my being that somehow I was being tested by a force that I didn't understand, by events that overwhelmed me, and I didn't understand what was happening. I knew that if I was not strong enough to love Tina, love her enough to let her go, that somehow I would be failing a test. Intuitively, I knew it, and I wished to God I didn't know.

Tina wanted to move back home to Chico, to be around the familiarity of family. "I want to live with

Charlie Mom; I don't want to live here anymore." Charlie had been part of our family since we first met in junior high school. Our friendship became cemented by a makeup mirror passed between the two of us until our math teacher; Mr. Roberts leaned over my shoulder with his foul breath grabbing the mirror from my hand. Who would have thought she would have become such an integral part of our lives. Tina was a sickly baby, cried constantly and seldom slept for any length in duration. When all else would fail we'd pile her in the backseat of my Volkswagen Bug and drive her through Chico Park until the vibration of the car put her to sleep.

This wasn't the first time Charlie would come to our rescue. When Ed and I broke up and I was such an emotional mess living in Sacramento it was Charlie who said, "Let me come and get Tina while you get yourself together, she can live with me and go to school." That was one of those rare times that my wisdom knew it was the right thing to do and I was ever so grateful at her intervention in such a tough time. She loved Tina and Tina loved her. In most ways she was the mother figure for my daughter, and I knew Tina looked at her through those eyes. Now, Tina had called Charlie and the wheels were in motion, the bags being packed. I wanted her here with me but it was too late. I called Stephen to see if he would go to the airport with me. I thought I'd fall apart if I had to do it by myself. I was desperate. Three times I dialed his number, and three times the line went dead.

My sister Susie called from San Francisco; when I answered the phone, I knew she could hear the turmoil in my voice. She said with concern, "I'm worried about you. Are you going to be okay? Why don't I fly down and go to the airport with you?" I could feel the floodgates begin to open up again. "No, Susie, I can't explain this to you. All I know is that somehow, I'm being tested, and if I don't do this alone, I'll fail. I don't understand what is happening and I am scared."

With daybreak, I tried to steel myself for the inevitable. What I knew to be familiar was no longer recognizable. The facade had been stripped away, the ugly truth of who I was and what I wasn't or never had been was exposed for what it was: sad, frightened, and out of control. The real truth was, I had always been out of control.

It was time to leave for the airport. All the way there, I prayed. "Please God, just let me make it back home. I can't fall apart there. Not there." Once Tina's luggage was checked in, we went to the gate and waited in awkward silence. The state of unease was unbearable, and when her flight was called, my heart began to race. We hugged goodbye and I told her, "I love you." It took everything I had to hold back the tears. If I couldn't control my emotions like an iron vice, I felt I would fall to the floor and lay there sobbing like a strand of limp spaghetti.

She looked so small, yet at the same time strong, as she walked towards the entrance of the gate. Before she entered, she paused, then slowly turned around and gave me a long look. If a picture could paint a thousand words . . . her face said it all. Tina never opened her mouth, but I heard, loud and clear, every word she was thinking. "Are you going to be okay, Mom?" I forced a smile and waved, "God help me, I don't know . . . . I don't know." I damned near ran to the car, and when I reached home, I couldn't get that key in the lock fast enough.

I threw myself on the bed and sobbed out sixteen years of garbage. I didn't know how to right the wrongs, how to rewind the clock to start over again. I don't know what is worse, living with the feeling of disappointment or knowing that I had been the source of so much disappointment and pain for others. The bedspread was soaked with tears; I was exhausted. Tina's gone, Stephen's gone. I must have fallen asleep, for the next thing I knew, I found myself climbing straight uphill, completely vertically up the side of a cliff. I hung dangling by my fingernails, dug into the dirt an eighth of an inch from the top of the ledge. I felt myself begin to slip. There was no strength in my body; my muscles were weak and burning, and I wanted to let go and freefall through space. "I can't make it. . . . I can't make it. . . . It's too hard. . . . I can't make it."

This wasn't a dream. I don't know where I was but it was lucid, real and I was in another dimension. All of a sudden, I pulled myself up and I found myself standing on a new plateau, where everything looked unreal and different, for it was unlike anything I had ever experienced on Earth. The beauty was indescribable. It was green, lush and alive. I stood there for a moment looking around. I don't know whether I was in shock or awe, or perhaps a bit of both. I turned my head to my right, and there, some thirty feet away, I saw my father walking towards me. There was a calm about him, and his eyes held a peace and radiance that I had never witnessed before. In my sorrow and despair, I knew he was aware that I was hanging on to life by a thread. He opened his arms to me, and as I entered them, I was enveloped like osmosis in his compassion of understanding. I laid my head upon his chest, and as he held me close, I could *feel a light* emanate from his presence. As it entered my body and touched my heart, it flooded every part of my consciousness, mind, body, and soul with a light of pure unconditional love—and that white light held within it absolute knowingness of how much he loved me, and always had. "Daddy! You really do love me!" I woke up sobbing.

My father had been dead for thirteen years.

The following day, swollen eyes covered by dark glasses, I stopped for a cup of coffee in a tiny restaurant in Westwood. I sat at the table, thinking about all that had transpired. I didn't know how to make sense out of it or anything else that happened within the last 48 hours. *Where was that place that I went,* the place in which my father dwelled? All I knew was that it was the most beautiful place I had ever seen, and I didn't want to come back. It was lush and green, and the foliage was filled with a shimmering radiance and light that made everything more translucent, vivid, and luminous. There was a heightened sense of awareness, a fluidity of thought and feeling, and everything seemed to be responsive to that connectedness.

The waiter brought my coffee, and as I lifted the cup to my lips, my eyes glanced above me. To my surprise, I found I was sitting directly under a large poster of Edward G. Robinson, the actor. I caught my breath and turned to a mass of goose bumps. My father, the spitting image of Edward G. Robinson, even down to the cigar in his mouth, had been asked on more than one occasion for his autograph, and whenever a film would come on with Edward G. Robinson, it never failed to make me feel wistful and sad. I always felt my father's struggle of feeling like a failure; my father, Diamond Jim, who once lit his cigars with hundred-dollar bills, died a pauper with a $1.38 in his pocket. I paid for my coffee and I glanced one more time at the poster. I wanted to soak the image into every cell of my body. I reflected back to my father, leaving the house with his suitcase in hand. He didn't know where he was going back then and now, neither did I.

Der Ruth, after i arive too Red Bluff sign that too go too work the onle Pay $12 a day dockot. Plees sanme my clos. too creyhound Pres Tobot. poot my name

J V James

It was an awful time. It seemed as if I had backed myself into a corner and there was not a sixteenth of an inch to move, turn, or maneuver. I was afraid of going back into that dark place again, where I couldn't be reached, and I felt as if I was being dragged down a black vortex and the suction was too great, for my psyche felt as atrophied as the muscles of a paraplegic. I wanted to keep feeling . . . and I knew that if I didn't have the truth to make sense out of it, then I couldn't make it. I never fought as hard for my sanity as I did then. The easiest thing in the world would have been to let go and to go back to what I had been.

I called Stephen and told him that I had to talk to him. Driving down the coast to his house was a blur, driving home was a blur, and what had transpired in between was a blur. Jesus, only to have some clarity. He sat in a chair, almost like he was afraid to get too close to me. "Help me, Stephen," I cried, "I am begging you to give me a reason, tell me something that makes sense out of all of this. I have to know why, or I can't make it, and I am afraid. I want to keep feeling, but I feel as if 99% of me is slipping into a black hole that I'll never be able to climb out of. I don't want to turn off again. I am begging you to help me, tell me something, please help me."

He stared at me, his eyes full of fear; then he said slowly, choosing his words carefully, "A relationship between a man and a woman is very difficult. A relationship between two men is much more difficult." I heard him, yet I didn't hear him. I couldn't focus, my mind was whirling in a vortex of confusion, and I felt a feeling of anxiousness and impending doom take over my psyche.

I grabbed my purse and ran for my car. I could feel him standing there in the driveway, watching me drive away. I wanted to keep driving forever. Anywhere other than home, where I could escape the inevitable of being alone with what I had done. I was grateful it was night; I was grateful that people in other cars couldn't see my blotchy red face, and I wanted to drive forever. I replayed his comments in my head: "A relationship between a man and a woman is very difficult. A relationship between two men is much more difficult." It hit me with full impact. "Oh my God,... he's bisexual!" I had heard him, but I hadn't heard him. I didn't know what to feel, what was real. Everything was too confusing. Once again, the statement, "It is what it is," played in my mind. What do you do with that?

"*What* in the world is going on with you?" Hildegard asked with concern. She sat back in the chair and listened intently. "You know," she said, "for three-and-a-half years, I never thought I could help you. You were the toughest piece of stone I ever tried to crack. Maybe your judgment in men *is* all fucked up." "No!" I screamed at her. "If you have tried to teach me to go with my gut feelings, and I felt that this was a good, kind man, then in God's name, what was all the pain for?" I never saw her again.

There was absolutely nothing in my world that was familiar to me. Nothing. I couldn't stop crying, deep gut-wrenching sobs, half the time just repeating to God how sorry I was. "Just make the pain go away," I cried, . . . all the while, still not believing in him. It is such a horrible feeling to feel lost.

I was fighting for my sanity in a new way that didn't make sense. I could sense that things had changed and that my life would never be the same, but I didn't know how to make it stop long enough to catch my breath. I felt like some black demonic force was trying to steal my soul, and I knew I was walking a tightrope and all it would take was one fragile breath to blow me off into a dark abyss from which my soul would never rise or see light again.

I knew it with everything in me.

There was nothing to do but pray. It wasn't a prayer; it was a desperate plea for my sanity, bargaining and begging, a cry for my soul. I felt whipped and defeated and I prayed and I prayed. It became my mantra, my chant, like someone in a mental institution that continues to rock and repeat the same word or sentence over and over again.

"Please help me to feel; don't let me shut off again. Give me strength. Help me to feel," I prayed. "The Lord is my Shepherd I shall not want, he maketh me to lie down in green pastures, he leadeth me beside still waters, he restoreth my soul."

I sat on the couch, mentally exhausted, and then the strangest thing happened. I felt a veil lift as I moved into a trance-like altered state. I was no longer in my body. My soul was hovering, then expanding, feeling massive, held by some unseen force. I was part of the universe, full of star systems and planets, whirling nebulae of light and dark at the same time. Suspended in space, I was being shown far below me, what seemed like a galaxy far away, no bigger than a quarter, a dark planet, unfamiliar and frightening. The giant hand that had been cradling me let me go, and I felt myself tumble through the blackness of space. I found myself surrounded by darkness, treading water, frantically looking around, trying to see through the fog. Nothing but nothing felt familiar. "Sink or swim." The voice came through loud and clear.

The dark night of the soul. The shadow self. The initiation. The crucifixion. What I had begun to see was how I had become my own victim. All the time I thought that I was making other people pay for my pain, for what had felt like great injustice done to me. Push them away, don't let them close. Isolate. Keep myself safe. From what? Certainly not myself. . . . there is a lot of truth in the idea that one can be one's own worst enemy. I was living proof of that. I suddenly had no sure footing, nothing stable or solid to stand on. Why did life have to hurt so badly?

I stuck with my prayer morning, noon and night, "The Lord is my Shepherd." I couldn't stop crying and I didn't know how to cope with another loss, let alone two. I escaped through sleep as much as I could, hated it when daybreak came and the reality of what had become fully etched in my consciousness came rushing forward and I had another day to deal with.

I wanted the opportunity to make it up to my daughter, but the bottom line was I couldn't bring the time back. It was gone forever. It was what it was. Period. I never gave her my time, I never gave her anything of me. I was busy being strong and removed, a workaholic, burying myself in diversion so as not to feel.

It must have felt terribly lonely for her. She didn't have a father, and she didn't have me, so she threw her love into that which would give it back unconditionally, animals. I remembered the first time I watched her bouncing up and down on a horse fat as an old cow, her green windbreaker flapping in the breeze, her feet barely secure in the stirrups. She found her niche, and it was from that moment her passion for animals became her refuge and haven from the disappointment of human relationships. She excelled quickly, taking lessons whenever she could, shoveling horseshit and cleaning barns in return for lessons and for the opportunity to spend her time where she felt most safe. I never went to the horse shows and events she participated in, never was on the sidelines taking pictures or telling her how great she did. I felt horribly ashamed of myself, thinking what I would give now to wind the clock backwards. Hindsight. I was getting everything I deserved.

The next few months passed in a blur. I did what I had to do to get through the day, all the while praying constantly because it was the only thing I had. I was blundering my way through a maze in the night, being lured by some unseen force that was intelligent beyond that which I could comprehend. I wanted to believe in God, yet everything up to this point told me that "This Presence" was uncaring for allowing all to transpire as it had. Still, I couldn't shake the feeling of something new being birthed. I began *feeling* the strangest need to get my house in order and I wondered perhaps if I was preparing to die. If so, I welcomed the thought. Even so, it was necessary to make amends with others I knew I had hurt or lied to. I had hurt countless men with my cold and detached manner, setting them up, taking pleasure in witnessing their pain at the lack of my response. It was safer hurting them before they could hurt me. I made them, all of them, pay for Tina's father's rejection of me, for being born into a place I didn't want to be, and for that which laid buried deep in my subconscious, still to be unearthed. I wanted to punish the force I said I never believed in . . . God. *I wanted to punish God for making me live.*

I had innately known, even in my darkest state of ignorance and confusion, that if I committed suicide, I would have to come back and live my life over again. I don't know how I knew this, I just did. I knew it would be a horrific and unforgettable tragedy for Tina, saddling her young psyche with the weight of even more abandonment issues, not to mention the feeling of unfinished business left for her to resolve the best she could.

It was a saving grace, this inner knowledge.

I didn't need to make a list of those I had to make amends with; I carried them around as weights in my consciousness. No matter how much I tried to push back and bury the discomfort of knowing I had wronged another into some corner of my mind, I knew in my heart what I had done. I thought a lot about the clarity of the insight and vision I was shown: "What goes around, comes around." So I contacted them, one after another, and made amends, all face to face when possible. It was hard. I felt the fear, but I asked God, "Be every word that comes out of my mouth."

"Tell the truth and the truth shall set you free."

I began to *feel* something different. Peace. I began to feel a sense of peace. I had written ten years before, "If I had the power to change the things I'd see, I'd change the girl inside the mirror who's staring back at me." And now, here it was . . . the transformation I'd hoped for.

I kept a journal, writing down my feelings. There was such sorrow in my soul. Where do all the tears come from? Painful insights became a cleansing, a purging of my psyche. I cried myself to sleep, only to wake up and repeat the process again. However, I began to feel a little lighter somehow. This purging, as it continued, began to replace itself with something new. And one day I wrote, "I think I am beginning to feel the presence of God."

There is a synchronicity that is flawless in its seamless way of bringing an event full circle. I am not sure if it is because I am moving into greater harmony with all life; I'm not sure if it is simply part of tying up loose ends, or if perhaps it is God's way of saying to me, "Trust. There is more to this divine plan than what you are aware of, or are even allowing yourself to be conscious of. Here I sit now, some twenty three years later, writing about my daughter leaving, looking at her walk down the corridor to board the plane, to get away from me. My phone rings, in 2003, "Mom, I just wanted to tell you how much I love you. I have felt all these walls and defenses around you begin to melt, and I really need you."

I was stunned. That's what I mean; there's a seamless magic that only God can orchestrate. Someone said to me recently that things don't always happen in our time frame, but God is always on time.

11

The Teacher Appears

*I cannot be awake for nothing looks to me as it did
before, or else I am awake for the first time,
and all before me has been a mean sleep.*
—Walt Whitman

I stood looking into the bathroom mirror. I was a mess. I couldn't stop crying, and I had to get myself to work. The brush felt like it weighed a ton in my hand, and everything seemed to take such an effort. It was an effort to breathe. "I can't do it," I said, as my arm fell limp to my side. I felt so internally weak, whipped, and beaten. I crumpled to the sink, blubbering. A friend of mine stood in the hallway looking at me and said, "You know, when I first met you, I thought you were one of the strongest women that I had ever met." I needed to hear those words, and to this day, I have never forgotten the way she said them, the look on her face as she said it, the feeling of exhaustion in my physical body, and how broken my heart and spirit felt.

My life was about to change forever.

Sean Kenney was a messenger. I liked him instantly when we first met, for I sensed something highly unusual about him. There was something about his presence that I couldn't put my finger on, but whatever it was, it made me feel good and attracted me like a moth to light. I felt as if I knew him, beyond our first time meeting. I understood nothing about reincarnation, not even the theory behind it, so that wasn't even a reference point. I just felt like I had known him before. Sean was the famous Winston Man with the beautiful blue eyes, great mustache, and cowboy hat who was plastered all over billboards and magazine ads that left women all over the country fantasizing about him. He was one of the kindest spirits I had ever met, and there wasn't a conceited bone in his body. I remember every detail about him. You never forget the one who gives you a key to freedom.

"You are ready for this," he said as he placed three books in my hands. I was ready for something, anything that could make sense out of what I had been going through, that could make sense out of my life. I felt as if I was preparing to die. But there was something so mystical about the events that had transpired, and in some ways I felt as if I was almost being transported to another planet, for all familiarity had gone out the window.

I curled up on the couch, opened up the first book— *The Original Unveiled Mysteries*—read a few pages, and started crying like a baby. I wept for in it was everything that I had always felt in my heart and could never find verbalized. I knew at that moment that I had the tools to go home to God. Here it was, confirmation of that which I had struggled with and against and that which I innately knew as truth. It was the only thing that made absolute sense out of my existence. All life manifest in form was God in action. It was only through our ignorance and misuse of this energy that its pure state was constantly interrupted, for allowed to flow undisturbed, we would experience peace, love, harmony, and abundance for that was the natural state of life. We were given free will to direct this energy through thought and feeling in any direction we chose.

I could never buy into the concept of organized religion. The idea of floating up through the clouds to pearly white gates, cowering and groveling at the feet of some massive God with a long white beard sitting in judgment of me left me cold. I couldn't believe that God, if He did exist, would be vengeful or cast my soul, no matter how misguided or lost I was, into a burning hell. That kind of fire and brimstone, hell and damnation was opposite to everything that I felt in the recesses of my heart. Nor could I believe that one could be a bonafide asshole here on earth, die, and go to heaven to be met by Saint Peter and enter into a state of eternal bliss, unaccountable. Even I in my ignorance innately knew that accountability didn't involve the "wrath of God."

It was in nature that I sensed a feeling of peace and tranquility, sitting by the creek's edge at the covered bridge in Chico, pouring my heart out on paper, as I had done as a troubled teenager. If there is a God, I would think to myself, it has to be closer to this. It was a feeling, and if that feeling existed in me, then this was closer to the truth of what God was, for there was nothing about fear, anger, rage, deceit, distrust, loneliness, or despair that felt natural. These were the inverse of everything that I innately knew, and had been born knowing. That knowingness was within me. That was the relentless drive, the searching, the longing to connect to the greater All—to connect once again.

It was strange that growing up in a household where God was virtually undiscussed, the only mention being a prayer of "Bless the potatoes and damn the meat; now all of us hogs sit down and eat." I remember going to church only once. My little sister, who had forgotten to put on underwear, and I crawled up on the old wooden bench directly in front of the preacher, and he shot a disapproving look in our direction as she bared her little butt trying to hike her leg up to reach the seat. My feet stuck straight out in front of me, as I wasn't very big, but I remember that I didn't like what I heard— or maybe it was the way he said it. Whatever, I never went back. Still, there was that little black Bible that I pushed around in my baby buggy along with my doll. It was as if this little book was the carrot that dangled in front of the donkey's nose and left its indelible mark in my consciousness.

Now, reading the book that Sean Kenney gave me, I had begun my journey back home . . . consciously. I can't help but feel that deep within the heart of all is that desire to connect and to go back home, even if we don't know what home is. There is that part of us that knows we are part of something. I don't believe that there is a person on this planet who can fulfill that desire besides God. Struggling with desire is hard. I know that I have searched relentlessly, through trying to be loved, trying to find that fulfillment in relationships with men, and I am always disappointed. And the fault doesn't lie with them; it lies with me and my expectation that they can make me feel whole, when they can't. I don't think that any human being can fill that hole within the self but with God.

All I know is that what I read made sense in every level of my being, and it confirmed what I had always felt, questioned, and pondered. All life was God. All energy was God in action. And I was responsible for how I used that energy, how I directed it through my free will. It was like seeing with new eyes. The "I am that I am." *Be still and know that I am.*

In my own quiet contemplation I began to think about statements that I had heard or read that never made sense, yet now they were beginning to become a little more clear, and it was like another veil was lifted from my consciousness. I began viewing the world with new eyes. *Be still and know I AM God.*

What began as a pursuit of, trying to connect with, something that felt so far away from me, came to fruition in this; all the while, it was the energy of God, the presence of all life that gave me the ability to think and to feel. It was the light-energy of God who beat my heart. *I AM the light that beateth every man's heart.*

I thought about the movie *The Ten Commandments* and when Moses went up to the mountain and God was talking to him through the burning bush: "What do I tell them?" "Tell them that I Am hath sent thee, for that is my name, a living memorial to all generations." What I discovered was that every time I said, "I am," I was directing the God force through me. I began to look at statements that Christ had said in a new way. "Of myself, I can do nothing; it's the Father within, the I AM who doeth the work." I was fascinated with them. *I AM the light that lighteth the world.*

I had always had this resentment and jealousy of Christ that I never understood and I had secretly carried around since childhood. I never understood the source of it, or why I felt jealous of him, I just knew I did. I had found myself in my private reflections thinking, "Why would you be the only one who could heal people? Why couldn't I? Why are you the only one who could walk on water and I couldn't? Why? Why could you feed the people and I couldn't?" I couldn't look at his eyes, and any movie of anyone being flogged or any television show that was shown around Easter of the crucifixion would make me bolt from the room like a rabbit trying to escape from a snare. I never understood these emotions, yet I couldn't deny that I felt them. And to make matters worse, I felt tremendous shame at even harboring these thoughts and feelings. I never told anyone about this; I just struggled with it throughout the years whenever I would ponder what God was or wasn't and how elusive and out of reach it all felt.

I always had trouble with the limitation of organized religion in almost every area, and to me that God would create "just one" who would possess all of these qualities and god-like abilities just never intuitively made sense to me. Yet there it was again, "Great things I have done, shall ye do also, and even greater things." If there was ever a statement that held the potential of hope and of possibility, that was it, and in my heart, it settled in its perfect place, in perfect balance. It was something that I innately knew, deep inside of me.

I am God? I am a god in the making? I was born in that divine image? What I gleaned out of it was the potential of becoming aware that I could raise my consciousness, but only by the self-conscious effort of redirecting my thoughts, feelings, and attention. Tall order, and hard to do, but my life had sucked up to this point, and I wanted a way out.

There is a saying that "when the student is ready, the teacher appears," and this teacher, this master on the invisible realms, could not have waited a second longer, as far as I was concerned. I was ready, willing, and able. The love I feel for the Ascended Master Saint Germain is indescribable and the gratitude, beyond words. I want to learn from those who have mastered the human element. I began to meditate, applying the method that he taught, and as clumsy and foreign at it as I felt, just as he stated, I began to feel the difference. Meditation, he said, really meant feeling, and the more I learned that I could begin to quiet the chatter of my outer mind, the more I began to feel a growing sense of peace. I holed up and studied every free moment that I could, and my meditations began to take me deeper and deeper into the mystical.

I didn't understand all that was transpiring; I just knew that another world had opened up to me, and I wanted it to reveal more of itself to me. I sought answers; I wanted answers to everything I had always questioned, and I was going to continue to pull on this thread, as I had a hold of something that was producing results. It wasn't something that I had to believe in because I was told it existed; I began to experience firsthand the reality of it as a result of my application, and I didn't need any more than that. I had something viable to work with.

My world was changing rapidly, and my meditations, rich and deep, began to produce spontaneous visions that always held keys, not fully understood at the time, but somewhere down the line, the comprehension of what had transpired and why it transpired was revealed. I became quite adept at reaching that state of stillness quickly, and I had a series of past lives that were shown to me in rapid succession over a very short period of time.

I never entered into meditation with a specific goal in mind other than to quiet myself and to try to find a sense of inner peace. I needed to heal the fragmentation of my soul, and I wanted to feel a deeper connection with God, with the master within. Reveal yourself to me, I would invoke. Reveal yourself to me. Exploring the world of the unseen simply came with the territory, in my case.

I lay down on the couch one afternoon to meditate, and somewhere in the process, I had drifted off. I was awakened by a vibration that originated from the center of my being and, as I opened my eyes physically, I saw my astral body of pure light lift and begin to separate from my physical body. Although I couldn't move a muscle, I was completely aware, as I was somewhat caught between realms. It was like someone or something had tied helium balloons to my ankles, and my astral body began to rise feet first. I could see the density of my physical body and the surgical greens that I was wearing, and as I looked at the lower half of my body, its counterpart, a finer blueprint in pure white light, surgical greens and all, quickly floated up at a ninety-degree angle, the soles of my light body feet pointing straight up at the ceiling. I did what first came into my consciousness and that was to call to my father, and immediately, it stopped. I didn't understand what had happened, and it frightened me; however, it wasn't long before the experience would repeat itself.

I was floating at the ceiling, slowly bouncing back and forth like a big blimp, looking down at my body, which lay sleeping below me. I felt like the Stay Puft Marshmallow Man in the movie *Ghostbusters* as he bounced and lumbered his way through the streets of New York City: "Don't get scared," I thought to myself, "or you'll go back into your body." I had awakened on many an occasion in the middle of the night from the vibration of my astral body as it began separating from its physical counterpart. Slowly, I became more comfortable with the sensation and began to relax into the experience. I thought of my sister Judy who lived in Eugene, Oregon. "I want to see her. I wonder how you build up speed up at this," I thought to myself, as my body doubled over and floated through the wall into the kitchen. I floated back into the front room and saw my brother's soul, who obviously had come to visit that night, and I remember that there was a form of a panther in the hallway by my bedroom, but I knew that it was the soul of my cat, Paula.

It seemed to me that all kinds of doorways into the realm of the unseen were opening—not that I understood them, by any means, but I was excited about learning about this whole new universe, and I began to give myself over to it completely, but in a way that I think now wasn't really healthy, as my attention was not on people or bridging my discomfort there. Now it seemed as if I had just been given a glimmer into the mind of God, the brilliance of the universe—and I wanted more.

This series of books, *The I AM Discourses,* by Saint Germain, had given me the key. They contained step-by-step tools to change my reality. The stories of mystical events that had taken place at other points of time in our civilization, how and why they fell, rang true for me. *Everything* in me responded and reacted to the information. I just knew that somewhere within my soul, I had the capacity to become greater, to become more magical, to feel more connected, to obtain super consciousness, to become one with God—no matter how long or how many lifetimes it took—and to finally find that which resonated so deeply within me that felt like shouting, "Yes!!!! I knew it!" I could have climbed a mountain and shouted to my human self, "I told you so, asshole!" Somewhere in me, I knew this stuff. I was elated, and when that door cracked open and that shaft of light flooded through, it flooded my consciousness with hope and a sense of truth.

If it wasn't a possibility to become one with God, then what was the purpose to living? I couldn't believe that this was all there was to life living on the Earth, seeing the destruction and the hatred, the anger, the filth and degradation that we lived in, the sorrow, the pain, all of it—the garbage that is put out through the media, the lack of care and concern, the irritation and the god-awful loneliness, the isolation. I know for myself that I was tired of feeling all of the above, tired of all the times that I have wanted to crawl off into a hole somewhere and push people away from me, wanting to shout at them, "Leave me the fuck alone!" And hating it at the same time, not being able to say internally how much I hurt or that I don't want to be alone, that I am afraid that I will die and feel that there is nothing more to life than moving through one disappointment to another. I resonated sadly with Peggy Lee's song titled "Is That All There Is?" I was tired of feeling numb, and tired of numbing myself from feeling as a form of protection. I was tired of hurting, and I was tired of knowing that it was the easiest place of all to get to and stay in, and that, by far, was the scariest thing of all.

I couldn't get enough. I studied the information every spare moment I could. I wanted to go home. My meditations began to produce vivid visions and always to my surprise, for when I would enter into that state of silence, it was simply to keep open that doorway and explore more of that which I was seeking to understand. I would enter into meditation with the thought, "Father, take me deep within thyself, and there instruct me and cause me to retain perfectly clearly all memory of that which I receive." That prayer was a clear intent. I visualized myself standing in the center of the sun, holding as long as I could in my mind's eye the brilliant white light flooding through my body. Sometimes I would go to a lagoon that was private and safe, all of my own creation. There I would take off my clothes and swim in the pool of white light water, breathing it in and feeling it cleanse the darkness out of my being. Sometimes I would stand under the waterfall of bubbling effervescent white light and feel it cascade through every cell of my body. At times I could hear messages from my spirit guides, but most of all, I just felt more peaceful afterwards, and God knows how I desperately needed that.

It was around that time that a series of visions began to happen, like opening a book to different times in history, and it always happened with spontaneous clarity, almost like a living, moving photograph, full of color, full of life, and there was always an instantaneous emotional wash that would surge through my body at the same time. These visions would "jolt" me back from that alpha state and leave me mystified as to why I had experienced it. But I knew, somehow, there must be a reason for it, as my reaction with each vision was strong. Once I set my intent with the clarity of my prayer and invocation, I simply tried to quiet my mind by repeating, "be still, and know that I am." I didn't understand that statement fully, but I wanted to, and that was enough for me.

I felt the muscles contract and push me through the dark opening, into light. There was a orange-ish red haze that clouded my vision like a film over my eyes. There were two dinosaurs; one was eating foliage from the tree, the other, a tyrannosaurus Rex, was close by. Jesus! That was strange! What the hell was that? My heart was pounding, as it completely caught me off guard. Some years down the road I was told that was my first incarnation upon the planet earth. That gives a whole new meaning to the term "old soul."

Another time, I had entered into a state of meditation once again when suddenly I saw an African male get beheaded. Later that same day, a man that I was dating at the time came over and said, "I just had this fascinating reading, and she told me that I was dating a woman whose daughter I had known in Egypt." He continued, "She said, 'This woman you knew in Africa, she had lost a position in a village through competition and went out into the wilderness, built a hut—that's where you met her. The two of you lived together until . . .'" I interrupted Bob at that point and said to him, "If she tells you that you were decapitated . . ." He stared at me and slowly finished his sentence: ". . . until," he said, "I lost my life through decapitation."

Although it seemed to me that these were "shown" to me quite closely together, I had no idea as to why or the reason behind the visions. I wasn't really frightened by them as much as I was fascinated, but as they continued, what I did glean from each vision was a sense that "something about this feels way too familiar." Each vision had its own unique feeling that accompanied it, a different "emotional wash" of some sort, whether the feeling was that of sadness, intense love, fear, reverence, or confusion. It was as if a gateway from one dimension of my conscious mind into another had temporarily been lifted or set aside for my viewing.

I was standing at the top of the Parthenon at the Acropolis in Athens, my pitch-black hair pulled away from my face. I was leaning against a marble pillar, and I was wearing a long white gown, off the shoulder, gold ties wrapped around my waist. I looked below to a soldier who had one foot on one stair and his right foot on the stair directly above it. He was resting his right arm on his knee. His feet bore sandals with knee-high leather wraps, his toga was white, and there was red material draped over the top of his left shoulder, secured by a medallion of sorts. I loved this man.

Upon my first trip to Greece, when I stood at the base of the Parthenon, I couldn't stop crying. I took several rolls of film of it; one would have sufficed. I knew I was home. I felt that way then; I feel that way now. That vision held an important key for me in my healing, but it would not manifest for several years. Still, it stirred within my consciousness a knowingness of a deep love, of sadness and loss. It was a pull in my heart and it was physical. The memory of it, recorded in my conscious mind and stirred from the depths of the subconscious, now sat in the back of my mind, awaiting exploration. The following vision flooded my emotional body with terror.

I saw a peasant woman standing in a road, and she watched her husband sitting on the back of a wagon as he was being taken away by two men. She knew she wasn't going to see him again and watched in horror as they slaughtered him a short distance down the road.

Another vision once jolted me of crystal blue water that held the body of a little boy, around seven, who had just drowned. It was as if a movie screen was completely filled with the blue of the ocean and I was witnessing, from beneath the surface, his body as it floated downwards, his right arm floating straight up as a last cry for help. It looked peaceful. Perhaps that explained the fear I have always had of the ocean and of its massive power. As a young girl, when I was dropped off for swimming lessons and the instructor forced my head beneath the water, I remember the panic as I gulped in a mouthful of water. After that, I always sat on the grass at the top of the hill, hidden from his view until the lessons were over.

Once I saw golden steps that led upwards to a doorway, which was flooded with light. There, upon a pedestal, stood a crystal that contained an eternal flame that burned without a visible source. It just danced in all its holiness.

12

The Baying Of The Hounds

*There are nights when the wolves are silent
and only the moon howls.*
—*George Carlin*

Psychically, just as the clairvoyant had predicted, I took off like a rocket ship. I pierced veils in ways I didn't understand, and it was as if any latent gifts or talents that had been tucked away in areas of my consciousness or subconscious had been stirred awake. In retrospect, I realized I had always been a little sensitive, having strange premonitions at times and experiencing other phenomena, such as the time when I saw my father the night of his funeral. But I never gave them much thought beyond the label of "strange" or "weird." Who said that truth is stranger than fiction? I had a dream around that time of giving birth to a baby with a flap of skin over its face, also known as a cowl. My daughter had told me that she had read in a novel that it represented the gift of clairvoyance. To be born with a cowl was to be born with a calling.

Whatever the reasons, there they were: visions, premonitions, and visuals, crystal clear and bizarre as hell. It seemed to me that a door had opened. I did not fully understand the hows or whys; it just did, and in this case, it would have been better had it remained shut. Somehow I had tapped into a dark realm, and the bottom line was that I was not fortified with enough light, enough understanding, or enough protection, and somehow a demonic force grabbed hold, in subtle yet dynamic ways. I just showed up, "B, D, and H": big, dumb, and happy, as I like to say. I didn't understand this new world by any means or all of the different polarities contained within it.

With Tina now living in Chico, I told a friend that she could stay in her room while she was in transition between apartments. Annie had gone off to a weekend in Hawaii with her boyfriend, and I, in turn, went to Oregon for a visit with my sister Judy.

I so loved my time with her and had been thoroughly enjoying our visit together until something weird happened. "What's the matter with you?" Judy inquired as she watched me pace back and forth in her living room. "I don't know," I said, "but *something* is happening to someone I know." I couldn't shake this feeling of anxiousness. It was so heightened and raw that it felt as if my whole body was responding to a level of fear, but I knew this feeling wasn't mine. I was just connected to someone else who was experiencing it. It wasn't even anticipation of impending doom; the doom was now a viable experience in someone's world. My left arm felt like it weighed a ton, and I held it close to my body with my right arm in an attempt to support it. It felt as lifeless as putting weight on a leg that had fallen asleep. The fear and anxiety was almost unbearable, and I began to cry. Finally, after few hours, it all began to settle down.

Upon my return to Los Angeles, the moment I opened the door to my apartment and saw Annie, everything shifted and I saw within her aura a Hispanic man with oily, pockmarked skin. I knew instantly what had happened. I could see it. She began to relay the story to me, telling me that while getting into her car at the airport, he had forced her at knifepoint onto the seat, pinning her left arm underneath her. When he looked into her eyes, he saw something in them and took off running. I know what he saw. She was a beautiful Eurasian girl who had been adopted out of an orphanage at the age of five. Her adopted father (if you could call him that) would sneak into her bedroom at night and began molesting her, which progressed to penetration and sex. This continued until her mother caught him in the act. She was twelve. Her mother locked herself in the bedroom for a few weeks, and then sent her daughter away to another home after screaming at her repeatedly what an ugly child she was. He became a born-again Christian fundamentalist, she became screwed up, and I in turn, connected up with this wounded bird with a gentle child-like laugh, a deep love for children, and a dream to be a teacher, floating somewhere between reality and fragmentation. When the rapist looked into her eyes, I knew exactly what he saw. The eyes are the mirror to the soul, and I am sure what he saw was a feeling that said her spirit could not fight the weight of one more assault. I have no doubt about that.

"You have got to go to the police," I insisted. "You have got to get this maniac off the streets before he kills and rapes another woman. You've got to do it for other women!"

"No . . . no . . . ," she said, somewhat dazed. "I think I need to go lie down for awhile." She was already escaping into La-La Land. I understood that kind of fragmentation. But I was agitated and upset that she wouldn't go to the police and went into my room to meditate and quiet myself down. I slipped into the silence, and after some time, a visual image like a Polaroid snapshot flashed in my mind's eye, and I felt myself shudder at the feeling that accompanied it.

I saw a man standing against a shiny metal background, wearing a white tee shirt and blue Levis, and there were two gloves hooked somehow to his belt on the left side of his body. He had short, blonde hair and sunken, red-rimmed eyes with dark circles. His skin color had a sickly ashen appearance to it. I saw a blue van, parked in the alley behind a yellow horseshoe-shaped apartment building. I instantly sat up in bed. "Jesus! What the hell was that?" I knew I had viewed something. I didn't know why, but I had a sneaking suspicion that I had opened the door into something dark just by the feeling of it all. I couldn't shake the sensation or the image, and I had no idea what the hell it was or why I saw it. There was some weird-o killing women at that time in L.A., and some months down the road, I was hired by a photography studio to do the make-up for an advertisement for the Los Angeles Police Department. I asked one of the guys from the police department at the photo shoot, "Hey, did they ever catch that guy that was killing those women?"

"Yeah, they did," the man replied.

"Tell me," I said, "what color of car was he driving?"

"He was driving a blue van."

A few days later I sat across from the two detectives at the police headquarters. I gave them a detailed description of the man that I had seen. Periodically, they would stop and make eye contact with each other, the one detective stood up and went into another room and came back with a snapshot. My accuracy blew me away. There he was, exactly as I had seen. He had worked in a facility that had a big boiler in it—thus, the shiny metal behind him. "Oh, and by the way, I saw this apartment building . . ."

The detective shoved a piece of paper and pencil

towards me. "Draw it," he said. I drew the horseshoe shape and said, as I finished the drawing, that it was yellow.

"That's where we apprehended him," he said slowly.

I could tell by the way they looked at me that they were intrigued. They didn't understand it nor could I explain to them how I saw what I saw. Somehow, when I sought to quiet myself down from my roommate's attacker, I had tuned in to the energy of a completely different man; however, both were identical in their intent to do harm. The universal laws of energy, frequency and vibration were new to me. I was barely comprehending the concept that whatever you focus on, you bring into your world. It is like going to a muddy fishing hole and throwing in the line—you can reel out some pretty ugly stuff and it can open you up to the sewage of the underworld. Little did I understand that my attention alone began to draw lower frequencies and vibrations. Like I said, the sewage of the underworld.

The Atlanta murders had seized the attention of the nation and I, like the rest of the people, followed it closely, as the terror was enormous. Talk about a dark force. I found myself responding to a call they had placed on the radio for the help of psychics with any information or leads. Just pulling on a thread of it, placing my attention on it out of curiosity, began to roll that small piece of thread into a ball of twine, and it grew larger in scope. There were a number of visions that flashed in my mind: names of towns, country roads, streams of water, and bridges and it wasn't long after that they would find bodies in areas that I had seen in my mind. I am sure they must have thought in their dealings with psychics that they were dealing with a bunch of crackpots, depending on their own personal beliefs or skepticism around the subject of the unseen so I wasn't sure I wanted to share the information I was getting.

I was frustrated with my new ability for I didn't know what to do with it, or how to incorporate it in my life. It was like being thrown in the driver's seat of a Ferrari when I was just learning how to drive a Volkswagen and still popping the clutch. I called UCLA and spoke to someone in their parapsychology department. I found their attitude was somewhat condescending, which just added to my frustration. Intuitively, I knew that working in the area of crime was not something that I wanted to do. However, it was as if I stepped in a puddle of glue, and when my foot wedged opened that door, garbage clung to the soles of my feet and when I tried to shut the door, I carried some of that back into my world.

A friend and I had gone out to dinner, and upon returning to my place, the moment I opened the door, I could *feel* a dark negative force. It stopped me cold in my tracks. The hair on my arms and neck was standing straight up as Lori and I looked at each other. Her dark brown eyes were big as saucers. "Oh, my god," she whispered, "do you feel that?" My cat Paula bolted out of the room, meowing and hissing at the same time. We weren't the only ones whose hair was electrified.

"Jesus Christ! What the hell is that!" The room was ice cold. My instinct was to run, but I knew whatever it was would follow me.

"What are we going to do?" I walked in first, Lori followed, and we both clung close to each other. Strangely enough, the day before, I had purchased enough white candles for each room in the house. It was as if some part of my consciousness knew what was about to transpire.

"Quick! Grab all of the white candles in the kitchen drawer by the sink and I'll get the lighter. We have to place them in every room. We were both shaking as we began placing the candles in the rooms, neither one of us leaving the side of the other. We inched our way into the hallway. *Oh Mother Mary, it's in my bedroom.* My curtains were blowing, flapping from the force, but there was no wind outside. Whatever this was, it was massive.

"Dear God," I muttered, "don't let it manifest." It took all the strength and courage I had not to run. I knew it had to be confronted or it would take possession of my soul. I knew it was there for me.

"In the name of Jesus Christ and Archangel Michael, I command you into the light to be consumed! I command in the name of God, the I AM Presence . . .You have no power! Go into the light! In the name of the Brotherhood of Light and the Ascended Masters, go into the light to be consumed! The light of God never fails!"

After what seemed like a very long three or four minutes of commanding, the curtains settled down and the most beautiful fragrance of roses filled the room. We both felt a presence walk past us. Everything was fine now. Paula came back in the house and rubbed up against my leg, purring. We were both shaking and terrorized, but whatever it was, it was gone.

"I don't want to walk back to my apartment alone," Lori said.

"I don't blame you. Let's get the out of here." We walked and talked little, still shell-shocked, trying to absorb what had just transpired. All the while, the most ravishing fragrance of etheric roses enveloped us every step of the way. It was some time later that I read that the fragrance of a master is that of a rose. I knew one had taken on the cloak of invisibility and came to our aid.

Past life information was new to me, but certainly was the only thing that made sense to me. I, like others, would like to believe that in all my previous incarnations I was a healer, a high priestess, a queen, and only those of the most noble of intent, but that simply isn't true. I'm sure I had also been a murderer, a torturer, I had dabbled in other lives with black magic, and been a con artist, male and female—all part of the exploration of the human drama of moving back to God through experience. In my studies I had read that we turned away from God consciously and had to turn back consciously, and that the human part of us does a great job of creating chaos. Still, however, the musty odor of something lingered behind in the crevices, something that surfaced for a final house-cleaning—not that I understood it by any means, not at that stage of my "waking up," but I would understand it down the road with greater insight.

I had never seen the movie *The Exorcist*, for it would have played upon my fear of possession at that time. I still felt as if hounds baying in the night when I was most vulnerable were preying upon me. It didn't help that my attention was catapulted back into paranoia constantly by the vibration of my fear alone. I slept with the lights on, and just as I would drift off to sleep, it was as if voices, demonic, would come full force into my consciousness, and I would wrestle with them the best that I could. I felt as if it was a fight between good and evil. I was worn out and tired, and I couldn't speak to anyone about this. I knew they would think I was crazy. Hell, sometimes I felt like I was, but it was different than the times I had previously struggled for my sanity. *This was a force to be reckoned with.* It seemed as if everything was reaching an apex.

I had flown up to Vancouver one weekend for a spiritual workshop. I was so exhausted from fighting whatever this was, and it seemed as if my heart had become accustomed to a rapid pace of pounding. Fear is paralyzing. I had finally fallen asleep, only to be awakened by a deep guttural growl coming out of my throat.

My own fucking throat.

Yikes!

The workshop was spiritual in nature, and finally I

took aside Peter, the facilitator. "The messenger" was more appropriate. I told him of all that had transpired. He knew exactly what was happening, and I think he felt somewhat like the Cavalry charging in. He was a powerful being, full of light and conviction in his love for God, and he invoked two archangels to stand guard at my door, literally and metaphorically. It was the first night in months I slept like a baby. Now I know why I was so bound and determined to attend that workshop.

I was told once that I was tying up loose ends in this life, and it *feels* to me as if, before I was born, my guide and I walked into a large room that said on the door, "This garbage belongs to Athena Demetrios," and it was filled with past incarnation experiences like dirty piles of laundry, some whites, some dark, with lots of color and mismatches. *"Are you sure this is all mine?"*

"Yup!" my guide would have said, "It has your name on it. What do you want to do with it? You don't need to take it all with you this time around, you know. You're immortal; you'll be back again."

"Ah, what the hell, give it to me, I'll clean it up!" and threw them all in a big bag and carried them in with me like the hunchback of Notre Dame. I have a faint recollection of hearing someone in the distance calling after me. "And I don't want to hear you whine about it, either!"

Christ once said, "In my father's house are many mansions." In my house are lots of piles of laundry, but I'm working on it, God!

13
Kundalini Rising

He who looks outside dreams;
who looks inside awakes.
—*Carl Jung*

I had fallen to sleep meditating and was brought to conscious awareness by a vibration in the base of my spine. It was an amazingly sexual feeling, and it felt as if the vibration alone was almost levitating my hips off of the bed, it was so intense. I knew if I didn't open my eyes soon, whatever it was would shoot up my spine and out the crown of my head. I immediately called my friend Bill and explained what had happened. He began to laugh. "It's the kundalini waking up. It's great!" he said. "Nothing to be frightened of."

My meditation produced a spontaneous vision of a cobra. I wasn't sure what that meant, but I found out later that the kundalini energy is depicted in the Eastern traditions as a snake coiled up at the base of the spine.

It was around this time period when, on several occasions while deep in meditation, I saw the face of two different masters. Neither one of them was I very familiar with—at least, not on a conscious level. One was wearing a white turban with a turquoise jewel in the center, and he had the most beautiful blue eyes I had ever seen. The other I knew of—Swami Muktananda—although I had never followed his teachings. He flashed his face bigger than life, showing himself to me with the red dot between his brows. I didn't understand what it meant, but on the other hand, I figured all would be revealed when it was supposed to. If nothing else, these kinds of phenomena have always left me with a knowingness and feeling that "you are not alone—you're being watched over, and we are with you." What a feeling that is.

To say that there was luminosity about them was an understatement. If anything could ever come close to the visual description of my visions, it would be the movie *Contact*, when Jody Foster went into the other dimension and saw her father. The translucent and vivid colors are alive in their vibrancy; the energy in them almost dances. The study of the Ascended Master Teachings and meditation had become a part of my daily routine and, as a result, the continued focus was pulling me deeper and deeper into the mystical. I had gone down to the temple one afternoon when one of the women gave me a stack of books, and in the stack was a picture of the master that had shown his face to me. I had been reading a discourse or two by him but didn't know what he looked liked. "Who is that?" I inquired. "That's who I saw when I was meditating."

"Oh," she said with a smile on her face. "That's the Ascended Master El Morya." I will never forget those eyes.

I have experienced the vibration and sensation of kundalini twice in my life: Once when I was nineteen shortly after my Dad died, and several years later when I was thirty four preceding the visions of the Masters. I had no idea of what it was, but it frightened me back then. However, spirit was now waking me up. At times, while deep in meditation, I experienced a rhythmic contraction of the root chakra and my body began to move clockwise and then counterclockwise. I am not sure what it all meant, but I trusted it was part of the movement of energy, and I knew I would be guided to what I needed next. I adore the mystical. I adore God.

14

Back Off, You Ugly Slimeball!

"May the forces of evil become confused
on the way to your house."
—*George Carlin*

I sat up in bed. Something was terribly wrong. Just then the phone rang. It was my sister Judy. The moment I heard her voice, what had transpired *while I supposedly slept* came flooding into my waking consciousness. It wasn't a dream. It was one of those lucid experiences that I had on the inner realms in my "light body" while my physical body slept.

I entered into a room with great speed. It felt to me as if I was flying, for I came through the walls with a feeling of great urgency. My body was pure white light, and I could see before me a massive entity, almost touching the ceiling, perhaps eight feet wide. It was not completely without shape; it was thick, dense, and demonic, and this entity was pure, unadulterated evil. It was enormous and was hunched over a man, choking him. The man was on his knees, clawing at the hands clamped around his throat, trying desperately to free himself from the hold. I knew he was about to die. I extended my right arm in front of me, pointing directly at the mass, and with full authority, I gave the command, "I AM THE LIGHT! YOU HAVE NO POWER!" I watched as this thing released its hold and began to shrivel and back off.

I left the memory of what had transpired that night and came back to the conversation. Judy's voice was on the edge of hysteria. "Judy, what's the matter? What's wrong?"

"Ted tried to commit suicide last night," she said. "I was sleeping; I heard some noise. . . . I got up and found him in the front room floor, on his knees, choking on his vomit."

"Is he alive?" I asked. "He's in a coma," she said. "I'm on my way."

If a picture could paint a thousand words . . .

When I arrived at Judy's, the look on her face was pure panic. I was always the one she called when in a crisis, and she was always there for me. I know that just seeing me helped her somehow, for I don't think she felt so overwhelmed or alone. At least we could be overwhelmed together. She filled me in as we drove to the hospital, and upon entering intensive care, I noticed a nurse standing close to him. His heartbeat was irregular, and I knew that he was making a decision whether to stay or go. I placed my hand over his chest and flooded him with white light and began to whisper in his ear. "You are a strong spirit, you are strong enough to stay here and confront this. You are a being of light Ted. Come back. . . . Come back. . . . You are loved. You're strong enough. You can do this, Ted. . . . You can do this. Don't give up. You can do this."

He must have made his decision then, for his heartbeat became more stabilized and I remember the nurse looking at me funny, and I know that she wanted to ask what I had said to him, for I could hear her thoughts. I had read once that a coma was a deep state of meditation in which the soul was in a state of re-evaluation. I believe there is great truth in that statement.

Ted had discovered his ability as an artist and was just beginning to receive some notoriety when he found out he had multiple sclerosis. I don't think that he could deal with it. Everything in their household had become chaotic and crazy but divinely inspired at the same time. I felt strongly that for some time, Judy had been struggling with alcoholism. Her late night phone calls and occasional slurred words were a dead giveaway.

When we returned to her home from the hospital, she asked me if I wanted a glass of sherry. "No, I don't." I said.

"Come on, have a glass."

"No, I'm fine. . . . I don't want one." She walked past me with her commanding presence and sat on the couch directly across from me. I could sense she was about to plead her case.

"You know," she said very matter-of-factly, "alcoholism is inherited . . . . We come from a whole family of it."

She was pissing me off. "That's bullshit! The bottom line in life is you either get it together or you give up!" She stared at me as if I had just hit her between the eyes with a two-by-four. Upon my return to Los Angeles a week later, I had an incredible lucid dream. I was sitting with my arm around Judy. Her face was full of fear, and mine was very calm and serene. We were in a house that was caught in a tornado and was spinning in circles, just like in *The Wizard of Oz*. The house slammed down on the ground but not on its original foundation. I saw the Ascended Master Saint Germain and said to him, "Saint Germain, isn't there anything we can do?"

"No," he replied, "it's in the divine plan."

And it was. Ted came out of the coma, and Judy joined AA. Wonders never cease to exist. In my newfound study, I had also become aware that when we sleep at night, many times in our "finer light bodies" we are of assistance to spirit in a myriad of ways. That experience has remained deeply etched in my consciousness, not only for its lucidity, but for another reason as well.

I can still see that black mass full of hatred and evil shrivel and back off like a slug that had been bathed in salt. It reminded me of a snail that was retreating back into its' shell, but it was the way in which it trembled at the authority of the light, knowing full well that it was finished, that I remember most. I *need* to remember it even more when at times I "buy into the fear" that is so prevalent within the daily waking life of the human drama. I do so love those experiences in which I am shown the grandness of my soul, however brief it might be, because it gives me a knowingness that what I experience in my journey in the "earthly plane" is nothing compared to what we are truly capable of becoming—and what a challenge that becoming is. There is no greater truth than the statement by Pierre Teilhard de Chardin that we are not human beings on a spiritual journey but rather *spiritual beings on a human journey.*

15

Meeting My Mystical Muse

In all the paradox of human emotion, remember that a wee bit of humor is necessary if not wise; simply seek enlightenment and simply lighten up.
—Dr. James Martin Peebles

My first encounter with Dr. Peebles was in 1982 when I heard him through his medium Thomas Jacobson on KABC talk radio. His effect on my psyche was electrical and thrilled me through and through. I once said that was the beginning of our love affair, and it continues to this day. I really doubt if I would be here if our paths had not crossed.

As my brothers and I gathered around the radio that night, I was absolutely mesmerized by his message and his humor. I remember when a woman called up and complained to Doctor Peebles that she had all kinds of things missing, he paused and then said in his sing-song Scottish brogue, "Maxine, ya got leprechauns." "SAY W-H-H-H-A-T?" she replied. You could just see in your mind's eye this woman's eyes grow big as saucers—it was the way she said it—and my brothers and I lost it. We laughed so hard. "Ya got leprechauns," he chimed again. "They're here to tickle your funny bone. You take life too seriously. Just because you don't see them doesn't mean they don't exist. There are billions of life forms that you don't see with the naked eye, but that does not mean that they don't exist or are of less value."

I had no idea of mediumship, what it was about, or even the dynamics that were involved with it, but something in me responded with an excitement and a thrill that just rang through every cell of my body. It intrigued me to no end, fascinated me, and I simply wanted more. As synchronicity would have it, the following day, while working on a commercial, I experienced an instant rapport with the actor. The conversation flowed effortlessly and easily around metaphysics, and then he said, "I just had the most incredible reading by this character named Dr. Peebles." I could hardly contain my excitement, and I immediately contacted Thomas Jacobson.

I was curious about certain writings that just seemed to flow through me with great ease after meditation. There was something ethereal about them. I wasn't sure where they were coming from, but it didn't really seem like me—not in my conscious awareness, anyway. Some of them felt angelic in their message and delivery; some of them felt as if they were inspired and coming from my "higher self." Higher self, lower self, fragmented self, whole self—who knew. All of this was new to me, yet at the same time, *it felt deeply familiar* in a way I couldn't put into words. In no uncertain terms, I was going to pull on this thread.

I called Thomas, and he suggested that I might want to participate in a group channeling that would be taking place at his house in Topanga Canyon. I jumped at the opportunity. I was excited and nervous as I drove up the winding mountain that evening, full of anticipation at experiencing this spirit coming through this man. What would that look like? Did his face change? Certainly his voice on the phone was completely different than the boisterous presence I had heard on the radio that night.

I was intimidated by his presence when he opened the door, and I think he felt that from the moment he met me. I, like many people, thought he was almost God-like in his ability to do what he did. I know it made him uncomfortable, and rightfully so.

There were about ten people at the house, sitting on the floor in a semi-circle, and I joined them, feeling nervous and unsure of what was about to transpire. He sat in his chair and, after a moment or two, looked like he was almost dozing off. You could hear a pin drop in the room. He whispered an invocation to spirit, and all of a sudden, he bent forward and Doctor Peebles came through with a bang!

"God bless you. Dr. Peebles here! It is a joy and blessing when man and spirit join together to increase our truth and awareness. Might I offer encouragement, my dear friends, as you strive to understand your rights to receive and give inspiration, in this your given and chosen life, for you are upon the school called Earth, hand in hand with all humanity, each and every one a student, a student of the divine. And in that journey to the heart you will discover illusions, illusions of separation. We offer to you the following principles to be used in tandem: Number One, loving allowance for all things to be in their own time and space, starting with yourself.

"Number Two, increased communication with respect to all life, starting with yourself.

"Number Three, self responsibility for your life as a creative adventure, for never in your soul are you the victim, always the creator.

"God bless you each and every one, and would there be question or comment?"

I sat there completely mesmerized by what I was witnessing. I loved this spirit; I loved his answers to people, and it seemed to me no matter how relevant the information was to the one he was speaking, there was something in every response with which I could identify.

"Dr. Peebles?" I said, somewhat hesitantly.

"God bless you."

"My name is Athena, and I have felt the desire to write." He jumped right in with the following answer.

"This is a channeling state, and we encourage you to write about your own growth in life personally; ahhh, . . . this will prepare you for the channeling you'll be doing down the road after confrontation of change towards the end of the decade."

"Thank you," I replied. I was somewhat stunned by his answer, and at the same time, it felt so right. But channeling? Me? It gave me a lot to think about. I heard someone else ask a question, but I was still replaying his words in my head. He was a few paragraphs into their answer when he turned back to me.

"You see, my darling, we already know about your books down the road . . . give or take a decade or two, and spirit wants to be a little greedy and wants to be acknowledged as your motivating factor for writing your book."

"I already have," I replied.

"Good girl!" He said with great warmth in his voice. I just felt like I had received a gold star from the teacher. I had been receiving subtle whispers to write, fleeting thoughts, and I remember two separate clairvoyants had spoken to me of writing. I had written the dedication prior to my meeting the Doc that night, and it still remains the same to this day, and is the one that graces this manuscript, for God only knows what will happen with this. It may wind up in Grandmother's musty old trunk, something my grandchildren will read one day and say to my daughter, their Mom, "Mamo was weird . . . huh, Mom." Or it may wind up at a garage sale, or it may get published and who knows whose hands it might fall into, but this much I do know: My dedication has never faltered, nor have I ever desired to change it. As I write these words, I am in the second decade with "the book that wouldn't wrap," and my relationship with Dr. Peebles is rich, fertile, and growing. He has taken out his "spiritual boot," as he calls it, and used it on me on more than one occasion, in particular as to writing this odyssey.

When I finally told him that I was going to finish this, that I was bound and determined to do so, he replied, "Wait a minute, one of your spirit guides just fainted, and another is chiseling your words in stone; we are bearing witness to your words."

Who wouldn't love this guy?

16
Those Who Hear Not The Music

Those who hear not the music think the dancers mad.
—Friedrich Nietzsche

I looked through the window of the small plane as it began its descent in final preparation for landing. *What an unusual twist of events,* I thought to myself. If Mom knew what I was about to do, she would have strapped herself to the wing of the airplane with anything she could get her hands on—a garden hose, piece of twine, even an old worn-out pair of support hose, if need be. Anything that would guarantee she would be able to witness what was about to happen—that which intrigued and fed her soul.

Some fifteen years had passed since I had driven my mother up the incline to a small church in Paradise, California, a tiny town some twelve miles from Chico. I hadn't been particularly interested in taking her that night. Watching some documentary on aliens and a psychic surgeon was not high on my list. The operation was bloody and gory, and I winced as I watched the surgeon's hands penetrate the massive bullfrog-like goiter that was protruding out of the man's neck.

On the way home, Mom had me pull over and park

the car in a turnout on one of the bluffs before heading back down the highway to our town of Chico, which was nestled below. She wanted to watch for UFOs, and we were far enough away from the lights of the town that we could get a good view. The black night provided the perfect backdrop, for stars were in abundance, and if nothing else, perhaps we could spot a shooting star. She inhaled on her cigarette, munching away on a bag of pork rinds, talking excitedly about what we had just witnessed, full of life, hoping beyond hope she would see something out of the ordinary.

What a turn of events. Now it was I, feeling that same sense of excitement at the anticipation of having the identical surgeon I witnessed so many years ago work on me. I had received a phone call from a friend who had moved to a small town in Alaska with his pregnant wife a few months prior. "How's your arthritis?" Bill inquired.

"Funny you should ask," I replied. "I was just saying last night that I would rather work with a spiritual healer than get pumped full of medication."

"I wanted to let you know that the psychic surgeon from the Philippines is here," Bill replied. That's all it took. I was packing my bags and making a reservation. I love how spirit works. I love the orchestration and synchronicity of events when something falls into place seamlessly. This was one of those times that left me shaking my head, half laughing, yet at the same time, completely full of wonder at the magic of it all.

I had been diagnosed at 32 with rheumatoid arthritis, one of the worst cripplers, and yet despite the amount of medication the doctor wanted to put me on, I sought to the greater degree to work with it through meditation. Something in me innately knew if I fully accepted that diagnosis, I would be in real trouble. Around that time, I had a lucid dream where a young girl walked up to me and held out her hand for me to heal. There was something on the top of her hand, a dark, green-black energy that looked like the lobster-type thing that attached itself to a man's face in the movie *Alien*. I tried with all of my might to lift it off her hand, but the suction was too great. It felt as if this energy was almost cemented to the bone.

I got off the plane and hugged my friends Jan and Bill. I liked them both immensely. I was glad that Bill had followed the impulse to call me. They were a handsome couple. Jan, a pretty woman, more than a few months pregnant, with big blue eyes and blonde hair, was the more pragmatic and logical of the two—a role reversal it seemed, as men were usually by far the more logical in those days. She struck me as the kind of person who had no problem getting in the face of any instructor at a seminar with a sincere "Why do you say that?" and who would stand there blinking her big, blue eyes with child-like curiosity, until she was satisfied with the answer. Bill, on the other hand, seemed to be led more by his gut-level instinct and intuition. If it "felt right" to him, then that was good enough. There was something about Bill, a quiet melancholy. I had the feeling that his path in life had been arduous and trying. He was a sensitive man with a deep reverence and love of the Native American and it felt to me as if some part of his soul was seeking to bridge a distrust of the white man from a past life on levels he wasn't aware of, despite his engaging nature.

The following morning we pulled up to the condo where the healer was staying. I was feeling a slight bit of apprehension. Jan and Bill had attended a gathering the night before and observed what was called an "operation" by the healer himself.

This morning, there were several people in the room standing around chatting, awaiting their appointed slot. I recognized two well-known celebrities. I looked at a woman who was sitting on the floor with her legs stretched out in front of her, ankles crossed. There was room next to her, so I sat down. She was watching a video from the night before of the master healer performing surgery. Completely relaxed, she smiled at me and said, "They're playing this for me. . . . I'm the one lying on the table." She turned her head back to watch the monitor.

I watched in awe as the healer took his finger and made an incision as if with a knife, splitting her from below her navel to her pubic bone. He inserted his hand up to his wrist and began pulling out "black gunk." I don't know what in the world you would call it, but that's what it looked liked. The young woman lay there, completely relaxed, with her eyes open, while other people stood close by, huddled together, their heads straining to get a better glimpse, observing the operation. When he removed his hand, her skin closed up.

When it was our turn, we went into the room together. I remember the grin the healer had on his face when he saw Jan and her swollen belly. Bill told me that I could "request a scan" in which the healer would hold his hands over my body and would thereby be guided to whatever needed attention. Being the control freak that I am, I went with four specific requests: my arthritis in my right hand, my left breast, my right knee, and last but not least, I wanted him to work on my third eye.

He was not a big man, rather slight in build, with golden brown skin and a full head of shiny, black hair neatly combed in place. His eyes were like two black olives, but they shone with a light that revealed a serenity and reverence for life. He seemed to be without ego, and I remember how humble and almost shy he was. He was a man with a gentle demeanor and simply radiated a sense of peace and well being. I could *feel* his deep love for God. Sometimes you don't understand what it is about a person that is so unusual; you just know something is, and you have only to be in their presence to feel it. He was that way. He was fascinating. I wanted to crawl inside his journey and understand what revelations and insights had enabled him to become so aligned with the God consciousness that he was able to be a pure conduit for that "Presence" to work through.

Intuitively, I had been feeling something was the matter with my left breast—the beginnings of cancer, who knows—but it was a sensation, a thought, a gut feeling, and that was first on my list. I went behind a curtain, put on the robe, and crawled on the table, pulling the sheet up, covering my chest.

He stood off some seven or eight feet from me, and I watched as he dipped his hands in what I assumed was holy water. He walked over to the table, made eye contact with me, and then placed his fingers on the left side of my breast. I felt a pressure, like trying to penetrate firm Jell-O. I could feel his fingers moving into the tissue in my breast. He had his eyes shut, like he was being completely guided by his God-self or some guide. I could feel the blood trickle down the side of my breast, but I felt no pain. His wife took a paper towel and wiped up the blood, cleaning off my breast. He smiled at me and said, "You're healthy now."

This I thought to myself *is beyond cool.* I told him I wanted him to work on my third eye. I know penetrating the skull took more energy, and I could feel when he had found entrance. Again, his wife wiped the blood off my forehead. I quickly sat up. He was going to work on my hand. I watched, with my eyes glued to the procedure. He gathered his fingers together until the tips were touching one another. There is a smell when the body is opened up, and I was completely intrigued with how he was able to lift and "magnetize" some liquid, which he dropped into a bowl. He did that a few times and then my skin closed up. He pulled out something black from my knee, and I know to this day, it has never bothered me since.

I looked at Jan and Bill both standing close by watching. I shot them a grin that went ear to ear. They both laughed at the look on my face. I sat there, dumbfounded but elated, then quickly got dressed. I wanted to witness what he was about to do.

An obese woman sat on the edge of the table across the room. Bill leaned over and whispered quietly in my ear, "She has a brain tumor." We watched as he inserted two fingers through the base of her skull and a few moments later, through the socket of the eye, and proceeded to pull out a mass of gunk. That seemed to take it out of him, and he sat down in the chair and said to her in broken English, "There, big mama. You're okay now."

I stared at the house as we drove away. "My God, it really is whole new consciousness coming forth on the planet."

Upon my return to Los Angeles, I immediately made an appointment to speak to Dr. Peebles through his medium. I wanted feedback about my recent experiences with the spiritual workshop in Canada, the psychic surgeon in Alaska, and my dream with the young girl.

"Was I seeing with inner-vision what the energy of arthritis looks like?" I inquired.

"Yes, you were," he replied. "The young girl was you in another life. Your arthritis," he continued, "runs parallel to your anger." *Parallel to my anger.* I hadn't even begun to tap into that. Certainly I had been wrestling with it, wrestling more so not to acknowledge it. There was so much below the surface that was feeling like a volcano. I could feel it churning, but I rarely allowed myself to express it. I felt like I wouldn't be able to survive if I pulled the cork. Not only that, but if I pulled the cork,

I wasn't sure what would come out, and that thought alone terrified me. There was so much I had no memory of, unexplored terrain, a journey upon which I was about to embark. It was, for me, a matter of timing.

I had been struggling with and trying to fight what felt like demonic forces. I slept with the light on at night and searched to find ways to heal myself on all levels. It felt as if I were reaching my arms to the light, but no matter how hard I stretched and strained, something dark had me by my ankles, trying to pull me back into a black place that frightened me beyond words. I didn't know if I had the strength to fight its weight, to keep from being pulled into the belly of the beast.

Whatever this was, it was something that was keeping me from the light inside myself. I felt as if I were bound in cords of invisible barbed wire, like a snake trying to shed its skin. This energy was dense and dark, vibrating at the lowest of levels, and I was being pulled backwards and sucked up by quicksand.

Dr. Peebles said the following words to me about it: "This was an exorcism of your own soul of the places within yourself that you had termed and judged as dark and black from other lifetimes where you did play with black magic. The psychic surgeon was like tying a final knot, a surgeon's knot, and that is why you feel a sense of equilibrium and balance."

That statement made complete sense to me, for I have yet to meet another who can judge me more harshly than I have judged myself. Somewhere in our path, judgments do come forward to be healed through forgiveness. I still struggle with that, and it is one of the hardest areas of my life, for I can beat myself up unmercifully. When the dark energy reared its ugly head, it was part of a cleansing process, one that would unfold in myriad ways down the road, but not all to be revealed to me just yet. The metaphor of peeling an onion is most appropriate to the evolution of becoming conscious—and it seldom happens without tears.

Over the years, I have had two other experiences with the Philippine surgeons, but never the master healer himself again. I had to laugh, though, at my last visit. When I walked into the room and told the healer I wanted him to work on my third eye, he started laughing. "Ahhh," he said, "you want to see spirit!"

17
Queen Of De Nile

How often it is that the angry man rages denial
of what his inner self is telling him.
—Frank Herbert

I had never realized how strong of a need I had to "save" people. And if anyone had tried to point that out to me, I would have turned a deaf ear in a heartbeat. As much of a "Hard-Hearted Hanna" as I had been, there was always the part of me that felt deeply for the poor, the underdog, the underprivileged, the abused. I felt as if I had just come upon the truth, and I wanted to enlighten the world with it. I had been in prison all my life, so what better place to start than with the penal system itself? I began feeling this pull to work with prisoners. The desire, subtle at first, became stronger, and finally, I made contact with a prison within the Los Angeles area.

"Great! We can utilize your expertise in grooming classes for pre-release men and women." I followed the warden around as he showed me other areas of interest and programs that they had in place for rehabilitation. But I drove home feeling depressed. "I don't want to teach friggin' 'grooming' classes," I thought to myself. I wanted to give them hope, to explain karma and the laws of the universe. Although these concepts were all new to me, I had been shown that life did have purpose and it did operate on laws, and I wanted to change their world. I still felt that I had been let in on this secret that few knew about, and if I could get this information out to people, then I could give them the tools to set themselves free.

Three months passed and they did not respond to my invitation. I was crushed, although I couldn't say why. I could no more have explained the growing desire to work with prisoners than I could have explained the fundamentals of algebra. I didn't understand where it originated; all I knew was that it was a pull, and it was strong, and it wasn't going away. One night, after I had been meditating, I poured my heart out into my prayer and I gave God an ultimatum—and I meant business: "Look, God, you either remove the desire from my heart or you open the door. Your choice."

The next day, the phone rang. "Can you come teach a class on grooming to 45 pre-release men?"

"Ahhh,...sure," I stammered.

"You'll have them for three hours."

Oh, shit!

I didn't take notes, didn't make an outline, and I had no idea what would transpire. I decided to just turn it over to spirit—for three hours. I was nervous driving out there, and even more nervous when I pulled up to the gate. *What the hell am I doing here?* I turned off the ignition and sat in my car, trying to soothe the butterflies in my stomach. I quieted myself and invoked the Light. *I speak to the God within. I AM presence; come forth. You speak through me and do it your way.* I surrounded myself with white light and sent it before me.

All eyes were on me as I was being introduced. A few were slouched back in their chairs with that "too cool for school" look, and others just looked curious. The nervousness left and I took time as I completely surveyed the room, making eye contact with each one of them. I don't think I saw what most people would have seen. I saw lost souls, but most of them looked like scared little boys to me.

"They wanted me to come teach a class on grooming," I said. "I want you guys to wash behind your ears and brush your teeth. Now we're going take your hearts out and dust them off." That got their attention. They just stared at me as I continued. "I don't believe there is one of you in this room that has the balls to walk up here and look me in the eye and tell me that when the lights go off and you are lying in your cell at night that you don't hurt inside, that you don't want the love of a woman and the respect of a family and community, the respect and the love for self."

You could hear a pin drop.

Words just flowed effortlessly and easily. We talked about the concept of Earth being a school, experiences as lessons, free will, and choice. I shared with them that I read once that meditating meant feeling, quieting oneself and that it was the outer self going against the still voice within that created the chaos in our lives. I asked them if they would like to listen to a guided meditation. The majority responded with a nod of the head. I had brought along a tape player and inserted the tape into the slot. I adjusted the volume so it would be audible but not distracting. I watched as they closed their eyes, and I could see the tension begin to leave their bodies as their breathing became slower and more relaxed. I thought back to something Dr. Peebles had said to me recently when I shared with him the desire to work within the penal system. In his answer to me, it was as if he were personally speaking to the men. He said, *"All people upon the planet Earth have anger. Even the Judge and Jury have anger and discontent. Perhaps you, my associates here in prison are more honest with your discontent.*

I would invite you to make contact with the master within you, so brilliant in choice and clarity." The meditation came to a close and they stretched and yawned as they became more conscious of their surroundings. They were relaxed. It showed on their faces. It was time to wrap up for the day and with a half-hour left, I passed around paper and asked them to write out their desires or dreams. A "positive prayer," I think I called it. They took their time writing, focusing on those parts of self that they kept hidden from others. At the end of the class, 44 men and I stood in a circle holding hands. "Too cool for school" sat alone in his chair watching. It was impossible not to *feel* the light that erupted in whoops and hollers at the end of our allotted time. I drove home feeling elated, feeling as if I had touched them in some way, and by God if I couldn't change the world!

Karma is an interesting thing. I was thirty-five at that time and had absolutely no idea of the draw or the magnetization that drew me into that experience. I had an understanding of karma, the law of cause and effect, but how that was applicable in my world at that time with that which had manifested in my heart as such a "pull" was not to be revealed in its fullness for some years. When it hit, it hit home with full force, and there was really *nothing* about me that wasn't touched by the experience. As a rule, we see things from one perspective only, and what lies beneath the surface speaks volumes about the *real purpose in life.* I have always felt that this place called Earth is a disguise for what is really going on. We wear such blinders to the inner truth that we fail to see the inner workings of an experience as something that is being brought to our attention from the God self as a tool of self-revelation, and is always an opportunity for a healing of some sort.

I had gone to work in a salon after I had left Revlon, and just as the clairvoyant had predicted, it allowed me the opportunity to go out on print jobs, where I could "get my feet wet" applying makeup to models for various magazines and catalogues. The salon afforded me a regular paycheck that I could count on to pay my monthly bills and I was ever grateful for that.

It was the middle of the week, and the salon was quiet. It was late afternoon, the clock was creeping along, and the manicurist and I were both bored, trying to fill the time before we could call it a day. I was rearranging the makeup in the display case and Linda was reading out loud the want ads. "Oh, here's a good one," she said. "Sexy blonde with good figure seeks wealthy professional male. I love moonlit walks on the beach, romantic dinners (don't we all). Must be financially independent . . . yada, yada, yada. Yeah, why doesn't she say it like it is: Gold-digging bleached blonde with boob job seeks wealthy man to take care of her. Looks not important. Bank account is."

She read, I commented, we laughed—until she read the following:

> Outlaw, motorcycle tramp.
> My years of wondering aimless
> and wild have come to an end.
> No family or friends,
> A prison cell and loneliness are
> my only companions now.
> My heart is broken, spirit heavy.
> I am in need of someone,
> who will care . . .
> if only a little.
> I love the sun's warmth
> in my face,
> the wind in my hair,
> a country stream and
> mountain place . . .

If any of you are out
there and can relate,
I hope you'll write and
fill this empty space.

Neither one of us said anything for the longest time. It was one of the saddest things that I had ever heard, but it was the most honest as well. I can't imagine anyone hearing those words and not feeling the authenticity of the feelings behind them. And who can't relate to feeling as if your spirit has been broken? I knew exactly where he was.

"Give me that," I said, as I read the ad again. "I am going to write him."

Driving home from work that night, I couldn't get the poem out of my head. The word "weird" was about to take on a whole new meaning. My whole life was becoming weird. There was a synchronicity to events that was uncanny, supernatural. The mundane was quickly being swept aside, for I had entered into a new state of consciousness, a level and a plane of experience that fascinated me. I had already made the decision that I was not going to reveal anything about myself. I curled up on my bed and with pen in hand I began,

Dear Mark,
I felt the weight of your words on my heart.
It's easy to wall off and become hard . . . tough
to be vulnerable . . .

It was a long letter, and I simply wrote what I felt guided to say. I didn't anticipate receiving a response, but I did. He had received a few hundred replies, but there were only two that he responded to. I was one.

"You don't know me from a can of paint," he said, "yet again you have hit upon everything that I am feeling. You're right. It was easier to wall off and become hard. When my father was beating my mother, I hid in the closet and prayed to God to make him stop. He just kept beating her. And when he wasn't there to beat her, she'd beat me. I figured God was a real creep for letting that happen."

I was moved by his honesty, and his letter was almost a purging of sorts. I could tell he felt that someone understood his feelings and he was taking the opportunity to give voice to that which he had had so much time to reflect upon. I honestly don't think that he thought I would write back, but I did.

I was continuing my work as a volunteer in the prison, and I began writing Mark on a regular basis, as it seemed a natural evolution. I have never liked to think of anybody as a lost cause or beyond redemption, and still to this day, I am a die-hard at believing in the ability of the human spirit to rise out of great adversity. I told him nothing about me personally, and I know that his having another person he could write to was cathartic for him. The more he revealed about himself, the more intrigued I became by his life—and he was a hell of a writer. He didn't embellish; he was just honest and clear in his ability to express himself. I began to look forward to his communications, and I encouraged him and shared with him in his victories of confronting himself in ways that would turn his pain into tears of release.

Mark was a fighter. He was a scrapper, and under all that anger was a lot of hurt. He was a Vietnam vet, a tunnel rat—Special Forces—who did three tours and came home to get spit on, and he was a sensitive man. Too sensitive, he said. He had found himself on the streets making drug runs when he was twelve. His mother insisted that he become a ward of the state. He was placed into an institution that was eventually closed down for abusing the kids. One of the many forms of punishment he relayed to me was being forced to kneel for eight hours on a hard wooden bench while still in his pajamas. You know that some sick bastard with unresolved issues from his own childhood was taking out his aggression on those who knelt before him to assert his position of authority. No wonder Mark hated God—and that, I could relate to.

I am sure his addiction to drugs was aggravated in Viet Nam. I think the pain of what his life had been was too much for him to handle. I remember him telling me once that he had killed over a hundred and twenty-five people, and I can't fathom what it must be like to reconcile that and find any level of peace or self-forgiveness with it—especially when, upon your return, you are spat upon and called a baby killer. His anger at God, the world, and himself became all-consuming. I remember that his favorite song was "Running Against the Wind," by Bob Seger, and I think that's how he felt—as if he had been running against the wind. He rode with a motorcycle club, produced crystal meth in a lab, and eventually, with the law looking for him, he went to church one day, listened to the sermon, stood up and gave his own, and then went to the police station and turned himself in. He was an unusual man. The judged said he was beyond redemption. His reply was simply, "Do what ya got to do, man."

Walling off and becoming hard I understood. It is easy to go to the place of no return. His anger eventually landed him in the hole, and there a guard named Warren would sit outside his door and read to him. I think Warren saw the same thing in Mark that I did.

I encouraged Mark to participate in therapy sessions and to begin to deal with his pain and anger. When he finally let go, where Vietnam was concerned, he lost consciousness of the whole event, he was so deep in the experience of it. That was a breakthrough of great magnitude for him, and I was a cheerleader in his corner.

Once he said something in a letter about "if we had the power to change it today." The following, my response to him, flowed like water, and I could barely keep up with the words, they were coming so fast.

If We Had The Power To Change It Today

We would look into ourselves first—into the recesses of our very souls, for therein lies the cause.

We would gaze upon the less fortunate, and would not use his ill fate to feed our ego, and induce self-inflated smugness for the possessions we have gathered. We would bless him instead and wish for him the courage and strength to rise out of his limitation, that he, too, might become abundant.

If we had the power to change it today, we would see that we have created a world of distrust and raging emotion of destructive thought and feeling, carried through to full fruition in our lives individually. We would look courageously at our own relationships first, and would see that they reflect exactly what we are willing to give.

If we had the power to change it today, we would speak words of truth, encouragement, and kindness. We would give hope where there is void, faith where there is despair, wisdom where there is ignorance.

If we had the power to change it today, we would take a stand for truth, integrity and peace. We would see with eyes that can see, and lend the ear that can hear the silent voice inside our hearts.

People O People, I AM the love that sets you free.

Athena Demetrios 1983

I married Mark in prison. The events around that were strange. I had gone deep into meditation, beseeching, *Show me a sign, Father. If I am to marry him, show me a sign.* And some time later, out of the depths of silence, I heard a voice say, "Matthew 25, paragraph 36 . . . Matthew 25, paragraph 6. I got up, walked over to a bookshelf, and picked up the tiny black Bible that someone had given me. *It fell open to Matthew 25, paragraph 36*: "Naked and ye clothed me. I was sick and ye visited me. I was in prison, and ye came unto me." Then I read paragraph 6: "Behold the bridegroom cometh."

I stood there shaking. I have never been a Bible reader and had never even opened that book, nor can I remember who gave it to me or how it came to be in my possession. *But the truth is stranger than fiction.*

To him, I was the sunrise and the sunset all rolled up in one—not a good thing to be for anyone. I remember the first time he held my hand. He touched it with the sensitivity of handling a fragile robin's egg. I guess if it were reversed, that is how it would appear to me: as if the person was a savior. And I liked the role. It gave me a feeling that I was worth something. That struggle alone, the struggle to ascend to my own worth, has been the most difficult and tumultuous climb of my life. If I could control the world of another and make them happy, make them feel less pain, then all would be right.

It seemed to me I had spent my whole life trying to do

that anyway—visualizing myself as someone who could "save." Save what? It exhausts me now just thinking about it.

Here's the kicker: I knew it was the wrong thing to do when I married him, because I wasn't in love with him. But I did it anyway. Although it would be a few years before he would be released and come home—and much was to happen before that time—I was going to save him, and in doing so, I would redeem myself in the eyes of God and my subconscious. Who knows, but perhaps that feeling of being so flawed and worthless would go away.

18
Busted On My Garbage

Have you learned the lessons only of those who admired you, and were tender with you, and stood aside for you? Have you not learned great lessons from those who braced themselves against you and disputed passage with you?
—Walt Whitman

"I thought you were full of bullshit the first time I laid eyes on you." Thomas's words stung deeply. I felt myself begin to panic as I scrambled to find a defense. "You don't know a damned thing about me or my life or anything that I have been through!" I shouted back at him. "I've never felt as if I was judgmental of people," I continued. His wife Joanna interrupted. "LISTEN to me, YOU are judgmental as hell! You walked in here this morning with a bunch of books under your arm for everybody, like you are going to CHANGE us by forcing your TRUTH on us. Like thinking that we NEED you to change us. If that isn't judgmental, then I don't know what is."

I felt bewildered and exposed. I looked at Thomas. I could sense that he was getting ready to unload both barrels at me. The onslaught continued, "I think it's pretty damned sad . . . no," he paused as he searched for a more descriptive word. "No, not just sad—tragic. I think it's tragic that the only time you feel alive is when you are working with prisoners. I think it's tragic that you can't feel that same sense of aliveness with life."

I could feel everybody's eyes on me. I wanted to run and hide, anywhere. I just wanted to be anywhere except where I was. There was nothing I could say. I felt the tears begin to run down my cheeks. I walked into the bathroom to grab a tissue. His voice followed: "And another thing: You're constantly leaving the room to blow your nose."

"Jesus Christ," I screamed back, "what the hell do you expect? I've been sick. I've had a hell of a cold!" I walked back into the center of the room. I could feel the eyes of the other group members on me. I didn't look at them, just Thomas. I hated him. I wanted to hit him, to slap that smug look off of his face. I hated his fucking guts. We just stared at each other. I felt my eyes narrow and the muscles tighten in my face as I silently shouted obscenities at him.

"I'm going to ask you to do something and you have a choice. You either do it or I'm asking you to walk out that door and leave this class. You do it, or you leave." I felt a sense of panic surge through my body. "Oh God, what now," I thought to myself.

"I want you to stand in the center of this circle of people. I want you to walk up to each of one of them, look them each in the eye, and let them see you totally vulnerable. You can't have any Kleenex for your nose. I want you to let them see you totally fall apart . . . without always stopping to wipe the mascara from your eyes, without always trying to look so perfect."

"Jesus, Thomas, that's not fair!" I shouted. "I've got a cold! I can't help it if I have to stop to blow my nose." God, I hated him. *Who needs this shit? I've paid money for this abuse? You son of a bitch, you can take this class, this "Journey to the Heart" as you call it, and shove it up your ass,* I thought to myself as I glanced at the door and wrestled with the multitude of thoughts that were racing through my mind. I wanted to run for it, to get away from him and all of the eyes that were transfixed on me, waiting for my response. The silence in the room was unbearable, and so was the panic inside of me. I was beginning to feel like a caged animal. If you walk out of that door, Athena, he'll win, I thought to myself. God, I can't let everyone see me like this, I know I'll start crying the moment I look at Taryn, the moment I connect with her eyes, I'll crumble and there I'll be, black streaks of mascara running down my face as well as snot coming out of my nose, and I can't wipe it away. I'll be a disgusting spectacle, and I'll still have nine people to have to confront in silence, to move slowly around the circle holding full eye contact with each of them, saying nothing, just feeling total humiliated and degraded.

Thomas began pacing behind me while he waited for my decision. "You are always so concerned that you look so perfect, you show up every week with makeup on, always looking so perfect. Let us see you a complete mess."

"Damn you, Thomas!" I shouted. "All of the other women wear makeup, they all wear lipstick. Why are you picking on me? I can't help it if I do a good job putting it on. It's what I do for a profession, damn it!" I could see the corner of his mouth tilt up with a sarcastic smile.

"You're worried about people seeing you with snot running down your face? Here, let me help you," he said, as he wiped the back of his hand across my upper lip.

"All right! I'll stay!" *You're not going to win, you son of a bitch,* I thought to myself as I yanked my head away from him. My breathing was rapid and shallow. I was filled with rage that made me want to obliterate this man from my universe and rip him apart in any manner that I could.

I stood in front of Taryn, forcing myself to hold eye contact with her. I don't know whether it was pity or compassion that I was reading in her expression—perhaps a little of both. I felt myself begin to break down. I stood there, not saying a word, just looking into her dark eyes. I felt the tears begin to flow down my face and along my nose. I began to cry. I tried to hide by turning my head and burying it in the only place that held any refuge, the place that was closest, Thomas's chest. He grabbed me by the shoulders and shoved me back, at the same time turning my body to face the next person in the group. I was frightened and defeated, a total blubbering mess with snot running down my face, humiliated, without defense or dignity. I stood there and cried like a baby, walking and stopping in front of each person, letting them see me out of control and feeling like I wanted to die.

Thomas motioned the group to come close, and all of a sudden I was being held and hugged as I sobbed. "You see," he said, "how the universe responds to you when you allow yourself to be totally vulnerable?"

I felt a great sense of relief that the ordeal was over and fell into the chair totally exhausted. Thomas's voice broke the silence. "Someone get her a box of tissue." I sat there, feeling too weak to pull the tissue out of the box. I wanted to curl up into a ball and just shut my eyes, thankful that I was no longer in the center of the circle.

Thomas began speaking, "I'd like to find out how all of you felt about what just happened. What was your response? Shawn, let's begin with you."

"I know one thing I was feeling," Shawn said. "If Athena decided to leave, I was going to block the door.

I didn't feel sorry for her at all when she was angry. I could feel the walls and the defenses. But, when she began to cry, I felt really close to her. I'm glad you decided to stay," he said, with a genuine smile on his face.

The response was basically the same throughout the group. People felt a lot of love for me towards the end of the exercise, especially when I broke down. I just sat in the chair, listening, not responding. I was just so damned thankful that it was over. I felt proud of myself for not leaving when it would have been the easiest thing for me to do. But I know it would have been nothing more than saving face. No matter how hard it was to remain and to confront a situation that was unbearably uncomfortable and frightening, knowing that I quit would have been worse.

Thomas concluded the class. As everybody was circulating and saying their goodbyes, it felt to me as if all who were hugging me held me a little longer and tighter than usual. It felt good, but I just wanted to go home, crawl in bed, and lick my wounds like an injured animal.

Driving home that warm afternoon, I experienced the strangest sensation that, to this day, I've never forgotten. I know that since that time, I've never felt it again. I became acutely aware, not just through my senses alone, but from the feeling part of my nature, that I was connected to everything around me. There was no illusion of separation. It was as if I felt a part of every tree I was passing on the road, part of every cloud in the sky, part of the dirt and the cement. As I steered my car on Pacific Coast Highway, I felt the tears start again. It was such a beautiful sensation. I wasn't really thinking about it; I was living it, with every breath I was taking—like osmosis.

Driving among the mainstream of traffic that Saturday afternoon, like an army of ants, one following the other in their frenzied state of "getting there," wherever that is, I was no different. I was the form and the formless. For once in my life, I was a part of it all.

I had experienced that exact same type of crystal-line clarity ten years ago. However, at that time it was at the extreme opposite end of the spectrum—a feeling of complete and total separation. I thought it somewhat strange that this memory would present itself to me at this time for comparison. It had happened at a time in my life when shoving down the impulse to commit suicide was becoming too much work. I found myself succumbing to the thought out of sheer exhaustion. I remembered driving down Sunset Boulevard on my way to see a therapist. I knew I needed help. I also knew that she was my last hope. Shortly before, I had a dream in which I was standing on an island. There was nothing else alive but me. I knew I had to get off of the island, but I had no idea how I could escape. I looked up at the sky, which had become a threatening mass of black. It was the eerie quiet, the deadly silence that I was so afraid of. I knew that the wrath of God, a storm which nothing could survive, was about to be unleashed. I could feel it. All it would take was the prick of a pin. I felt so isolated and alone. The storm of my emotions had been suppressed, shoved down through the fear, and was gaining the momentum and strength of a hur-ricane. All that was needed was a microscopic opening through which it could unleash all of its fury.

Driving that night to the therapist's, the lights from the oncoming cars were blinding. I felt as if I was in a Plexiglas bubble. Everybody had some place to go, rushing home after work. All of those faceless blurs passing me on the opposite side of the road. They didn't know each other, yet they all looked like they belonged to something. What did that feel like, to belong? To know where you were going? I wanted to be part of them, but I wasn't. I didn't know how to be part of them. Physically, I was there in that stream of people, but I was so separated from them. I wanted to belong. I wanted to be a part of something. Yet I felt like a speck of dust that was being carried aimlessly on a current of wind.

As my mind came back to the present, the sensation of total oneness had vanished. I was more aware of the exhaustion within my body. I wanted to escape through sleep, to shut my eyes and forget about the humiliation and embarrassment I had experienced that afternoon.

I could no longer deal with the frustration and anger. Anger was an emotion that I never gave myself permission to fully express. I felt that it was wrong, that I wasn't a "nice person" if I couldn't control my anger. So I just never let myself feel it. Instead, it would take its toll in the form of deep-seated depression, or I would try to meditate it away—anything but to feel and acknowledge it. Well, here I was, so full of an emotion that to a great degree felt foreign to me that it was eating me alive. I was afraid of it.

I had an appointment with a new therapist the following week after Thomas's class. The moment I walked into her office, she immediately picked up on the fact that I was in pain. "What is going on with you?" she said, with genuine concern.

"Oh God, it's a mess!" I replied. I was aware of the tears that were beginning to sting my eyes. I hated to let people see me cry. I hated even more the fact that I couldn't control this emotion. Normally, I would just take a deep breath to cut off the feeling before it had a chance to surface, but she was too quick for that. "Just sit quietly, stay with that feeling." I sat Indian-fashion on her couch, shredding Kleenex in my hand, feeling uncomfortable with her eyes on me, uncomfortable with silence in the room.

I liked Patricia the first moment I met her. She was

a pretty woman in her early thirties, with long brown hair and a kind face. She was spiritually aware. The white candles that she burned before starting a session with anyone gave me a sense of safety, as well as peace. I remember thinking to myself, or I should say feeling, that I had indeed been guided to the right person to help me. She made me feel safe, just from the presence that emanated from her being. Her green eyes held compassion and concern, not sympathy or pity. I had the feeling that her own life had held more that its share of turmoil, but that she had come through the other end bringing to her clients a greater understanding of the healing process, based on both therapeutic knowledge and personal experience.

Her office was small but comfortable. All anyone had to do was look around to see what Patricia was all about. Large crystals sat on the table, and pillows were placed around the room for the client's comfort. Soft meditation music, barely audible played in the background inviting relaxation. I liked it here, and I liked her.

I explained all that had happened the previous week with Thomas's class. She listened intently until I finished my story. "Whew!" she sighed, as she relaxed back into her chair. "He hit hard!"

I just sat there, nodding my head in acknowledgment. I had not shared this with anyone. I was too embarrassed. I felt a sense of relief that someone knew.

"I want to try something," she said as stood up and pushed her chair out of the way. She made a larger clearing in the middle of the room. Then she bent over and grabbed a pillow and tossed it on the floor.

"Here, lie down, stretch out, and get comfortable. I have an idea." I began to feel uneasy and vulnerable instantly, not knowing what she had in mind. I never did like lying on my back. I folded my hands across my stomach. I didn't feel so exposed that way. "Hands down by your side," she said gently. "I want to take that little girl part of yourself back into the center of the circle with Thomas."

Instantly, I wanted to get up off of that floor. I didn't like this exercise. I did not want to do it. I didn't want to cry anymore. I was afraid. I hated feeling out of control, and I didn't know where this was going.

"Breathe slowly and deeply. I want you to be aware." She began to speak slowly and rhythmically as she guided me through a relaxation exercise, with guided imagery, back to a time when I could see myself as a little girl. She probed gently with seeking questions, trying to help me to see that child. "What does she look like? Where is she? What is she doing?"

As I listened to her voice, I felt myself begin to go into a deeper state of relaxation. I felt the tears roll down my cheeks. I was uncomfortable with the feeling of blackness I saw in my mind. It wasn't blackness from a void; it was blackness that the little girl part of me was entrapped in.

"Where is she?" Patricia asked quietly.

"It's all black down there; she's hiding."

"I want you to reach for her hand. I want you to put her in the center of the circle at Thomas's."

"NO! I can't! She'll get hurt, and I have to protect her!"

"So you feel that you have to protect her, and so you have to be in control, is that right? What felt so bad is that you lost control, and it was your little girl that got attacked."

"Yes." I was crying harder now. There I was, once again, exposed, vulnerable, and hating the feelings.

"How do you feel right now?"

"I feel like a house that's been burnt down to the ground, and the only thing left standing is the fireplace."

"That's a good analogy," she replied.

"I feel vulnerable."

"I want you to put that little girl on your lap and tell her that it is okay to be afraid. Tell her it is okay to feel vulnerable. It's okay to feel fear. Life is scary sometimes, we don't always know what is going to happen, and it's okay to admit you are afraid. You don't always have to be strong."

Patricia's words touched something deep inside of me, and I began to cry harder.

"What are you doing right now? What is going on inside?"

"Quick! I have to build the walls back up!" The words tumbled out of my mouth so fast that I had no time to censor them. It was like something had escaped from deep within my subconscious so quickly that I was totally stunned for a moment.

"Oh, my God," I cried, "did you hear what I just said? I have to build the walls back up!" I searched Patricia's face for an explanation. She just sat on the floor and nodded her head in recognition. I didn't need an explanation. It was all contained within the sentence I spoke.

I sobbed and sobbed while she held me, rocking me back and forth like a mother comforting her child. "This man, this Thomas Jacobson, he gave you a gift," she whispered.

19
Another Delightful Opportunity For Growth

There is an eagle in me that wants to soar, and there is a hippopotamus in me that wants to wallow in the mud.
—*Carl Sandburg*

I can't remember the exact moment when I began to realize that my running around trying to "save" people was a futile attempt, in a sense, at trying to save my own drowning ass. That realization had been struggling to surface on its own for quite some time, but it was the last thing that I wanted to look at. Thomas Jacobson served as the catalyst and brought into full focus that which had already begun to stir within my soul. He poked a red-hot iron into the layers of scar tissue and reopened a wound that had never healed properly, and I screamed and bellowed from the pain.

I do, however, remember sitting on the couch in my living room, staring out the window into the courtyard and crying. It was a feeling of overwhelming sadness that throbbed from the inside out. There were so many issues that I had to look at and address now, whether I wanted to or not. I couldn't shove these things to the back of my mind simply because it was easier and much more comfortable to do so.

I kept hearing Thomas's words in my head, playing over and over again like a broken record. "I think it's sad . . . no, not just sad, I think that it's tragic that the only time you feel alive is when you are working with prisoners. I think that it's tragic that you can't feel that same sense of aliveness with life."

I couldn't count the times that I've sat on this couch, staring for hours, thinking, not thinking, drifting—just staring through my window. If only that window weren't there, and I could reach out my hand and touch all of "life" out there, to *feel* it, *really feel*, instead of feeling so separated and isolated from it. If only I could do that.

Now I was beginning to see who was really imprisoned. My front room window somehow represented my own internal bars. Although I could see life, every time I stretched out my hand to touch it, I came up against an invisible barrier. God, I can't even put into words the sadness I felt, or the sense of loss that these realizations held for me. I had to give up the only thing that made me feel good, that gave me a sense of worth, that said to me, "I am an okay person. I'm not so bad. I'm worth something." Working with prisoners, I felt like *something*, like my life had purpose and meaning. It gave me a sense of power and identity, like trying to prove to the world as well as myself that I was a good human being, instead of feeling like nothing. A "no thing"—that's how I had felt most of my life, like a "no thing."

The hurt and loss stemmed from my awareness that all of it had engendered a false sense of power. If I *needed* this volunteer work to make me feel whole and good, to make me feel okay about myself, it meant to me that I was nothing more than a vampire drawing my life force from others. Everything was still outside of me, and inside I still felt vacant. I felt ashamed of myself for being so manipulative, for using people in order to feel good about myself, to feel good about being alive. Who was that wise old soul who said, "We teach what we need to learn"?

The trouble was, I'd never felt good about being alive, and I guess as hard as it was to admit, as long as I kept my attention on others, on their pain and their problems, I didn't have to look at my own, on the deepest levels necessary for my own healing. This may be a crazy analogy, but at this stage in my life, I felt like there had been a pot of beans sitting on a stove, in full view, waiting to be cleaned out, but out of my own laziness and unwillingness to dump out the contents, it had fermented and spoiled. And now it felt as if I was edging my way slowly towards that combustive monster, trying to build up enough courage to lift the lid before the pressure of its own gaseous poison blew up and splattered me from head to toe.

I've resisted like hell being honest with myself. It has been so much easier to blame others for my feelings of emptiness and inadequacies, and I still do it. I can feel it through anger and outbursts of irritability that make me want to shove everything and everybody away from me. Half of the time I want to scream, "Screw it! It's too much work," go in my bedroom, shut out the world, curl up in a ball, withdraw from everything, and escape through sleep.

I wanted to scream at the top of my lungs until everything in the universe recoiled from the sound. I felt a guttural almost primal cry from the depths of my frustrations trying to escape and find release, while at the same time; another voice reprimanded me with, "Jesus Christ! Control yourself!" I didn't want to be conscious of the fact that the neighbors might hear my outburst. "Fuck the neighbors! Fuck it all! I'm so pissed!" I screamed.

I wanted to have the freedom to lose all control and not give a goddamn about the results. Just once, I wanted to *feel* the peak of my anger, without restraint, without the wide-eyed look of shock on anyone's face that happened to be in my path when my anger reached a climactic level of pressure. I picked up an ashtray off the coffee table and started to throw it through the front window—through the pane of glass, through my prison, almost as if to break through that invisible barrier. I caught myself and hurled it at the wall instead. I watched it break into three pieces. I felt my adrenaline like liquid fire, pumping through my veins. *Not enough noise. . . . not enough noise! Son of a bitch! I want to feel it! Really feel it!*

I threw open the cupboard door in the kitchen and grabbed an ugly fucking green goblet. I stood back and threw it as hard as I could. I watched the goblet hit the refrigerator and smash into an explosion of green fragments. "Fuck everything in this cocksucking world!" I screamed and threw myself onto the bed, letting all of the frustration come in waves of sobs. "I hate myself! I say that I am writing a book and I don't fucking work on it! I'm a goddamn phony! I hate my smoking. I need to lose weight. I say that I want to paint, but I don't even take a fucking art class! I am so filled with self-hate and I'm *afraid*. I'm so damned tired of feeling withdrawn and separated from life. I can't stand it anymore. I feel like I'm going crazy. I'm sick of all the anger that I've been feeling this past year. I don't understand where it is all coming from." I felt drained and exhausted. I wanted to sleep and never wake up.

The next day, I felt better. I cringed a few times when I looked at the dent that I put in the refrigerator door, but what the hell, what's done is done. I figured I'd just hang a potholder over it and no one will notice.

At least I was starting to write my book. I thought, *It may be nothing more than a pile of shit, but it's a start*. It all seemed so overwhelming, such a major undertaking.

20
I'm Sick Of Being So Nice

You did not come to the earth to become perfect; you
came to the earth to stop condemning yourself
for not being perfect.
—*Dr. James Martin Peebles*

I let my mind drift back to May of 1986. I remember the sensation of anticipation I was feeling as I drove down Pacific Coast Highway towards Palos Verdes. It was a clear day, unusual for Los Angeles. The yellowish haze was at least nonexistent at the coast. I felt the cool ocean breeze against my face and was thankful that if I chose to live in LA, at least it was at the ocean. Somehow, in this transient time, the beach held a sense of space and peace for me. Not that I spend a lot of time on the beach—I don't—but what has always felt good to me is the feeling of not being closed in by cement.

My excitement grew as I steered my car down the tree-lined street, slowing down as I double-checked the address of Thomas Jacobson's house. I turned on the radio, hoping to catch the time. I didn't want to be late for this appointment. I rummaged through my purse for the list of questions that I had carefully pondered and put in order of importance. I picked up the cassette recorder and hit the eject button, making sure that the blank tape was in correctly. "I don't want to miss a word of this," I thought to myself, as I opened the car door. The air was filled with the smell of fresh cut grass. I inhaled deeply as I glanced down the street. This neighborhood was occupied by people who took pride in their home and surroundings. That was apparent in the well-manicured lawns, and the splashes of vibrant flowers in full bloom, carefully planted for all of the passers-by to admire. Their fashion show was not in vain. I, for one, admired them dearly. Fresh flowers have always been the one luxury I allow myself. I would rather be able to pick a bouquet of wildflowers than to pick out a new piece of jewelry.

Thomas and Joanna had moved recently from Marina Del Rey. We had begun the class called "Journey to the Heart" while they were living in Topanga Canyon. I was beginning to feel that they either had a little gypsy in their souls or that they were being guided to new locations because of reasons perhaps they weren't even fully aware of, but they followed the impulse out of trust and a knowing that it held a purpose. That first class had been over for quite some time and, though I was able to view it as a real gift, I still did not feel totally comfortable around Thomas.

I rang the doorbell and waited impatiently for the response. Part of the nervousness that I was feeling was the uncomfortable sensation of my own insecurities, I suppose. I had always wanted Thomas to like me. Although the class certainly proved to be a great lesson in how hard I fought to protect my own vulnerability, it also made me feel extremely exposed in his presence. It's like having a knock-down-drag-out fight with a mate, in which real mud-slinging occurs. Even though you resolve the issue and make up and are thankful that everything came to a head, you can never erase the experience in your memory. Thomas had labeled me a "bullshitter," not only in front of others, but, more importantly, to myself. It had left me with intense feelings and questions about the level of my own sincerity and honesty. He had the eerie ability to cut to the core quickly to assess what was really happening on levels one could not see with X-ray vision. Thomas was not your normal, run-of-the-mill kind of guy. This man was different. He was just downright powerful. Your senses told you that—your gut intuitively felt it. His whole psyche commanded respect, whether or not you felt like giving it. It didn't matter, you just did it.

Thomas was a man of large stature—six feet and some odd inches, with sandy blonde hair and attractive features. The most endearing quality about him was a laugh that was downright infectious. He could laugh at himself. That's what I always enjoyed the most—the moments when that impish grin broke out on his face. You knew something good was about to follow. Just when you were dealing with something serious in nature, he'd jump in with something off the wall. Before you knew it, you were laughing because of *his* laugh, the way it sounded. It was contagious as hell.

He opened the door and stepped forward to give me a hug. He was wearing a pair of sweats and tennis shoes, looking comfortable but tired. "Hi, Thomas," I said as I embraced him.

He stood sideways with his back pressed against the door and, with his left arm, pushed it fully open, so that I could enter first. Once inside, he took the lead and I followed him into the front room. It was well decorated, spacious and comfortable. He stopped, turned around, and just looked at me. Tilting his head slightly, he paused and squinted his eyes like he was somewhat perplexed and was trying to figure something out. I started to say, "What? What is it?" when he said, "You look different.

You look more alive. That's it. You look more alive. You look younger, too."

I felt awkward and embarrassed. I stammered, "Thanks, I guess I do feel more alive."

"It shows," he said, "Shall we get started?" I nodded my head and followed him into the hallway that led to a small bedroom that had been converted to what felt like a cross between an office and a meditation room. I chose not to sit in the chair, but immediately removed my shoes and lowered myself onto the floor, sitting Indian fashion. I set the tape recorder in front of me and began to survey the room for an outlet. "There's one right behind you," he said. I leaned sideways with the cord in my hand, stretching my arm until I felt the prongs slip securely in place. I pushed down the record button, pulled out my list of questions and, placing the sheet of paper on my lap, I began to relax a little.

Thomas sat across from me, about seven feet or so away. His body looked out of place in the small blue wicker chair he sat in when he channeled. "It must be of importance to him," I thought to myself. "This is at least the sixth or seventh time I've watched him go into trance, and he always uses this chair."

The process seemed to take three minutes or so, starting with his settling into the chair and getting as comfortable as possible, while at the same time breathing a little deeper, until he began to yawn. I watched him slip deeper and deeper into trance, fascinated by the sudden jerks that seemed to jolt him awake again. It reminded me of the times when I had almost fallen asleep, but was reawakened by a spasm or a jerk of my arm, and felt temporarily disoriented for a split second as I awoke.

He looked as if he was almost asleep. His head fell back slowly, when once again the jolt brought him back to semi-consciousness. I listened to him as he spoke in an almost inaudible voice, affirming the love and one-ness with all life everywhere. It was a brief sentence he always spoke as a part of the ritual of preparing him-self, and all of the space around him, to become the doorway in this dimension that the spirit of Dr. Peebles could enter. Another minute passed while I waited in suspense. I could begin to feel the energy in the room change. I felt a quickening, almost like an acceleration within myself. Three more affirmations followed, as he called upon the spirit to enter and become one with life and truth. Thomas was in full trance now.

With full impact, his body fell forward, slightly dou-bled over, and for a moment it seemed as if all life had left him. Then, like a drowning man whose lungs were ready to burst from lack of oxygen, he breathed in life to the maximum capacity that his lungs could expand. I had the distinct sensation that every cell in his body had been collapsed and instantaneously re-expanded with more life and oxygen than it had previously held. A marriage of consciousness had taken place, it ap-peared to me. The facial features that were so uniquely Thomas's no longer looked the same.

"God bless you, Dr. Peebles here! It is a joy and a pleasure when man and spirit join together to increase our truth and awareness. Might I offer encouragement, my dear friend, as you strive to understand your right to receive and to give abundance of love in this, your current and chosen lifetime?

"Greetings my dearest friend, Athena. This is a time of celebration within your soul, for 1986 assuredly is your time of greatest birth, where you will experience your finest love for self in the presence of life everywhere. You are here, Athena, to understand the Goddess, not only within you but within life around you—also the Goddess

in relationships, the Goddess in communication between self and all life everywhere. You are effectively
understanding the nature of purity now as something
that does include all colors, all vibrations of life and all
experience. You are opening yourself in the midst of life;
you are allowing life to penetrate you. You have felt moments of severe and great anger. We wish to assure you
that this is success, not failure, for it is allowing you to
know that inner pain that you were able to cover over.
It is allowing you to know the inner truth—that truth
which includes not only forgiveness for others but your
own temporary bias. It is allowing you to know, then,
enlightenment . . . , enlightenment as something that
can be at hand, rather than in the eternal distance.

"We encourage you, for you are a healer, a healer for
life everywhere, and now you are truly, for the first time,
Athena, healing yourself beyond your wildest dreams
and imagination. Thereby, do not be discontent, my
dear, do not feel afraid in moments of great change in
your emotional nature, for it is only helping you know
truth, the truth of your relationship with yourself, the
truth of your relationship with all life, which is the only
reason that every spirit is here—to study the nature
of relationships in your own personal, your own self-
image. God bless you, my dear, and would you have
questions or comment?"

"Yes! Dr. Peebles, the last four months I have felt like
I've been blown apart in ways. Is this that process taking place?" I asked.

"Absolutely! And it's not completely over yet, but you
will feel less and less like you are being blown apart by
outside forces, you will feel more and more that it is
your own internal fuel igniting."

"Recently, I've been entertaining the thought that
I've been real controlling and manipulative. I haven't
wanted to look at that or acknowledge that. I think this

running around, trying to save everyone else, has been a way of trying to save myself."

"Good girl!" he replied with great enthusiasm. I felt like a kid in preschool that had just been given a gold star by a favorite teacher. "As a healer," he continued, "as the old healer, my dear, I know . . . you want to take care of everyone else, you want to control their reactions, you try to anticipate their best interest. Free yourself from that. Instead, communicate your best interest with respect, love, and oneness with life around you, and don't presume what's best for others. Allow them to respond as they must respond. Even though you were doing it from love, in the experience of others, it feels like you are trying to control them, and manipulate them, for what was best for them, you see?"

"Yeah, it's beginning to become clear. I have felt so much, almost like, inner turmoil. It's been hard for me to understand and see and get to the surface."

"All of that desire to serve others has certainly been an act of love that is legitimate on your part, but it is especially a cover, a camouflage that allows you to ignore your greatest fear of serving yourself—your greatest guilt from the past of serving yourself too much. When you expressed your demands, then you were rejected, beaten, cut off, killed and denied, starved to death. And your need is to express yourself, but this time there is a difference from when you did it in the distant past time—there is a difference. This time it is allowing others to express themselves any way they want in response. The way you can understand how you are controlling, Athena, is you try to say the right things, you try to say them in such a way that others will not feel pain, so that they will not get angry at you, so they won't think that you don't love them. So instead of speaking the truth of how you feel, exactly how you feel, you contort it, even distort it, trying to anticipate what others' needs are.

Now imagine someone doing that around you—always trying to anticipate your needs in their terms, distorting their communications, as if they know what you are thinking, and feeling what's best for you."

"I don't think I'd like it very much," I replied.

"You might feel obligated to say 'thank you,' but you wouldn't feel very free in their presence would you?"

"No, I wouldn't. And lately I've started to become aware of the fact that I haven't really been very honest with myself."

"I know," he replied. "I believe that the channel confronted you with that in his class. You haven't had the time to be honest with yourself, because all of your attention has been on others. The reason your attention has been on others, Athena, is so that you could avoid putting your attention on what you really want in all honest truths."

"Where does that guilt come from? From feeling unworthy?"

"Absolutely!" He paused a few moments before continuing. "Well, it's a long series of lives. More than unworthy, Athena, you were shattered by pain when you came from another planet, when you came from another place. And pain, as human beings experience, was quite abnormal to your experience. So, right from the beginning, Athena, you wanted to take pain away from everyone, for everyone. You felt that you failed utterly, over and over again. There went life, on and on, having pain—relatives, friends, family, community— and you banished yourself and said, 'I am a failure, not in technique, but in desire. I didn't want it bad enough.' You made strong commitments, over and over again, that you were going to love people, take care of them, heal them and get rid of that pain. The pain, of course, which is really in you. The pain which is the result of your judgment and your assumption that the way Earth works is not proper, that God didn't plan this quite correctly—something is wrong here. So, if you can surrender that Earth is fine, just the way it is—shocking though that may be—and that God is already present, and heaven on Earth and fruits of the labor simply have not been translated yet by each and every human being incarnate . . . but God is present."

"Well, it is all new. It's beginning to become a little clearer to me now. I feel like it is foggy, but I'm starting to see something underneath there and I understand it."

"It's valid to be concerned and compassionate about pain, it's valid not to have pain, but there is an entirely other approach that has reverence for the pain, rather than fear of it or judgment of it. More of a curiosity of it, rather than a surgeon cutting it out."

"Well, I've noticed that I haven't been talking about spirituality to people as much as I did before the class with Thomas."

"That's because they are already spiritual. One who would be master is simply to retranslate what spiritual means. When spirituality is limited, then it is impossible to avoid changing others. It is a sincere act of love to try to change others so they can be spiritual and be good, but when you expand your concept of spirituality instead, you can allow other people to be with you, which feels good and feels like you are being loved fully for the first time rather than needed. Life takes on a new color, more of a celebration rather than avoidance, and it all begins with expressing yourself publicly, and vulnerably. The second step, equally important, is to allow life to respond back in any way in which it wants, and to see that as spiritual and equal."

"Okay, that helps a lot." I replied. "Dr. Peebles, I have another question. When I was young and was molested, did that happen only once?"

"No." He replied without a moment's hesitation.

"It happened more?"

"Yes."

I sat there shocked for a brief moment before I could respond.

"Good Lord!" I heard myself stammering as I tried to ask him a question. "You mean . . ., you mean . . . that's interesting . . . you mean . . ."

"And I don't mean less than a dozen times either."

"You mean more than a dozen? With the same man?"

"That's all I'm going to tell you now. You need to explore it. I can tell you for sure, that the same man was more than a dozen . . . yes."

"Did he physically enter me?"

"Yes."

"Oh, my God. Can you tell me the age? The year six keeps coming to me."

"Have you explored this in regression?" He asked.

"Pardon me?"

"Have you explored this in regression?"

"No, I haven't."

"Well, that's why we are a little reticent to tell you everything. We'd like you to experience it, so when you experience it, you won't feel like you are just making it up, replaying what we told you. So you can feel the spontaneity of it from within you. Will you consider that?"

"Yes." I answered back, still stunned.

"With any source you wish," he continued. "Anyone you want to help you and it will be wonderful. It will be wonderful, and it will help you understand amongst other things part of the healer in you in this life. Well, that's all I'm going to tell you."

"Okay, I'll definitely trust your wisdom on that."

"Yes, I strongly encourage that."

"Ahhh, . . . was this a blocking?"

"Yes, definitely."

"So, that's why I don't remember?"

"You will see and experience how and why. How and why you created that and techniques you used to do it, . . . the decisions you made. You will experience them again. You'll experience some inner decisions you made that were very firm that have had an impact on your entire life. And you must not judge yourself or others if you do allow that to take place and feel it and accept it, and eventually you must forgive yourself and others, and see how you have learned from it."

"Well, that makes sense. Was I under six? Can you tell me that?"

"No, no, no, no, no. That's all I'm going to tell you. At another point and time, if you wish confirmation, I'll tell you then, but your teachers here and myself, we would like you to go through it."

"Okay."

"Because you see what will happen, Athena. You'll go through the experience and feel like you made it up because Dr. Peebles told you so—and instead, if we tell you a little bit and you go through it yourself, you won't be able to say that."

"Well, I want to get this thing resolved, and if that's what I have to do to grow then that's okay."

"I believe it's that strong that you have to do it."

"I know I have to, so I will definitely do that. Dr. Peebles, for the last few years, I don't know why, but I have found myself thinking about the pirates Blackbeard and Bluebeard. Can you tell me why?"

"Oh, yes," he replied quickly. "Many times while you were in the sleep state you would come up here on the spirit side and you would stomp your feet on the ground with your hands on your hips yelling, 'I'm sick and tired of being so nice all the time. Can't anyone help me?'

"You attracted many wonderful spirits to you, but the

two that you were most attracted to are these two notorious, colorful characters who have long since learned the errors of their ways, and they have been helping you to explore your anger. Incidentally, you love their costumes."

21

When Evil Finds Its Root

Sure I am of this, that you have only to endure to conquer. You have to persevere to save yourselves.
—*Winston Churchill*

It seemed to me that everything was coming up to the surface to be looked at and healed in all areas of my life. There was little breathing room, as my experiences seemed to be tumbling over each over for conscious acknowledgement. The good, the bad, and the ugly emerged, and Ed aka "the troll," the perpetrator, was "the ugly." It was impossible for me to think of him without shuddering within every cell of my body from repulsion. I wanted to heal, but on the other hand, it's hard to heal something when you simply can't remember it. So I called my sister Judy.

"Hello?"

"Hi Judy, it's me. Is this a good time to talk?"

"Sure, what's up?"

I stammered within my discomfort, trying to make my request easily understood. "What can you tell me about Ed Dahlberg? I really need help in remembering. . . . Is there anything you can tell me? I can remember specific things clearly and then it is like it all goes to snow.

Nothing. I can remember him sitting on the side of the bed scratching my back. I was sleeping on my stomach on the outside of the bed. Connie was in the middle, and Susie was sleeping next to the wall. He was drunk. He told me to get up and come into the front room. I remember him sitting me on his lap and forcing my hand on his penis and cramming his tongue down my throat. He pushed me back on the couch. I don't remember a thing after that. Judy, I have made a decision to see someone professionally. Would it be possible for you to record your thoughts for me on tape? It would help, and this way I could have this for the psychologist if I need it."

"Oh God, I don't know if I am ready to get into that crap." She sighed from the depths of her toes. "Okay, well, maybe, because you are asking."

"I love you, Judy."

"I love you too." I hung up the phone, knowing I had now set things in motion. What in God's name would be unearthed was yet to be seen.

A few weeks later I received a tape in the mail.

I put the tape in the recorder. *Here we go,* I thought to myself. I hit the play button.

"Nothing, but nothing, prepared me for Ed," Judy began. "I was stunned, I really was. When I walked into the house, here was this man who looked like somebody who would be sleeping on a doorstep on Seventh Avenue in Klamath Falls—that was the town's skid row. That, and Klamath Avenue. He looked that way. It didn't seem to matter how much he cleaned up; it didn't seem to matter. He had horrible teeth; he was missing some in front and the others were rotted. Unkempt looking, he wasn't clean-shaven, was in need of a haircut. He wasn't neat looking—there was nothing neat about him, and he drove this ratty old car— and he was a part of our lives.

"I was so thoroughly repulsed, if I would have had

somewhere to go, somewhere to run, I think I would have," Judy continued. "Because, I just couldn't believe it. I didn't trust him. . . . I didn't trust him. And I thought, well, after I thought about it for awhile, I thought, gee, I'm judging. . . . You know, how you rationalize and justify on a gut level what you know is not so, and yet you rationalize and justify and say, 'I'm being unfair to this person,' and I wasn't. I was right dead center now as I look back.

"Ed was . . . disgusting, in my opinion. I never liked the man. I didn't trust him, and I had good reason. He and Mom drank an awful lot, and boy, that's when her alcoholism was, I mean, really out of control. She said, from time to time, that she was with him because the family needed the money. That wasn't it at all.

"She was just out of control—an out-of-control alcoholic—and for some reason she always needed a man in her life to validate who she was. And I don't find that hard to understand. She, like the rest of us, gets her identity from other people.

"Anyway, it was not unusual for them to go out, and when they came back, for her to be covered with bruises, have black eyes and teeth loosened. She kept going back for more. She would take responsibility for it, lie about it—'she fell' or, you know, a whole lot of crazy shit. He was violent, he was sick, he was an alcoholic . . . , a real low-level skid row drunk," Judy recalled.

"One weekend when they had been drinking, they had gone out, and I was babysitting. We had all gone to bed, and I woke up at one or two in the morning. I was sleeping in the front bedroom, and you kids were all awake and screaming. I went into the girls' bedroom. Johnny was sleeping in the crib. Everybody was awake, the lights were on, you kids were screaming, and Ed was choking Mother, and she was turning blue. She was half on and half off the bed. Bill was beating on his back, you and Connie, Paul, everybody was on him, and I kept trying to break his hold," she said, her voice filled with emotion.

"I couldn't get his hands off her throat. I kept trying and trying and finally, I went into the living room and grabbed a piece of firewood. I can remember this incredible rage building up inside of me . . . , and I didn't want to hit him, so I said, "Let go or I'm going to hit ya!" He wouldn't let go. Finally, I *had* to hit him, and it was *hard* and that wood seemed to weigh a ton.

"I got it up over my head and came down with it, but it didn't seem to do any good. I lifted it up again and I hit him again . . . and it didn't do any good and I hit him again, and I hit him again . . . and finally, he let her go and she fell to the floor.

"He looked at me with this strange dazed look and kind of went down to his knees, then got up and staggered down the hall through the dining room and into the kitchen. The door closed and I heard him fall. It was awful . . . awful is not the word for it. The feeling that I had . . . I wanted to kill him . . . *I wanted to kill him.* And that rush of adrenaline . . . I can still remember that feeling of banging the wood against his head and *feeling* the concussion run up the wood into my arms . . . and this awful rage . . . like all I wanted to do was kill him, and when it was over, I knew it was possible. Then I was *afraid* I killed him . . . What if I killed him?

"Everybody is still screaming . . . Mom is not moving, and I started to try to revive her . . . She was still breathing. What she was, was passed out. I got her up onto the bed, got you kids quieted down, and didn't know what the fuck to do next," Judy continued.

"We didn't have a phone, it's now three o'clock in the morning, Ed is on the floor in the kitchen. The door is closed, so I can't see in there; all I can hear is him thumping and bumping around, trying to get up, falling back down, mumbling, what he's going to do to that 'bitch that hit him on the head,' mumbling how he was going to kill me . . . me or Mom. I don't know who he was talking about; I thought it was me . . . I ran over to the Steinbrooks' and woke 'em up, used their phone to call the police . . . I couldn't get anyone to go back to the house with me to go in. I knew you kids were alone and Mom was alone. I was so afraid to go into that house, because I didn't know what was going to happen to me.

"I got in and it seemed like it took forever for the police to finally get there. I met them and told them what had happened. They wanted to see Mom.

"I'll never forget the look that they gave each other when I told them that she had been sick . . . like, *ah, yeah . . . oh sure,* and I hated that! I hated that feeling of trying to defend something that was indefensible . . . the pain you kids were in . . . It was awful trauma.

"They brought him in, and I had to face him, and they told me I had to tell him that he was under arrest. He had blood running down his forehead. I had bashed him pretty good. I was relieved he wasn't dead, but I was deathly afraid of him then, and full of hate, just full of hate. That hate followed me around for years before I could release it.

"I got everybody settled down . . . got you kids to sleep, and finally fell asleep myself."

"Mom didn't remember this, had difficulty believing it. She was mad at me that I had him thrown in jail—'He's not that bad you know,'—and I came unglued! All of the resentment that had been building up came out, and I know that it really shocked her, shook her, and I think my total rejection of her and what she was doing got through. She cooled it with her drinking from that point on for quite awhile . . . At least, if she drank, she didn't drink at home."

Judy went on, "Ed kept trying to come back into her life, and I know she was still seeing him, but because of the way I felt, I told her if he came back, I was not only going to go to the police, but I would go to the authorities because I was afraid for the kids. I think she believed me. I don't know what I would have done, really didn't know that much about the workings of the system. Of course, all this time, you know, I've got friends, and I didn't talk to them about it. . . . I was too ashamed. I just couldn't let anybody know that I had these kinds of feelings."

"At some point after that, probably a couple of weeks, I think you must have gotten comfortable then or began to believe that he wasn't coming back, and that's when I found out, when we were talking . . . because you had been asking on a daily basis, 'Is he coming back? Is he coming back? Is he coming back?'

"I thought you were just afraid. Shit, I was afraid. Son of a bitch, he used to come and park out in front of that street light in front of the house . . . and just park there all night because my bedroom was in front and he knew I could see him. I didn't dare go to sleep because I didn't know whether he would come into the house through the basement. Mom would be at work, and he would sit there. He would come down to La Points and park his car right in front of the window where he knew I would be working . . . psychological terror. He was a very sick man.

"I had to go testify against him that he had attacked my mother, and Mother wouldn't come and back me up, so he got off. Some time after that, he stayed away, but I am pretty sure that they were still seeing each other. He finally came to the house. This was after you had told me what he had been doing to you."

"I had told Mother; she didn't want to believe either one of us. She was worried how she was going to make ends meet financially; she didn't want to hear it. . . . She didn't want to believe it. I threatened her again. I told her that nobody was safe with him and that she'd better take a look at herself and what she was getting the kids into. I was just so thoroughly disgusted with her, that I almost hated her as much as I hated him, for letting such a thing happen . . . for not believing, for not wanting to believe. I realize now it was because she was so deep in her alcoholism and couldn't help it.

"Ed came to the house, and I confronted him. You kids were all behind me. I remember that you answered the door, 'cause he rang the doorbell. You came back and your eyes were big as saucers, and Bill was right there guarding the door, and I confronted him and I told him if he ever came back that I was going to make sure that they threw his ass in jail and threw away the key, because of what he had done to you—and it stunned him. He just couldn't believe that I knew.

"You could just see it registering on his face that I really did know, and that he hadn't covered his tracks. He knew, he knew that it was over, and he never bothered us after that."

I have no memory prior to the police taking him away although some of my siblings have great recall of that violent event. I remember that Judy's friend came over to the house to help restore a sense of order. I plastered myself next to his leg as he stood in front of the stove stirring hot chocolate and buttering toast. I could feel the warmth radiating off the porcelain of the oven door and the security of a human body. I felt safe.

Some time after, Judy moved to San Francisco to start her new life. It must have felt like walking out of prison after being in "the hole." I don't remember her leaving, which doesn't surprise me, as I found a way to compartmentalize anything that was scary. It must have been traumatic for all of us who looked to her for whatever consistency we had. I can only imagine her guilt at wanting to be free, and at the same time, her apprehension and fear of what could take place if she wasn't there. It must have been a torturous decision to reach.

From sunrise to sunset, most of the time we would fend for ourselves without Judy, looking to empty cardboard boxes to build forts on which we would write dirty words. We didn't understand what they meant, but we knew that voicing them was bound to evoke a response. So we girls would yell our profanities at the boys and throw rotten fruit at them and duck as we were hailed with flying debris in retaliation. It was, of course, okay if we tormented each other—we were kin. But God help anyone who would harm another of our clan; the battle between the sexes would instantly disperse as we all joined forces like a pack of wolves, running after the source of the threat. That's all it took to remind us that we were, after all, family.

Seldom bored, we found a myriad of ways to occupy ourselves. Manicured lawns on summer nights were the site of flower raids: We would gather in a platoon, plot our attack, and then slither through the grass on our elbows and bellies like a bunch of snakes in the dark, grabbing flowers by the fist-full. It must have looked like a swarm of locusts flew over the neighborhood yards come daybreak, but to us, it was great fun, and our biggest challenge was to find an empty jar of any kind to hold our limp-necked prisoners of war. Mother, arriving home from work, never did scold us but instead seemed more moved by our gesture to "pick her something pretty," and her comment, made with a half-smile, was void of any cautionary words about the virtues of respecting someone else's property. More

often than not, the evidence of our antics was met with
a giggle and a "Good God! It looks like someone died
in here." I am convinced to this day that she had more
kid in her than we did and that her "reasoning adult"
took a hike somewhere in her youth.

22
Pandora's Box

My psychiatrist told me I was crazy. I said I wanted a
second opinion. He said, "Okay, you're ugly too."
—Rodney Dangerfield

I listened to the slow, rhythmic voice of Dr. Daniel Slavin describe to me, in microscopic detail, the sensations and visual imagery of the ocean. I could smell the salt and the seaweed in the air, I could feel the wet ocean spray against my skin and, as I slipped deeper and deeper into hypnosis, I could feel the grains of sand slipping between my toes. My muscles felt heavy with relaxation. Gone was any resistance. I felt as if I were sleeping on a cloud made of cotton.

"I want you to split off now, and become two, just like you are observing yourself sitting there on the sand. Can you see that?"

I wanted to speak, but there was a feeling of over-bearing control from another part of me. I felt and saw myself as the adult me begin to circle a small girl. I was witnessing both. I felt frightened as I watched myself stalk and be stalked. The adult me paced in a circle around the little girl me, looking at me with a scowl on her face, both hands clasped behind her back like a general in the army. She stared at me with intense displeasure and began to assert her authority.

"Why, in God's name, do you want to do this? Why do you want to go back and dig all of this up? Why?" she shouted. "Haven't I taken care of you all of these years? Damn it! Is this the gratitude that I get for protecting you? Can't you be content to leave things as they are? I am so angry at you! Why now? Do you know what would have happened to you? Well, do you? Is this the thanks I get for making you safe?" She was furious, and I, as that little girl, was afraid of her. I felt small and powerless, and my heart began to beat faster.

My attention diverted back to Daniel's voice. "I want you to walk over to a cave. You are at the entrance looking in. What do you see? Can you go in?" From the sand, I stared off into the distance towards a cave-like dwelling. Everything became black and heavy, and I felt as if I were being suffocated by a weight that I couldn't get out from under.

"He's hurting me! He's hurting me!" I felt myself pull my body into a fetal position. I could hear myself begin to cry. I couldn't stop the panic. It was overwhelming.

"I want you to breathe deeply and slowly. You can breathe effortlessly. It's okay. I'm going to count from zero to five, and when you awaken, you will feel very soothed, with a sense of well-being, like you had a nap, and I want you to remember consciously what you can. Zero . . . one . . . two . . . three . . . four . . . five."

I felt disoriented as I looked into the dark eyes that held their focus without deviation. "You okay?" I nodded in response, as he settled back into the chair, which he had positioned next to the couch. "Well, something definitely happened. What did you see?"

"God, it's such a strange sensation. It's like being two places at the same time. When I was sitting on the beach, I was a little girl, five or six years old, but at the same time, I was an adult—my age now. The adult was stalking me, the little girl, like a general in the army, with her hands clasped behind her back, and she had this really mean, angry look on her face. It was like when you did something when you were little that you knew you were really going to get in big trouble for. She walked around me in circles not saying a word, just staring at the sand like she was trying to take in the magnitude of what I had done, and then she stopped and glared at me with this look, like I had no control over her power. I wanted to speak, but I was too afraid of her. Then I heard your voice describing the cave to me. As I stood at the entrance and looked in, I felt a horrible panic. I couldn't go inside. I felt like I'd die in there, and never come out. I've always been afraid of caves. They're too black. Fear. A lot of fear, that's what I felt, and I couldn't breathe. How do you know when to pull me out?" I asked.

"I watch your pulse beat on your neck. When that starts beating fast, I know that there is a lot of fear going on. Look, Athena," he said with a growing sense of excitement on his face, "I don't mean to make light of your tragedy, but it's going to be very exciting for me to work with you."

"How so?"

"Well, you're one of a very small percentage that goes under so deeply. Have you ever heard of the word 'somnambulistic'?"

"No, what does it mean?"

"It means . . . the deepest level of trance obtainable."

"I never thought that I could be hypnotized. It feels so weird," I replied as I sat up and adjusted my clothing. I became self-conscious of how I must have looked, to wonder if I had smudges of mascara under my eyes. "Shit," I thought to myself. I wished I hadn't agreed to have dinner with my friend, Karen. I was exhausted and wanted to go home. I wanted to crawl under the covers and curl up in a little ball.

Daniel ejected the tape from the recorder, and held it up for me to see. With a parental tone in his voice, he said, "Look, Athena, I do not want you listening to this, not under any circumstances. Do you understand me?"

"Daniel, that tape is my property. . . ." He interrupted me, "I know that, but I want to hang on to these until we are through. Can you absolutely promise me that you won't listen to it?"

"Okay, hang on to them, but when we are finished, they're mine." I knew sure as hell that I would have taken it home and replayed it. I felt like a flake because I didn't have the self-control to tuck it away in a drawer until some future date, and more so because I wouldn't have kept my promise.

We agreed to night appointments, as it was impossible for me to schedule anything during the day because of my work as a freelance make-up artist. Most commercials were shot during the day, with early calls, and so we would wrap in plenty of time for me to keep my appointments.

"How did it go?" Karen asked, as she stood up to hug me.

"Good, but I'm tired. I feel like I've been through the mill. I want a cup of coffee—and a cigarette."

"You've got lipstick on your face," she said as she wiped it off with her thumb.

"Oh, that's cool. He let me walk out of his office like that? That's like smiling at someone with spinach in your teeth, and no one tells you."

"It's gone. God, Dr. Slavin's really cute," she remarked, as she waved her hand at the waiter.

"Yeah, he is good-looking, isn't he? I never expected him to be so young, either."

"I bought you this," she said, as she handed me a bag. "I was so nervous, waiting for you. I could feel some intense things were going on, so I tried to pass some time. It's not much."

I felt my eyes begin to tear as I looked at her little sack of love. White candles, incense, and bubble bath, all items of thoughtfulness that were so typically Karen.

"So tell me—I want to hear all about it," she said.

"It's like being in two places at the same time. I felt like a rubber band that had been stretched to the max. One end was like the past, and the other is the now. What feels so strange is being so acutely aware of both, simultaneously. It's weird. I can remember every movement I make, every word that is said, every sensation, but I can't stop it." I told her about the cave and the fear. "I wonder what's in the cave. It terrified me. I just wanted to speak out loud, but I couldn't. All of these thoughts just kept whirling in me like a hurricane."

We ate dinner and talked for a few more hours. Finally, I complained, "Karen, I don't want to talk about it anymore. What I really want is to sleep and forget about it. I'm sick of all of it right now." I felt myself becoming irritable and angry—and pissed off at myself for not knowing why.

At home that night, I had the distinct feeling that I was about to take a ride on a roller coaster, and I wondered at the wisdom of opening up this can of worms. "Fuck me. Another delightful opportunity for growth." I threw back the covers and climbed into bed. "Look, God. I don't want to think about this, dream about this, or talk about this. Why in the hell are all of these lessons so damned hard? I don't like you tonight, either . . . so there."

I began to drift off to sleep, when I was instantly jolted by an image of Ed Dahlberg staggering towards me, with his pants down and his penis exposed. He was drunk, and just appeared out of the blackness. My heart was racing, adrenaline shooting through my veins. I hated images that seemed to fly through my subconscious with no warning, scaring the hell out of me with their total spontaneity and clarity. *The cave . . . maybe . . .* I fell back asleep.

I sat by myself on a bench, feeling isolated and separated from the small groups of people that were busy milling around the park. "I don't feel like a part of them," I thought to myself, as I sat there observing them. "I don't feel much, one way or the other."

I watched the man guide a boat through the groups of people, with great speed and skill, as he headed towards me. "I'm going to help you," he said, as he picked me up and carried me to the boat. "Wait a minute," I thought to myself, "I'm going to another country, and I don't have a passport. How am I going to get in?" I decided to go on trust. As he rounded a corner, the people disappeared, and it was pitch black. I was completely alone now. "I'm going to be cold where I'm going," I thought to myself, as I reached over the side of the boat and grabbed a blanket off of the ground. It was pitch black and I was in a hot air balloon that began to rise off the ground with great speed. "Where am I? I'm afraid." I looked over the edge of the basket that was quickly rising in the night. I saw something huddled on the ground, covered in a blanket, in the fetal position. I couldn't tell if it was dead or just in a state of hibernation. It's my daughter! "Tina!" I screamed. "Up here! Look up! It's me, Mom! Tina! Wake up! Look up here! Look up here!"

She raised her head and started to quickly look around, trying to find the source of the voice. She was a little girl again, no more than six. "Up here!" I screamed. "It's me, Mom!" I was feeling a growing sense of panic. *It's so black down there, she can't see me.* "Look up!"

"Mom!" she screamed, "what's happening?" Her eyes were filled with terror as she frantically searched the darkness to find me. I was almost out of sight when she spotted me. "Mom! Don't leave me! What's happening? What's happening? I'm afraid!"

"Tina!" I shouted back, "I don't know how, but someday I'll find you again. Somehow, I'll find you!"

"Mom! Don't leave me! Don't leave me!"

"Tina, I'll find you somehow! Somehow, someday we'll find each other again. Somehow we'll be together again!"

I was almost out of sight. My daughter, engulfed in that hellish blackness, was almost a speck, invisible to my eyes. I heard her voice echo in the darkness, "Don't leave me. . . . Please, don't leave me."

Oh, God, what do I do? I'm almost out of sight now. If this balloon rises any higher, I'll be out of the earth's atmosphere. I'm afraid. If I jump, I'll die. . . . There's too much distance. It's so far down. Quick! Jump! Jump! If I die in the fall, at least she'll know that I loved her and we'll be one in spirit.

I felt myself tumble through the blackness. When I hit the ground, I became the six-year-old girl, and I began to run. "He's chasing me! He'll kill me! He'll kill me!"

I ran into a cave-like dwelling and frantically began pushing the dirt in front of me, trying to make myself invisible to his view. I could see the legs of people walking past me. "I know these people. They'll give me away. They'll tell him I'm here." I felt his hands reach for me.

I shot upright, like a bolt, awake. I could taste skin and blood in my mouth. My heart was pounding out of my chest, and my skin was clammy, sweaty. "Jesus Christ! What a nightmare!" I couldn't stop shaking as I lit a cigarette and turned on the lights. It was three in the morning, and I knew that I couldn't go back to sleep.

I wanted to call Daniel, but I fought back the impulse and grabbed my journal to write down the dream.

"So, how was your week?" Daniel asked, as he sat down in the black leather chair.

"It was okay. A lot of stuff came up. Did you have a chance to read the dreams I put in your mailbox?"

"Yes, I did," he replied. "That dream was incredible."

"It scared the hell out of me. I almost called you, but it was three in the morning."

"That would have been okay. This work brings up a lot of stuff. I want you to call me if something like this happens again. It's important to work with it while it is still fresh. I would have wanted to see you the next day. So, what is your interpretation?"

"I think that the groups of people were events in my life, and that me sitting on the sidelines observing is what I've always done. Never participating or feeling a part of anything. I felt kind of blah . . . nothing one way or the other. You were the man in the boat, and what impressed me was the way in which you guided the boat through the groups of people, or the events in my life. When I felt fear at not having a passport, and decided to go on trust, I think that represented going from the conscious to the subconscious. One country to another. But the passport was the key, and I alone didn't have the knowledge, so I decided to trust you. The hot air balloon was the vehicle of hypnosis, because I knew I was going on a trip and that I had to go alone. I don't know what the blanket means, but I do remember as a child getting up in the middle of the night, making my rounds through the house, making sure everybody was covered up and warm. If they had a blanket, they were safe. I was obsessed with it, even my naked dolls. I can't stand to see people cold. It drives me nuts. As stupid as it sounds, if I see a naked doll, I have to cover her to make sure she's warm. It just drives me crazy. Stupid, isn't it?"

"How long did this go on?"

"I don't know, as far back as I can remember. A few years ago, we were filming at night, and it was really cold. I remember seeing this little girl dangling a doll by her hand. I walked up to her and wrapped her and the doll in a blanket, and said, 'Here, honey, your baby is cold. Let's make her comfy and warm.' People must have thought I was nuts, but I can't help it.

"Anyway, I'm not sure what the blanket in the dream means. The child on the ground wasn't my daughter, she was me. I think that's pretty self-explanatory. She looked dead, but I'll tell you one thing: When she finally saw me, Van Gogh or Rembrandt could never have painted the terror in her eyes. I'll never forget those eyes.

"Jumping out of the balloon was a decision to confront the past, to unite with what has always felt dead to me. The skin and blood in my mouth . . . Do you think he forced his penis in my mouth?"

"I think that's highly probable," Daniel replied. I shuddered. "God, how repulsive." I felt that all-too-familiar convulsion vibrate through my body. "Well, what do you think?" I asked.

"I think it's right on."

"You know, Daniel, the other night I was rummaging through some old writings, and I found this scrap of paper that I had written a dream on. It was dated twelve years ago. I walked down some stairs into a dark basement to rescue this little girl. I tried to get her to leave with me, but she was too afraid. She just hid behind a chair. Finally, I picked her up. She fought and screamed and kicked. Then her body went limp, like she was dead, and I felt this incredible fear. Finally, she moved her arm slightly, and I cried out of relief. I tried to give her a bottle, but decided to nurse her, because that felt more natural. I gave her a naked dolly, and a blanket to keep her safe and warm. I didn't want to leave her there—it made me feel so sad. I wanted to bring her into the light, to get her outside into the sunshine, but my mother and another dark figure without a face were blocking the top of the stairs. I screamed at my mother, "Don't you touch her! If you hurt her, I'll kill you! I'll kill you!" You know what is really strange? I had written, on that scrap of paper, "I'm not strong enough to get her out yet, but someday I will be." I think it's really strange that this thing would pop up at this stage of the game, don't you?"

"I must say, there is a certain synchronism to it. Where did Ed stay in the house?"

"In the basement, in the root cellar. Judy said that it was cave-like and made out of dirt and that the back of it was sloped so that you couldn't stand up straight."

Daniel shook his head in bewilderment. I can't even imagine someone living like that, like a mole."

"Well, from what Judy told me, Mom slept on the couch in the basement; it's where they used to do a lot of drinking, and when she worked, he would baby-sit us and that was a period of almost a year. You know, Daniel, I've been thinking—if I felt such incredible fear at the thought of entering the cave, then I know that something is in there. I'm scared to death; in all honesty, it scares the shit out of me, but I know that I have to do it."

"We will take it slow and we will never do more than what you are capable of handling."

"Yeah, right!" I replied. *I had thought that I'd come in, get hypnotized and it would be over in one session.*

"You're obviously strong enough to deal with this now, at this point in your life, and just the fact that so many issues have been surfacing concerning this leads me to feel that on some level, you're seeking to confront it, that the timing is right." He looked at me seriously. "Okay, let's get started. Stretch out on the couch and get comfortable." Daniel pulled up a chair and set it next to the couch by my head.

I took off my shoes and looked at Daniel. "I hate wearing shoes. If you want to get comfortable, feel free." I watched him hesitate. I knew that he was wrestling with the whole professional issue, but comfort won out. He leaned over and, with a grin, untied his tennis shoes, letting out an "Ahhh, that feels good," as he wiggled his toes.

I rummaged through my purse and took out a blank tape and a small white candle. "I would like to light this. Do you mind?" I felt a little self-conscious at my request, wondering what he must have been thinking. But I felt much more comfortable in dim lighting, especially when I was under.

I took out my lighter, lit the candle, and said a quick prayer. "I'm calling to my own higher presence, the God within, to come forth. I'm asking that all of my spirit guides and the presence of Dr. Peebles come forth and be with us tonight. *Help me remember.* Daniel, do you mind if we shut the shades and dim the light? I know it sounds crazy, but it makes me uncomfortable knowing that people are having dinner in the courtyard below us." I was aware of the fact that I thrashed about and moaned too loud, and I felt self-conscious as hell about it.

"No, that's okay," he said, as he pulled the shade.

I could feel the cool, wet moss beneath my feet, as I floated down steps, going backwards in time. "The cave . . . Oh, God, there he is, stumbling toward me . . . He'll kill me . . . He'll kill me . . . ! Ju . . . Ju . . . Ju . . . Ju . . . Ju . . . "

I was powerless to speak. I couldn't even push out

the name 'Judy'—it was tangled up in terror and pain. I tried so hard to form the word, my body tried to push it through the fear into a sound that could become the word, but I couldn't get past the horror of the physical pain that was taking place inside of me.

"Oh, God, it hurts . . . He's pushing himself inside of me . . . I can't breathe . . . I can't breathe . . . He's choking me . . . JU . . . JU . . . JU . . . JU . . . JU . . ."

"Are you calling for Judy?"

"JU . . . JU . . . JU . . . JU . . . JU . . ."

"Tell him to leave. Can you do that? Can you tell him to leave?"

"Leav . . . le . . . le . . . leav. . . JU . . . JU . . JU . . . he's ch . . . ch . . . ch . . . ch . . . me . . ."

"He's choking you? Is he choking you?"

"I can't br . . . bre . . . breathe . . ." Help me, som . . . somebody help me . . . It hurts! It hurts! It hurts! Ju . . ."

"Judy? Are you calling for Judy?"

"Ju . . . Ju . . . Ju . . . I can't bre . . . breathe . . ."

"You're safe, you're safe. . . . Athena, I want you to take a deep breath. Breathe deeply, effortlessly and easily. . You can do that because you're safe. I'm going to count from zero to five . . ."

"Just stay still, relax. Do you want some water?"

"Oh, God."

"Shhhhh . . . don't try and talk yet. There's plenty of time." After a few minutes of silence, he asked gently, "What happened?"

"Terror. A lot of terror. I could hear myself stuttering, but I couldn't form the word—I couldn't push it out of my mouth. I was calling for Judy. He was choking me with his hands. I couldn't breathe. I felt a lot of physical pain when he was trying to push himself inside of me, and I felt like I was being suffocated to death. I couldn't breathe. Can I have some Kleenex?"

"Sure," he said quietly, as he stood up and walked to his desk, picking up the box of tissue, while he turned on the lamp with his other hand.

I felt naked, raw and fragmented. It was a feeling that I would experience week after week; the feeling of total exhaustion and vulnerability left me drained to my toes. I had dreams of myself giving birth, and physically, I felt the same sensation every time we worked together. I could no longer be confined to the couch, for I thrashed too much and could feel him at times grabbing me, so that I wouldn't fall off. We began working only at night when all other clients, including the secretary, had gone home for the evening. I could hear myself cry and stutter, scream and gag at times, and I knew that it must have sounded like someone was getting killed in there. Usually our sessions were an hour and a half, sometimes two. I knew that they exhausted Daniel as much as they did me. It took all of the strength I had to drive home and crawl into bed.

I was grateful that God gave me a day or two to recoup between my sessions with Dr. Slavin and being booked to film a commercial. I needed it. Everything was being brought to the surface, and I felt so close to extracting the venom from the wound. I thought back to the time I had made a decision to explore this, and I remember wondering how in the world I would find a therapist that would be qualified to do this kind of work. I wasn't willing to just turn this over to anybody, for something in me on some subliminal level knew that I would need to find someone who would have a sense of intuition, not just theory, and would be able to work with and trust that part of me that seemed to be orchestrating from a sense of knowingness within my soul. I prayed that God would guide me to the right person. I had interviewed two other therapists, and the moment I heard Dr. Slavin's voice, something in me knew on a gut level that he was the one.

He was highly qualified, his background and credentials impressive for his age. I knew instinctively that it would be a co-creation from the higher realms between spirit, forces of the unseen, his skill, and my willingness and determination to heal. I needed someone to be open to the probability of mystical events, as I knew that somewhere in the natural evolution of our discovery process, most likely, stranger things would unfold. They did.

23
Waking The Giant

Courage is almost a contradiction in terms.
It means a strong desire to live
taking the form of a readiness to die.
—Gilbert K. Chest

"This week, Daniel, I don't want you to pull me out when the fear begins again. I want you to leave me there and let me experience it from start to finish." I could see the look of growing concern, but I cut him off before he had a chance to respond. "Look, I know and you know how intense this is, and believe me, Daniel, with all of my heart I appreciate your concern, but I know that I'm strong enough to handle it. I want to experience the rapes from front to finish. I really feel strongly about this, and I've given it a lot of thought. It's frustrating to me to be pulled out when I'm so close. Is it a deal?"

"Athena, you've got to trust my judgment, and there are times that I have to exercise that, as a trained therapist."

"I know that, and I respect that, but trust my judgment that I can handle it. Will you? Will you leave me under?"

Daniel let out a sigh and then responded, "I can't

promise you. We'll see how it goes."

I unfolded the thin, blue Afghan and spread it out on the carpet while Daniel dimmed the lights and pulled the shades shut. I lit the white candle, and silently said my prayer while Daniel sat down on the carpet next to me. He barely started speaking when I felt the familiar heaviness and deep relaxation spread through every muscle.

"I want you to be aware of the basement. It's cold and dark . . . , and as you walk down those stairs, you will become six years old again. . . . What are you seeing?"

"He's got a kn . . . kn . . . knife."

"What's he doing? Can you tell me what he is doing? Breathe comfortably. . . . Take some deep breaths.

What do you see? I want you to become the observer now. This isn't happening to you right now. . . . What do you see happening to Athena?"

"He's got . . . he's got . . . got . . . He's got a butcher knife."

"What does it look like?"

"He's got . . . he's got . . . got . . . got . . . it has . . . has . . . it has a bl . . . bl . . ."

"What does it look like?"

"It has a bl . . . black handle and it's wo . . . woo . . . wood. . . . It has silver . . . silver in it and he's . . . he's . . . got . . . got . . . it up at my . . . th . . . th . . . thr . . . throat."

"He has it up to your throat? Is he threatening you? What are you afraid of happening?"

"He's going to ki . . . ki . . . kill me."

"I want you to see the knife, and next to the knife I want you to see the adult. I want you to be able to both feel the fear and to know that you are going to survive."

"He's goin . . . goin . . . he's going to . . . to . . . k . . . k . . . kill me."

"What are you scared of . . . What are you seeing? It's okay. He's scared. He's not going to kill you. It's all right. What are you scared of?"

"He's goin . . . going . . . to . . . to . . . to . . . to . . . k . . . k . . . k . . . kill m . . . me."

"What is he telling you to do?"

"Be quiet . . . don't . . . don't . . . don't te . . . tell . . . don't tell . . . don't tell . . . I won't . . . won't tell."

"And you're not going to tell anyone right? So you have nothing to fear. What are you seeing? What are you seeing? Now he's hurting you?"

"It hurts . . . it hurts."

"Okay, I want you to be the observer now, to step out for a second and to watch, just watch. He's telling you not to tell anybody, right? Your neck is free. . . . You can breathe. . . . You can breathe."

I motioned that my hands were tied together and then gagged.

"He's tying your hands? He's in your mouth? Is he in your mouth? Okay, I want you to breathe. . . . I want you to tell him 'no,' that you won't tell anybody. . . . I want you to tell him 'no'. . . you won't tell anybody. . . . That's good. . . . Just breathe. . . . Breathe easy. . . . It's over. It's over, it's over. . . . He's going upstairs, it's over. You've seen the whole thing, the fear was visible. . . . Breathe comfortably.

"Now you're in the basement by yourself. What happens now? What happens now? You're in the basement and you are going to come up the stairs . . . , right?"

I felt myself separate and detach from the body of the little girl and float to the ceiling. I just lingered, hovering, . . . looking down at the event taking place below me. I watched, unemotional, completely void of all feeling, feeling no connection, as the man raped her.

I wasn't connected to the pain anymore. I was free.

"What's going on?"

I felt myself respond to the voice that seemed to be in another dimension. The whisper was almost inaudible.

"He's raping her."

"What? He's raping her? What's he doing to her?"

Again I whispered from the ceiling . . . .

"He's tying her hands and taking off her clothes."

"Okay, just breathe easy and tell me what he's doing to her."

"He's tied her hands . . . raping her and threatening her with a knife."

"What would you tell her to do to protect herself?"

"To die."

"To die? Is that what you said? To die?"

"To die."

"To die so he can't hurt her anymore? Can we let that little girl die?"

"I'm not going back."

"What? You're not going back? Okay, I want you to leave him, to leave her, to leave the observer and to come back out . . . to close it up. You have seen the whole thing, you have realized the abuse, you know that he has lived a miserable, decrepit existence, and he's paid heavily for it. So has that little girl. She's back down there. She was able to pick herself up."

I floated, observing, pure consciousness, looking at the body of the child, hearing the voice trying to coax me back in. . . . I was free. I fought to free myself further into spirit.

"I'm not going back. I'm not going back."

"Okay, you don't have to."

"I'm not going back into the body."

"What? You're not going back into *what* body?"

"I'm not going back into that body. I'm not going back in. . . . I'm not going back in. . . . I want to die. . . . I want to die. . . . I'm not going back in. . . ."

"You don't have to . . . you don't have to."

"I don't want to. . . . I want to . . . I want to . . . I'm not going back in that body. . . . I want to die! I want to die!

I want to go back and be in spirit. . . . I don't want to go back into that body."

"You don't want to go back into *what* body?"

"I don't want to go back into that body."

"Of the little girl?"

"Yes."

"Why?"

"BECAUSE IT'S TOO HARD! IT'S TOO HARD! I DON'T WANT TO GO BACK INTO THAT BODY!"

"Why don't you want to go back into that body? Look at what you've done. You were able to survive! You were able to live and he hasn't. You have been able to survive."

"Mama . . . I want Judy. . . . I want Judy. . . .

Help me . . . Somebody help me. . . ."

"Judy? You want Judy? What do you want Judy to be able to do for you? Protect you from him? He's gone. He's *gone.* You're safe. He is leaving you alone. . . . He can't harm you anymore. You want Judy to protect you, don't you? You want her to cover you up and protect you, don't you? That makes you safe from him, right? You want her to cover you up, just like you have covered up everybody else your whole life to protect them, to save them, to keep them from the same fate. You wanted to protect the dolls, . . . the people that you love. You have wanted to protect Tina. You've wanted to protect everybody, and you have, . . . by giving them the care that you didn't have . . . , by protecting them the way your mother didn't . . . , by protecting the way your sister tried, and couldn't. By protecting them from people like Ed.

"You have tried your whole life to give, and to give, and to give, to get what you weren't able to get. You have arrived. You have been able to get that type of protection for yourself and from other people. You have given enough. You need to give to yourself. You've given and given.

"You've given to Tina, you've given to total strangers, all in trying to protect that little girl, that sad little girl that's been released. You've come out the other end, you've been able to see all the horror. You have a chance at life. You do. You can see that, can't you? You've protected them enough. *You've covered up everybody's pain to cover your own pain.*

"Your neck is free, you can breathe, you can open yourself up with no fear, because nothing is going to happen to you. Now, instead of being fearful of something around your neck, you can feel a freeness.

"I want you to relax . . . , relax. I want that to feel all right." He put his hand on my shoulder, and I jumped. "It's just my hand . . . , it's just my hand. It's not a knife . . . , it's not danger. People can give you warmth. The people that you love can give you warmth. You don't have to be fearful. You can open yourself up. I'm going to run my hand across your neck five times, and each time I want you to become more comfortable. One . . . it's okay, it's warmth . . . two . . . three . . . breathe deep . . . four . . . five."

"Go ahead and cry. You don't have to cover people up anymore. You don't have to cover yourself up. You're safe. You can open yourself up without the fear of losing control. You've chosen very sensitive people around you. . . . You attract warmth. . . . You attract trust. I want you to lie on your back . . ."

"I don't like to lie on my back."

"I want you to lie on your back and to take some deep breaths. . . . You're safe. You're safe, and you're open and you're very vulnerable. You've seen the worst and gone through it. . . . You can feel the breath going through your body and feel the openness."

"I can't."

"You can't feel it?"

"I can't feel. I can't feel there. . . ."

"Can you breathe up through your feet and have it come through your whole body?"

"I don't feel there."

"You don't feel a thing?"

"I only feel from my waist up."

"Breathe and exhale down through your body. . . . Feel it pass through your body. . . . It will take some time. I'd like you to be able to do this, before you're with anybody, or, by yourself, I'd like you to be able to breathe, and pass through, with no fear. No fear. . . . You don't have to be covered up or closed. Lie on your side and breathe deep, with no fear. . . . Then lie on your back, open and vulnerable, with no fear . . . , no fear. You'll still need some time. You've seen the whole thing, and you will still need some time to have the feeling come back."

"It's hard."

"It is hard. I want you to do this . . . to curl up on your side and to allow yourself to breathe through the fear, and then to lie on your back, open and vulnerable, and to breathe deeply, . . . feeling the breath pass through your entire body. Don't ever let anyone rush you. . . . Take your time. I want you to do this once a day. You can go back down the stairs any time you feel fear, and breathe through it."

"I don't want to go into the basement again."

"I'm not talking about the basement. Okay, I want you to walk up the stairs now. I'm going to count from zero to five . . ."

"Where is the little girl?"

"What do you mean, where is the little girl? She's here."

"No. I don't want to leave her down there. . . . She's so scared. Where is the little girl?"

"The little girl is here . . . , right here."

"No! SHE'S DEAD! He killed her! He killed her! She's

dead. . . . She's dead! He killed her! She was just a little girl . . ."

"Yes, that is very sad. You're angry, aren't you? He killed your little girl."

24
Summoning The Warrior

The real war will never get in the books.
—Walt Whitman

God! I was tired. The timing of all of this sucked. Dr. Slavin had known I was leaving for six weeks to do a film, and in his wisdom, had said that it was against his better judgment to explore what we were exploring at that point in time. But me and my big mouth said, "No, I'm strong enough; I can handle it."

By the time I had gotten home from his office, it was eleven at night, and I had to be on the set at five a.m. I had been booked on a commercial which meant no time off to catch my breath before leaving for Pittsburgh where the film was to take place. I didn't sleep at all, and my eyes were damned near swollen shut.

I put on my sunglasses at the first sign of light and pulled into the parking lot, thinking about what in God's name I could say. I was already embarrassed.

"You okay, Athena?"

"Yes, I'm fine." What I really wanted to say was that I just had my guts blown out. "Don't look at me cross-eyed or I'll start again." *Just leave me the fuck alone.* I hoped this director wouldn't go for umpteen takes. All I wanted to hear was "It's a wrap!"

People were wonderful, and the crew as well as the actors did everything they could do to make me feel comfortable. At times I had to swallow down the tears. I told the actress that I was dealing with something difficult, and if she could just allow me to be in that space, I would appreciate it. I was sitting next to the set, when I felt someone massaging my shoulders. The actor bent down and whispered in my ear, "I heard that you're having a hard time with something. I just want you to know that it's okay with me for you to be where you're at." That did it. I reached up and patted his hand, wiping the tears away with the other.

As soon as we wrapped, I drove home and stayed up all night packing. I felt as if I had been running ninety miles an hour in four different directions, and as grueling as the hours were going to be doing this film, I was looking forward to the break from my work with Dr. Slavin. I needed this time to let things settle into whatever they were supposed to settle into.

I barely made the flight that was departing for Pittsburgh. I felt a sense of relief as I fastened my seatbelt and the plane began to taxi down the runway of LAX. Don't do it. Damn it, Athena, get a grip. Don't start crying again! I took a deep breath and shut my eyes, hoping that the man sitting next to me would get the hint and leave me alone. It had only been thirty-odd hours since my session with Dr. Slavin, and I had not slept at all. When I returned home from his office that night, I laid in bed and rocked back and forth, in the fetal position, sobbing and sobbing—praying for God to make the pain go away. I hadn't expected any of that to come out. Hell, I didn't know what I had expected, but certainly not that. And to have it come out of my own mouth was unbelievable to me: "She's dead."

You've been dragging around this half-dead, tortured

little girl all of your life. He won. He had killed me. I had said it myself. All of my life I have felt like I've been swimming in an ocean of fog as thick as pea soup, being circled by a shark, following the sound of a foghorn in the distance that I could not see, only hear. Being thrashed about, mutilated, and dismembered by something that I couldn't see was bad enough, but to have the fog lifted long enough to watch it rip me to shreds— to feel the horror of the fight for survival and to lose that fight—was devastating.

I wanted, more than anything in my life, to feel whole and united—with what I hadn't known, but I knew now. The fear was visible. I had felt myself crawl around on his office floor, crying, stuttering at times just like Sally Field in the film *Sybil. I wanted to die.* Dan didn't know what happened, poor guy. I had felt myself splinter and project out of my body, floating by the ceiling, watching him rape her, just like when it happened. I was experiencing it all again. "I don't want to go back into that body," I whispered. "I want to die and return to spirit." I hovered and watched it take place, and I knew that I had had the power, as a child, to leave the body through shock, because as a grown-up, I was experiencing the state of shock I experienced as a child.

I had never wanted to be on this planet anyway. I liked the feeling of being free of the physical body, and of the pain that was involved in feeling trapped within the flesh. I was aware of the anger and rage I felt at having to go back within that prison, and I watched as Dr. Slavin struggled to understand *which* body I was talking about. I fought tooth and nail to free myself further into spirit, and then, it was as if some giant force slammed me back into the body of that little girl. I heard myself moan and groan in pain and agony again.

I couldn't accept that part of me was dead, that I had deserted her, only to leave her buried in the root cellar within the basement of that house in Klamath Falls, Oregon. I was willing to face any amount of pain to find her again, but to find her dead—I couldn't come to terms with that. All I could do was to cry from the reality of what seemed to be a missing link of my psyche, and as much as I wanted that piece, I couldn't have it.

"You're not very social, are you?" The man sitting next to me slurred.

"No, not today," I replied. I stood up and walked to the back of the plane, glancing at the "OCCUPIED" sign on the bathroom door. "We've been watching that man sitting next to you," the flight attendant remarked. "We don't have an empty seat to move you to. I'm sorry."

"Yeah, you and me both. I would get a seat next to a drunk."

I smiled at a little girl sitting in the seat directly across from where I was standing. "Is that your baby?" I asked her. She nodded her head yes, and started playing with the baby' arms in an attempt to mask her shyness. "She's pretty. Does she have a name?"

"Julie."

"Julie's a nice name. Is she being good on this flight?"

"Uh-huh," she answered.

"Well, I bet you're a good Mommy, and she loves you a lot. How old are you, honey?" I asked.

"Six."

I felt my heart swell with a feeling of compassion for her and for her little doll. I surrounded her in white light as I mentally said a quick prayer for protection for her. Julie wasn't wearing any clothes, only a diaper, and I wanted to reach above into the overhead storage and grab a blanket for her.

I found myself reflecting back to the ritual that I had

performed nightly after the house was quiet and all were asleep. I would get up in the middle of the night, making my nightly rounds, checking on each family member, making sure that they were covered well with a blanket, tucking it in around their bodies. It made me feel safer somehow. When my dollies went to sleep at night, I didn't want them to be afraid, and if they had a blanket, there were no monsters that could get them, and they could have something to hide under for protection until morning washed the blackness away.

Pittsburgh was hot and humid, for we were filming in the midst of the summer. The hours were long and grueling, and despite the schedule, I was grateful for the cast and the crew and the state of exhaustion that left me little time to focus on anything but that which was immediately at hand. The weeks passed quickly, and upon my arrival back home, I immediately called to make an appointment with Dr. Slavin.

"I can't deal with it, Dan. . . . I really can't." I sat in his office, making my case. "I've had six weeks to think about this, and I've made a decision. I've done a lot of grieving about the events of our last session. I'll be the first to admit that I didn't expect that he would have killed her, or for me to admit that. I'm serious when I say that I can't live with it. All of my life, I have never been able to relate to what it really felt like to be a kid. It's hard for me to have fun. It's pathetic when you don't even know how to have fun.

"I mean, hell, Mother never believed me. Why didn't she believe me? I can't leave that child in the basement. I can't. I feel like I've been going through my life with half of my body missing. God damn it! He isn't going to win. I don't care what we have to do; somehow I've got to get her out of the basement. I'm the only one she has. I can't live, knowing that she's buried down there."

"God, Athena. I don't know. I listened to the last tape

over and over again, and I think it was too much. I just don't know if it would be possible. Maybe you just need to accept it and grieve the loss."

"Fuck that! I can't accept that! I know about all of this parent/child/adult shit, and I want that child part back! I don't care how painful it is. . . . I don't care! She's mine and I want her back!"

I left his office feeling angry and sullen. The desire to push everyone away from me felt overwhelmingly like my only source of relief. I rolled up the windows in the car and just screamed to release my frustration. I wanted to pound on anything, rip something to shreds. I could feel the rage begin to build. "Do you hear me, you motherfucker?" I screamed. "You're not going to win! She's mine and you're not going to get her! You are not going to win! I hate you! I hate you!"

"Is there a lost child?" I looked at Susan the actress and fought back the tears. "I just say what comes to my mind," she said, "even if it doesn't make any sense or sounds off-the-wall. A lot of times when I'm 'reading' someone, I get these strong images and feelings, even though they don't make sense to me. I go ahead and say them, because they may be relevant to that person." She paused. "You need to be painting. Are you an artist?" she asked.

"No, not really. I think make-up is a form of art, but as far as painting, it's something that I've kind of always wanted to do but never have," I replied.

"Well, you should just start moving color, because you have a lot of artistic talent that wants to come out. Just start moving color; you won't feel so frustrated, either. It will have a calming effect on you."

I liked Susan a lot. It was one of those instant connections. When she first sat in the make-up chair, the conversation just seemed to flow around subjects we both loved and had in common. She was hysterically funny, with an uninhibited sense of humor that I envied and admired. And she was intuitive as hell. We had agreed to give each other mini-readings, so while they were lighting the set for the next shot, we headed back to the make-up trailer to do a quick touch-up and read each other.

But today she really threw me. Throughout the day, I kept hearing her ask, "Is there a lost child?" I ached inside for that completion, and I prayed fervently to God to help me, to guide me, and as much as I knew that I needed to pray for acceptance of "what was," I wanted to scream, "NO! I can't accept that she is dead!" So I struggled, moment to moment, with what I wanted, and what was.

25
A River Of Rage

To carry a grudge is like getting stung to death by one bee.
—Henry H. Walton

I was in the throes of my work with Dr. Slavin when I had a very vivid dream. I was a young girl and I was dancing the ballet. My mother came in the room and I immediately stopped twirling. In my dream I heard a commanding voice; "Confront her! Confront her!" I took my mother by the shoulders while looking her directly in the eye and I shook her hard. "Why won't you acknowledge me? Why won't you acknowledge me?" She looked past me with that drunken glazed-over look in her eyes. I felt myself being held down and raped.

When I awoke, I decided to make a trip from Los Angeles to Chico, to confront my mom. I knew that my guides and higher self had given me another piece of the puzzle. "Don't have any expectations of an outcome from her" Dr. Slavin cautioned.

I was on a rollercoaster ride with my emotions and at times I was so damned angry because I was fueled by feelings I didn't know how to process. I was just trying to let myself feel them. Dr. Peebles told me that the anger I was feeling wasn't quite over, that there was more to follow. Great. Here was the "more to follow" and now it was following me. I perceived this more as my own internal fuel igniting and less as if I was being blown apart by outside sources. It felt ugly and vile and I felt ugly and vile as I was experiencing it. Feelings were foreign and like a whole other language. When something crazy was going on, Mom usually said things were okay but in my gut I knew different. I didn't know how to trust my own instincts for they were seldom ever validated by anyone other than Judy.

When I arrived in Chico I picked Mother up and headed for Bidwell Park. I pulled into a wooded area and parked the car close to a picnic table next to the creek. We got out, and I started to talk to her about what had happened to me as a child. Mother was so uncomfortable with the whole subject, and I remember her saying with a heavy sigh, "Well, we can't cry over spilled milk. I don't know if that happened or not."

"Of course you don't remember, Mom, because you were drunk." She squirmed in her discomfort.

"You know, looking back at my own youth," she continued, "I came to the conclusion that my mother did the best she could."

"Well, your best wasn't good enough." I was pissed that I still wasn't getting the acknowledgement I had hoped for, despite trying not to have expectations. This felt like some half-assed acknowledgement. I felt good that at least I had confronted Mom but still unresolved that there was no closure with her. The hard part now would be coming to terms and accepting the fact that any resolve with her most likely would not happen. I also came to discover that my real anger was that my mother did not protect me. That was her job as my parent.

Mother's Day came and went, along with any desire to make contact with my mother. I succumbed to guilt, and picked up the phone a day late, making a mental list of weak excuses. I found myself amazed that I was harboring such intense feelings. Here was a woman that I had believed was so strong, and now it was as if I was seeing a completely different picture for the first time. I didn't know where to put these feelings, or from where they originated; I just wanted them out of my body, out of my world. At times I hated my mother for bringing me into the world. I listened to the phone ring, and felt that all-too-familiar feeling of weight in my chest.

After a brief, deceptive conversation, I hung up the phone, relieved to get off the hook, already beating myself up for lying. "Yeah, Mom," I had said dryly. "I love you, too." *Liar,* I muttered to myself. *Bullshit! I don't love you, Mother. I didn't call yesterday because I didn't want to hear your voice. I didn't want to hang up the phone and feel what I am feeling today—hypocrisy.* Someone needs to come out with Mother's Day cards that say it like it is. "Dear Mother, as a parent you suck! Thank you for bringing me into the world. With total detachment, Your Daughter."

Shame on me for being so honest. Ahhh, fuck it! It's real and it's how I feel. I could care less if you died today. I'm looking forward to the time when it will all be over. I'll feel a sense of relief, if anything. Then I'll have to struggle with the guilt of your death. Dammit all to hell! I shouldn't have called. I hate the way I feel.

I glanced at the kitchen clock and opened up the pantry door. I had taped on the inside of it two separate sheets of paper. One was a listing of meetings for Adult Children of Alcoholics, and the other contained the times and addresses of Al-Anon. *Twelve noon, I can make that one,* I thought to myself. I had never been to an Al-Anon meeting before. Like so many other things in my life, it was one of those things that I wanted to do but never really acted upon.

I pulled into the gravel driveway of the Unity Church

and glanced out of my window to the parked car next to me. *Keep your ass in this car until the meeting starts and don't you dare leave,* I thought to myself. I was feeling nervous and wondering if I would be able to talk about what was really going on inside of me, the anger and hate I was feeling towards my mother. All of this stuff was new to me. I had only been to three or four ACA meetings, and I remember wanting to throw up when the speaker read off the list of feelings that seemed to be the common bond between all of us who grew up in an alcoholic environment. "Christ, that's me!" I thought to myself over and over again with each new character defect that was read off.

The meeting was small, and I was grateful for that. I felt a sense of relief that it was all women. After the twelve steps were read, the speaker, a young woman in her early thirties, glanced at me and said that it was helpful to share your feelings with the group. I was aware that her statement was for my benefit. I wondered if I had that "newcomer look"—anxious, sullen, and confused. Surely it must have shown, because it was revolving in my gut. Mom always said that I wore my heart on my sleeve. The furrow lines between my eyebrows are always a dead giveaway, even in the times that I've said, "I'm fine, nothing's wrong." People knew better.

"Today," she began, "our topic for discussion will be on expectation and control. I hate the way I try to control my husband. What I mean is that I hate that part in me. I get so angry with myself. It's really sick. I even try to control the way he drives the car."

Christ! I thought to myself, *now I know why I am at this meeting.*

"Hi, my name is Athena."

"Hi Athena." They answered back.

"This is my first Al-Anon meeting. I am also an adult

child of an alcoholic household. If my dad were alive today, there would be six out of nine in my family that are alcoholics. I, myself, never chose alcohol as my destructive route in life—there but for the grace of God go I. But it has filled me with a fear, for I have seen the effects of it and that has been just as damaging. Nor do I want to go through my life as "damaged." I am feeling so much hate and rage at my mother. Mother's Day was really hard for me. I'm having a hell of a time coming to terms with it, and I couldn't care less if she died today. When I called her and told her that I loved her, I felt like a liar. It's a lie. I don't love her. Yet again, I'm afraid I'll be strapped with all of these feelings of guilt after she goes.

"I really identified with what was said about needing to control. I try to control everything and everybody around me. What I really need is to feel out of control—to lose control— and the thought of it scares me to death. I've tried to control the effects of the drinking in my family so that I don't have to feel the shock waves from it. I've been a 'people pleaser' all of my life and I'm sick of it.

"When I was six, I was raped repeatedly by my mother's boyfriend. He was a disgusting, violent alcoholic. He tied me up, strangled me, and held a butcher knife against my throat so that I wouldn't tell. Throughout my adult life I had a fragmented memory of him pushing me back on the couch but then I went blank. I couldn't remember anything about my childhood. I've worked really hard to understand this. "Now, I'm finding all of this anger boiling inside of me all over again. I mean, there she is, a blind, broken-down, pathetic woman, and I feel like I couldn't give a damn when she dies. I want her to, and that's not normal.

"Three months ago, I started to think about suicide again. I feel like I have brought all of the major circles in my life to a full circle. To be honest with you, I feel like, if the first forty years of my life has been this hard, I don't think I want to hang around for the next forty. I was thinking that maybe I could just get a disease that could take me out of the body and do it for me, so that I wouldn't have to physically do it myself.

"Because of my spiritual beliefs, I know that there is no such thing as victimhood, only creation. I know this in theory, yet I balk and scream at that, because part of me wants to stand on a mountaintop and shout for the entire world to hear, 'Victim! Victim! I'm a victim of abuse!'

"I'm beginning to realize that my whole outlook on life is tragic and melodramatic. I'm addicted to that whole dark drama. It's all I've ever known. I'm having to face a lot of things about my attitude and how I've chosen to *see* life, and unless I am willing to be really be honest with myself now, at this stage in my life, what will ever change?"

The room was silent for a moment. Then one woman, sitting directly across from me, spoke. With gentleness in her voice she said, "You know what kept coming to me as you were speaking? Let go and let God!"

"That's all fine and dandy," I replied, "but what do I do with these feelings of hate and anger? Shove them down and pretend that they don't exist? I've done that all of my life, so that I wouldn't have to feel. How in God's name do you just let go of that? It's taken me my whole life to learn how to feel. To not shut off, that's been the toughest. I don't want to start shoving down my feelings again."

I glanced at the end of the table where the speaker of the meeting sat. "Feel it," she said quietly. I felt glad that I had some form of confirmation that what I felt in my heart was the right path. Even if she had not been in agreement, that wouldn't have changed how I was feeling about this whole process. And healing, I was beginning to find out, takes on many different colors, like a chameleon. The meeting was brought to a close. We all stood in a circle holding hands and saying the Lord's Prayer: "And lead us not into temptation, but deliver us from evil." Hey, God, just deliver me from me, okay big guy? That's my prayer for the day.

I got into the car and drove home feeling bummed out and depressed. That night, I had a dream in which I was looking at the inside of my mother's house. The house was empty. There was no furniture in it, only dirt. There was no clutter, only the residue of the inhabitant who was no longer there. I had the distinct feeling that I needed to push up my sleeves and give this room a final cleaning.

26
When The Lilac Lost Its Bloom

Nobody was really surprised when it happened,
not really, not on the subconscious level
where savage things grow.
—Stephen King

Daniel sat in his chair, holding the piece of paper, re-reading the procedure that I had carefully outlined for tonight's session. Neither one of us knew if it was going to work or not, but I had to try. "This is not going to be easy," he said, as he laid the sheet of paper down on his desk.

"I know," I replied. "Do you remember that dream that I told you I had some ten years ago? The one about me as an adult going down some stairs to rescue that little girl? I said I wasn't strong enough at that time to get her out? Where she was blocked by my mother and a dark figure at the top of the stairs? I want to re-enact that dream and somehow, through visual imagery, I want to get her up out of that basement and out into the light. I don't care how you go about getting that part to happen, but I have to get past my mother, and I want you to describe to me white light at the top of the stairs.

"Daniel, white light to me is the pure essence of God, it's the essence of all life, and I know if I can give her that in spirit, then I can live with that. Once we do that, I want you to describe to me the willow tree in the back yard. I loved that willow tree as a child; it was like being enveloped in a giant umbrella, and there, underneath that tree, I want you to describe her body to me as being white light, and then I want to take her spirit inside of me. I'll be the one who rescued her and, in spirit, she'll know that."

I was afraid. As I spread the thin, blue Afghan down on the carpet, my insides were uneasy and anxious. I was afraid of it not working and of being left to live with that feeling that I had abandoned and deserted that part of myself that my mother didn't care about.

"Oh, no you don't. No lying on your stomach. On your back."

"I hate lying on my back."

"I know," he replied, "but too bad—on your back."

"Don't forget to push the record button down once we get going," I instructed.

"It's right here, ready to go. How are you feeling?"

"Nervous and scared." I replied, as I took a few deep breaths. "No one is in the office, are they?"

"No, they have all gone home."

"Good." I replied. *Please help me, God. . . . Please help me, God. . . . Please help me, God,* I chanted silently.

"Ready?"

"Yes . . . , ready." I barely had to listen to the sound of his voice, deep, rhythmic, and soothing, before my eyelids became heavy and I could feel my resistance let go, and his voice drew me deeper and deeper into a state of relaxation. I stood at the top of the stairs looking at the darkness that lay at the bottom. I began the descent . . . five . . . four . . . Each step took me deeper into the darkness as he counted down, three . . . two . . . one . . . zero.

"I want you to be aware of being in the basement and that it's cold and dark. . . . You can smell the dirt and feel yourself as a little girl, six years old, . . . feel yourself down there by yourself. I want you to be able to tell that Ed is coming down the stairs and that you are very scared; you're scared that he is coming down and that he is going to hurt you like he has before. . . . You're aware of that. . . . You don't want that, but you know that it is going to happen. I want you to keep breathing; I want you to be aware. . . . You're scared and you know that this is the time that you are scared for your life . . . and that he has a knife at times, and you're so scared of that knife. . . . You're scared of him, and you're so scared of the things that he does to you.

"Okay, . . . I want you to be the observer now. . . . Observe Ed and the little girl. Can you do that? Just tell me if you can see them as if you were above, . . . as if you were the adult and you can look down and see Ed and the little girl. Can you see that?"

I nodded.

"Now, I want you to be the little girl again. . . . Now you're scared. Okay, . . . now I want you to be the adult again. . . . I want you to observe them, . . . quick! Be the adult. . . . I want you to observe them. . . . Breathe easy. . . . You're not the little girl now. . . . You're not scared, . . . just observing. I want you to get the feeling of being able to switch back and forth. I want this to be a real person; I want this to be you watching the little girl and Ed. I want you to be able to actually have that happen, . . . to see that the little girl and Ed are in the basement and that you're standing next to them."

I stood in the black cave watching him tie her hands and hold a butcher knife against her throat.

"Now I want you to be the little girl again, and I want you to be scared that he's attacking you. . . . He's scaring

you with the knife and he's telling you that if you don't
do what he wants you to do, that . . ."

"I won't tell . . . I won't tell . . ."

" . . . that if you don't do what he wants you to do,
then he's going to hurt you with the knife. Okay, . . . now
I want you to be the adult. Switch! Switch! Switch! Okay,
that's good. Breathe comfortably . . . You are standing
there, Athena is standing next to and watching the little
girl and watching Ed. Breathe comfortably. . . . Separate
the two. . . . Now I want you to be able to see that there
is still light in the little girl's eyes. I want you to be able to
see that light and know that it is a scared light but you
can also see it, and you can see the evilness of Ed and the
innocence of that little girl. You can see the fun in that little girl; you can see that the little girl has that life. I want
you to see a live glimmer in that little girl's eyes. . . . Even
though it's dark, I want you to know that she is alive.

"Okay . . . , he's coming after you, and he's telling
you that if you don't do what he wants you to do, he is
going to hurt you with the knife . . . , so stop struggling!
Stop struggling!"

"It hurts! It hurts!"

"Where does it hurt?"

"It hurts me here (I pointed to my vagina). . . . *It hurts!*"

"Right . . . , it hurts you and you're scared."

"Stop!"

"You're afraid that he's going to kill you aren't you?
You're scared that he's going to kill you?"

"Yes . . . , he's going to ki . . . kill . . ."

"Okay . . . , I want you to now feel as if I'm Ed and
I'm telling you that if you don't do what I want you to
do, that you're going to get hurt, so stop struggling! Now
he's in you, and he's scaring you with the knife. . . . Now
I want you to be Athena! Switch! Switch! Switch! Breathe
comfortably. . . . You're standing next to the little girl,
who has a glimmer in her eyes, and she's alive."

"She's dead! She's dead! She's dead! She's dead! She's dead!"

"NO! She's not dead. . . . She's alive."

"She's dead!"

"No, she's not dead. You can see the glimmer in her eyes. But she needs to get out of the basement. You're the little girl now, and at the top of the stairs, I want you to see your mother. I want you to see your mother watching this."

"I HATE HER! I HATE HER! I HATE HER! I HATE HER! I HATE HER!"

"She's watching and she knows what it is that is happening."

"I hate her! I hate her! She's letting him . . . I hate her! He's killing her!"

"She's watching him kill her, isn't she? She's watching him kill her, and what is she doing about it?"

"Nothing! She's doing nothing!"

"Right. . . . She's just watching. . . . She's just standing at the top of the stairs."

"No, . . . she's drunk! She's drunk!"

"She's drunk and she's not saving you and you hate her. . . . You're very angry at her."

"I hate her. . . . I hate her. . . . I hate her. "

"Okay, I want you to imagine that the little girl becomes very limp and the little girl looks like she's dead, but she's not. . . . Now, I want you to become Athena, and I want Athena to pick up the little girl and to hold her in her arms and I want you to see that she's alive. . . . Pick up the little girl and just feel her limp body. . . . Just hold her. . . . Just hold her."

"She's not moving."

"She's very still . . . but she's alive. . . . Just feel her. . . . Feel the hate for your mother and the hate for Ed. Now, look at your mother, and I want you to see a white light behind your mother. . . . I want you to look up at your mother. . . . Can you see her?"

"Yes."

"And you're holding the little girl, right?"

"No . . . I can't touch her."

"Why?"

"She's dead."

"No . . . she's not dead. . . . She's not dead. . . . He did not kill her. I want you to pick her up and feel that she's alive. Okay, I want you to be the little girl again. . . . You see the little girl is not dead, is she. The little girl has a heartbeat. . . . You can feel the pulse. . . . You can feel the pulse, can't you? Okay, now I want you to be Athena. Athena, I want you to pick up that little girl. . . . Pick her up. . . . It's scary . . . and your mother is watching and there is a white light behind your mother. . . . Pick up the little girl."

"She's . . . she's mine! She's mine! She's mine!

"That's right . . . that's right. . . . Pick her up . . . She's yours."

"She's mine! You can't hurt her anymore! You didn't protect her . . . and you can't hurt her anymore. . . . You let him rape her!"

"That's right. . . . Pick her up!"

"She's not moving. . . . She's not moving."

"That's right. That's because she's knocked out and she's very scared, but she has a heartbeat. I want you to be the little girl again. . . . I want you to be the little girl. Can you feel the heartbeat? Can you feel? There is a pulse. . . . She's alive. She's alive. You can tell that she's alive, can't you? Can you feel a pulse?"

"A little . . . a little . . . just a little . . ."

"YES! That's right! . . . She's alive. . . . She's alive! Tell me she's alive. . . . Say she's alive. . . . Say it. . . . I want to hear you say that she's alive."

"She's . . . she's . . . alive."

"Now pick her up! I want you to pick her up NOW!

Athena, you have to pick her up. . . . She's very limp, and she's very weak, and she's very beaten, and . . ."

"And she's so scared. . . . She's so scared . . ."

"Yes, she's very scared. I want you to look up at your mother . . . Do you have her in your arms? Are you protecting her?"

"No, I don't yet . . ."

"Pick her up! Pick her up! I want you to bend down and pick her up! Pick her up and save her from your mother. . . . Save her from Ed. You've got to save her now. Don't let her down. She's been let down by your mother and by Ed and by a lot of people. . . . I want you to save her. Can you pick her up?"

"I . . . I . . . I have her."

"Okay, wonderful. Okay . . . I want you to look up at your mother and I want you to feel the rage."

"I HATE YOU! GET OUT OF MY WAY! I HATE YOU! I HATE YOU!"

"I want you to start walking up the stairs towards the white light. . . . Walk towards the white light behind her."

"I hate you! I hate you! I hate you! Get out of my way!"

"Smash her out of your way before she kills your little girl. Smash her out of your way. . . . Can you smash her out of your way?"

"I did . . ."

"That drunken bitch . . . who didn't care, who couldn't get her life together and she fucked up yours! I want you to get past your mother, past the white light, into the backyard, and under the willow tree. That's where I want you to get to, and I want you to work on that right now. You have the little girl, and she has a heartbeat. I want you to be the little girl in Athena's arms right now. You're alive, aren't you? You're scared, but you're alive. . . . Now, you're Athena. Where's your mother now?

Where is your mother?"

"She's on . . . she's . . . she's on the . . . the . . . fl . . . floor."

"She's on the floor where you knocked her?"

"Yes . . . I'm out . . . outside . . ."

"You're outside, into the whiteness, into the light. . . . I want you to walk over to the tree and I want you to sit down under the tree. Okay? Are you under the willow tree holding her? You're going to save her life. Are you under the willow tree?"

"I'm . . . I'm . . . I'm by the lilac bush . . ."

"By the lilac bush?"

"I like the smell . . . I like the smell of the lilacs."

"Okay, okay, I want you to be a little girl now, and I want you to be slightly aware of the smell of the lilacs. . . . I'm talking to the little girl, now. Can you smell them?"

"Yes."

"You like lilacs."

"I like lilacs."

"I want you to turn around and I want you to see your mother lying on the floor. I want you to turn your head and see your mother as you are walking towards the willow tree. I want you to be Athena now. You're carrying the little girl, you're holding the little girl and you're moving closer and closer to the willow tree, and when you get there, I want you to let me know when you are sitting underneath the willow tree . . . okay? You can feel her breathing. . . . You know that she is going to live and stay inside of you. . . . Breathe. . . . Where are you now?"

"I'm . . . I'm . . . I'm . . . un . . . under the will . . . I'm under the willow tree."

"Are you sitting down?"

"I'm hol . . . hold . . . holding her."

"Okay, I want you to be her now. I want you to feel that

she has a heartbeat, and she's alive, and your mother's on
the floor, and that Ed is passed out somewhere. You're the
little girl right now and you're breathing, you're alive. . . .
You're alive. Now I want you to be Athena, holding the little girl and knowing that you just saved her life. She's not
dead . . . breathe. . . . You saved her life. . . . You smashed
your mother and you smashed Ed. . . . That's right. . . .
Just breathe. . . . You're holding the little girl that you just
saved, and you're under the willow tree. I want you to feel
a wind passing over the both of you. I want you to feel a
wind passing over the both of you, combining the both of
you together. . . . The wind is passing the energy through
the both of you, passing the life from Athena into the little
girl and vice versa. Just breathe and see the breath going
into the little girl. . . . You're breathing life back into her.
Your cells are her cells, combining both of you together.
You're both under the willow tree, your mother's passed
out, and Ed is . . ."

"It's over . . . It's over . . . It's all over . . ."

"That's right . . . that's right. Just breathe easy."

"It's over. . . . It's over . . . all over . . . all over . . . It's
over . . . all over . . . It's all over. . . . It's over."

"Just breathe . . . The two of you are breathing . . .
I want her to melt into you. . . . Can you feel that? Can
you feel her melting into you? She's alive and she's in
you. It's over. I want you to become one now with the
little girl who is very much alive within Athena, who's
very much alive. . . . Breathe. . . . It's painful, but it's
over. You're out of the basement. You're under the willow
tree, into the light. . . . That little girl is very much a part
of you. You can feel the good portions of what that little
girl feels. . . . You still know what happened. I don't ever
want you to forget what happened, but it's not going to
be debilitating to you. Breathe easily. . . . Okay. . . . Just
breathe. . . . That's good, . . . that's good. I'm going to
count from zero to five and I want you to become Athena

now. If we ever need to, we can go back to this. . . . You may have some things that you are thinking about, but I want you to leave them alone right now. You're one with the little girl. . . . She's alive and it's over, and we may be able to come back some time for some special things that you would like to do, but right now I'm going to count from zero to five and have you open your eyes and remember everything. Zero . . . one . . . two . . . three . . . four . . . five."

I could hear Daniel's voice off in the distance, calling me back to present time. Sobs racked my body. All I could do was lay there and let the waves of emotion take me. I had no energy to focus. I had surrendered completely and fully to the process. I was aware that my arms were twisted beneath me, and I was soaked in tears and snot. I could hear his compassionate voice whisper, "Take your time, it's okay. It's all over."

I wanted to untwist my arms from beneath the weight of my body, but I didn't have the energy to move. My sobs had begun to subside, though still coming in waves and gasps. My head was throbbing. I could feel the rough carpet on my cheek. Every part of me felt raw, vulnerable, and exposed. I tried to raise myself off the floor by pushing up with my arms but felt myself collapse again. "Don't try to get up yet. Just lie still."

"Oh God, oh God," I whimpered, and I felt another wave of emotion pass over me.

I felt his hand on my shoulder, "Here's some Kleenex," he said, as he placed it in my hand. He helped me to my feet and then to the couch. We both sat in silence while I tried to regain a sense of equilibrium and balance.

It was over.

27
She Belongs To Me

You have to allow a certain amount of time in which you are doing nothing in order to have things occur to you, to let your mind think.
—Mortimer Alder

I have often heard that it takes a great deal of energy to shove something down. The bitterness and defensiveness, the constant need to push people away out of fear, the punishing of men, the isolation, the aloofness—all of it—the anguish, the hatred, and the rage, all were exposed for what the root cause was: the need to protect myself. I felt an exhaustion in every cell of my body, but in a strange sort of way, felt as if I had been cleansed, even if temporarily. I believe it was one of the few times in my life that I ever truly surrendered to anything. I wanted to sleep, just sleep. It felt to me as if the boil had been lanced and, although the infection was draining, it would still be some time before the healing was complete. I needed the time to let my emotions settle into whatever they needed to be. I had begun to trust myself as well as the innate sense of what it was that I needed. I have always felt, even from my earliest years as a teenager, that all pain *has* to have an origin, a source, a point of reference. I have known this intuitively, and it has driven me relentlessly in the pursuit of healing. My soul had taken me exactly where I needed to go for this healing, and I had, to a larger rather than lesser degree, followed that whisper.

I have known that if it hurts going down, it will hurt equally as much coming up, and that is okay. Things began to settle, and I did not look for "change"; I simply began to trust that whatever I would need next would come, and I needed a break from the work. I wanted not to think about it. I just wanted to be.

For the next several weeks, I saw Dr. Slavin very little. I knew that we had extracted the deepest source of the cancer, and since the wound was still so new, I needed time to reflect. I had sobbed while I was under more than I could ever remember in my life, and to a great extent, I felt as if all of my nerve endings were raw and had been soaked in acid. I cried out of gratitude and thanked God for guiding me to Daniel. I cried out of a sense of love for myself and for the little girl who was no longer trapped in that blackness but was now inside of me where she belonged. I cried from the reality of what I never had from my mother, and I cried out of frustration from the anger and hate I felt for the woman whom I had told, "When I grow up, I want to be just like you." I cried for feeling guilty for feeling that way. I cried because she had watched and didn't stop him. I cried because I still wanted to crawl on her lap and to have her hold me and tell me that she was sorry and to know she meant the words from the bottom of her heart. But most of all, I cried because she never believed me. That was the greatest source of pain of all, and by far the hardest to come to terms with.

Five or six months passed. I felt shaky, exposed and vulnerable. And then, as if my psyche handed me another key to the puzzle, I became increasingly aware of how symbolic my life really was; for whatever reason, it almost seemed to me that there were blatant signposts pointing "go this way," and I began more than ever to toss logic out the window. I had a very lucid dream, in which I was walking through the rooms of the house that I had been born in, and I walked through the kitchen and stood at the entrance to the basement door. This time, however, the door was open, and I hesitated before beginning the descent.

When I awoke, I lay there and thought about it, reviewing the dream, which was vivid and clear. I knew beyond a shadow of a doubt that another level of healing was surfacing to my conscious mind. I needed to slay the beast, once and for all. So I made plans to drive up to Oregon to physically reenact my dream, to relive and to actualize rescuing the little girl, the part of myself that had been trapped within the basement for all those years. Most of my life I have felt as if someone had tossed a bomb at me and I have been running around picking up the pieces of my psyche, attaching a foot where my arm should be but trying to make myself functional and whole. It was like learning to live with an emotional limp. I knew that it would take all the courage that I could muster, and I also knew that my imagination had nothing over the events that had already transpired. I had lived my worst nightmare, but I survived.

I contacted the person currently living in the house and told him that I was revisiting for nostalgic reasons, and that I was writing a book. I could tell by his voice that he was somewhat young, and he said it was not a problem at all; he was simply the tenant and not the owner. I hung up the phone, feeling almost as if I wanted to throw up. I wondered if he ever on some level "felt" something evil and dark there, for I knew that the record of that horror was still present. I began to think that perhaps I should leave well enough alone. I didn't know if I could actually go through with it, but in my heart I knew that it was my way of saying loud and clear, "You will not kill her spirit. *She belongs to me,* and I will go back into the depths of hell to bring her home. I did, I had, and I would. *She belongs to me."*

I made an appointment with Dr. Slavin, at which time I recounted to him the dream and my decision to return to the house. I had contemplated forgiving Ed; whether or not I would be able to do that was yet to be seen. I just wanted to feel better.

"Call me if you need me, and if you can't forgive him yet, that's okay, and if you are never able to, that's okay too."

"Thanks, Daniel. I appreciate that," I replied.

"You have so much courage," he said quietly, as he opened the door for me. " Driving home that night, Daniel's words kept resounding in my head: "You have so much courage." *It's the desire to be free,* I thought to myself. *It's the desire to be free.*

I had called my sister Connie and asked her somewhat lightheartedly if she wanted to take a trip down Memory Lane. I was thankful that she said yes, and so I made arrangements to pick her up in northern California before heading up to Oregon. I was glad for the company; however, I knew this was something that, ultimately, I had to do alone. I felt queasy at times, in anticipation of what I would feel, what else would come up, but most of all at the thought of actually being physically present— to smell the smells, to feel the sensations, to actualize the memory made my skin crawl with unease.

It was dark when we pulled out of the driveway. I

was still groggy and tired. It was a long drive from Los Angeles to Chico, and I was numb from the nine-hour drive. A few more hours' sleep would have been nice, but we both wanted to get an early start. I put on the headlights and drove down the sleepy streets. I love the predawn hours; it has always been my favorite time of day. It's as if everything is suspended in quiet and stillness. It's healing for me, magical and inspiring, with the chance to begin anew. I have always enjoyed watching life begin to stir into activity, and it has been in those few moments of watching the deep purple hues transform, as night turns into day, that I have felt, in some ways, closest to God.

I could tell that Connie was somewhat uncomfortable discussing any of the events, so we kept it more lighthearted and laughed about the absurdity of the times and the depth of our poverty, reliving humorous memories and events, and it was if the day was allowing this time of reflection, for it had been sunny and quite beautiful for our drive up interstate five. We took our time, stopping wherever we wanted, and pulled into Klamath Falls in the early afternoon. As we rounded a bend that revealed the town nestled below, I suddenly became aware that the blue sky, accented with puffy white clouds, had within moments become menacing and dark. I found it bizarre that the transition had happened so quickly. It caught me off guard, and I became instantly aware of a heaviness in my body and was flooded with the feeling of anxiety.

I had come home. I didn't expect what I found. In a strange sort of way, I felt as if I had entered into a time warp. Nothing had changed, only decayed. There was a sense of eeriness in the atmosphere that made my skin crawl, and I couldn't help but feel as if the house was almost alive, waiting for my return. I stood motionless across the street from it as I watched the screen door open and bang shut hauntingly by a wind that carried an undertone of evil.

A crooked "For Sale" sign protruded out of the grass, which had dying patches of yellow that now looked like a worn-out carpet. The tree that had provided shade on hot summer days was an amputated stump, and signs of its massive root system swelled like long arthritic fingers from beneath the earth.

"It looks spooky, doesn't it?" Connie stated.

"Yes," I replied, "it looks scary as hell." I took a deep breath and headed for the porch. I did not want to be in that basement at nightfall. My stomach was churning, and I felt that familiar feeling of nausea as I knocked on the door. I wanted to turn and run, and there was a feeling of dread and apprehension that seemed to ooze out of every pore in my body. I hated that feeling of not knowing what I was going to encounter, what the end result would be. But I knew that I had to do this.

The door opened, and a young man in his early thirties greeted us with a warm smile. *What a strange contrast,* I thought to myself as we followed him into the front room. I could feel my eyes dart quickly around the room, for to be back within the walls that held so much of my soul felt unearthly to me. Connie and I had agreed that she would do the talking to keep him occupied while we began to walk from room to room. I was mystified and amazed that what looked so big from a child's perspective now looked so small and cramped. How in God's name did we all live in such small quarters?

As we walked from room to room, Connie kept the tenant completely engaged in conversation, leaving me to gather my prayers and strength as we headed for the kitchen. There it was, the door that led to the basement, my descent into hell. My heart began to race, and I wanted to vomit. I took a deep breath and opened the door. I could feel Connie behind me, and I started to back up into her, as I was flooded with an indescribable energy. I was afraid. All I knew was that I had to get that little girl out of the basement. It would never come from anyone else. I had to do it for me. I had to do it for her. I wanted to live and feel more alive. I just wanted. And although I had done the work and had achieved so much, this felt to me like tying the surgeon's knot.

The Stairs

The light was somewhat dim as I made my way down to the landing of the basement. Week after week, I had walked down those steps, and to be actualizing that in the absolute physical felt no different, for I felt the same dread and terror wash over me.

As I stood on the bottom of the landing, I was immediately taken aback by the sight of a dark wool blanket, suspended and hung by ropes from the air ducts and pipes, creating a makeshift divider that separated the current tenant's daughter's area from the root cellar. I felt sickened by the thought that his young child was sleeping here, and I wanted to rip down the blanket and scream at her to get out, that it was evil here. I knew that she would be sensing, on an intuitive level, what still hung in the atmosphere, her conscious mind unaware that her soul was picking up the etheric record that still remained after all these years.

The Root Cellar

Salty saliva filled my mouth. I took a deep breath and walked towards the cave-like dwelling. A single bare bulb hung from the duct in front of the plywood door; its hospital green paint had years of dirt etched within the grains of wood. Chunks of wood were missing from the frame, leaving marks where padlocks had once been used. I wanted to turn and run. I forced myself to open the door. The smell of damp earth flooded my senses, and the musty odor was overwhelming. The dirt was hard and compact as I forced myself to sit on the ground in the darkness. I could feel myself shaking, and I began to cry. I fought the urge to scream out my hatred and rage: *You motherfucker! You sick bastard! How could you do that to a child? Do you have any idea what you did to me? Do you have any idea how much I have wanted to die because of you? Do you know how hard it has been to hang on to life, to feel . . . just to feel? Do you know how you have tormented me? Do you know the fear you caused me to live with? Do you know what you robbed me of? You took my childhood! You took the trust and left the fear of sex, the pain. I hate you, and I hate my mother as much as I do you. You haven't won, you sick fuck. I am alive! I am alive, and I survived! I have won! She is mine!*

I wiped away the tears that were streaming down my face and headed up the stairs. This time however, I wasn't alone.

The drive back to Los Angeles provided me time to reflect. Hell, I couldn't have stopped the process if I tried. Thoughts and images floated into my mind: fragmented events and comments, nightmares and reactions, statements made by frustrated boyfriends, impenetrable walls, and imprisoned feelings. My private thoughts of suicide, my lack of response, my feeling numb and *wanting* to feel. My fear of knives. My inability to have fun, my need to control the events and people around me. My need to save people . . . not wanting people to hurt. My need to save myself.

I shook my head in amazement. I had once said while under, "I just want to feel better and I want Mama to feel better and JuJu to feel better and him to feel better too." No six-year-old child should ever have to utter those words. It was hard to believe that I was here. It was hard to believe that I had survived. It was hard to believe that someone could be that evil. I felt a great sense of triumph and defiance at the same time and an intense feeling of having surmounted the odds. I had gone into the vortex, the black hole, and I was *conscious* I wasn't insane. I knew it was the only way for me to heal, and I was willing to take any avenue that spirit was showing me would help me feel more whole.

I was taking that child with me, the one I had seen in so many dreams, the one who hid behind a chair and never trusted, the one who was so afraid and shy. I remember how sad I felt once when I awoke from a dream in which I had tried and tried to coax a little girl out from behind a big chair. I could never get her out of that darkness, and I felt so sad at having to leave her there in the dark. All of my prodding was in vain, so I gave her a blanket to keep her warm and headed up the stairs.

I am not quite sure when the next episode came to surface, but some time had passed, and I was not seeing Dr. Slavin on a regular basis. I began to become aware that I was not isolating myself quite as much as I used to. There has always been a memory that has somewhat haunted me, and I felt as if it were time to go back to see what would present itself. I felt as if, on a grander level, we had slain the beast; however, I was completely shocked by the events as they began to unfold.

28

The Year My Feet Forgot The Dance

The meeting of two personalities is like the contact of two chemical substances; if there is any reaction, both are transformed.
—*Carl Jung*

"So, what are we going to work on today?" The one thing that I loved about my work with Dr. Slavin was that he always seemed to trust in my ability to know when something was brewing under the surface for me. I remember him saying to me once, "Your soul takes you where you need to go for healing." It never seemed to come from logic *per se*, but more from feeling, a whisper, a dream, a rapid heartbeat, a feeling of repulsion without voice. Whatever it was, I trusted it. I never really went into his office with an end result in mind, but I was willing to pull on the thread to simply see where it led. I intuitively follow feelings to their source, and I have often found the most dynamic are the ones that are subtle in nature but relentless in their ability to create absolute havoc in our lives.

"Where is your soul taking you today?" He said as he sat in his leather chair with his legal pad on his lap.

"I remember once when you had put me under, when

| 259

Ed was raping me, I remember a sensation like someone poured ice water through my soul. It was at that exact moment that I felt my fists clench and my muscles turned to steel and a I felt a wall fall down around me." I found myself thinking back to the time a boyfriend yelled at me out of frustration, "You've got a fuckin' wall around you that no one can get through!"

"What was the feeling, the judgment?"

"I can't let people get close. I can't let people in. I want to see if I can go back to that one exact moment and create a new belief system. Think we can do it?"

"All right, lay back and get comfortable," he said, as he began to dim the light. I listened, and as Dan began the familiar countdown, I felt the heaviness take over my body as I stood at the top of the stairs, looking at the darkness below. I began the descent.

"She has to do it for me."

"Who has to do it for you?" Dan inquired.

"She has to."

"Who is she?"

"That other part of me. She has to do it."

"That other part?"

"Yes, that other part of me. She has to do it for me. She has to go down the stairs. I can't do it; I'm too little, she has to do it for me. She never lets me come out."

"Ahhh . . . How do you come out?"

"By having some fun. She never lets me have any fun!"

"Tell her that she needs to let you come out and have some fun."

"I think she's mean! She's mean! She *will not let me have some fun.* You *cannot* have any fun! That's what she's says, all the time, all the time, that's what she says! You *cannot* have any fun! And she made me stop dancing and I loved to dance. I loved to dance. She's mean and I hate her!"

"Tell her. . . . Go ahead, tell her. Tell her that she needs to let you come out and have some fun!"

"I want to come out! I want to come out! I want to come out!"

"Tell her what you'll do when you come out."

"If I want to make mud pies and throw them at the house, I'll make mud pies and throw them at the house, and you can't do anything about it! If I want to play the piano and pound the keys, I'll pound the keys, and you can't do anything about it!' I want to come out! I want to come out!"

In a barely audible whisper, a voice then came out of me: "It's been me taking care of her all of these years. It's been me."

"Who said that?" Dr. Slavin asked.

"I said that. It's been me."

"Athena," Dr. Slavin said gently, "you have to let her come out."

"She would have died! He would have killed her! It's been me taking care of her! He would have slit your throat! Is that what you want . . . to die? To have your throat slit? He would have killed *you*. He would have raped *you*. It's been me protecting *you*!"

"I want to come out! I want to come out!" said another voice, coming out of my mouth.

Dr. Slavin addressed this voice: "Go on, tell her some more. Tell her what you are going to do."

"If I want to make mud pies and throw them at the house, I'll make mud pies and throw them at the house, and you can't do anything about it!"

"Tell her some more!"

"If I want to paint pictures and scribble on the walls with my crayons, I'll scribble on the walls, and I'll scribble, scribble, scribble, and you can't do anything about it! If I want to play the harp, I'll play the harp, and you can't do anything about it! And stop putting that food in my mouth because I don't want to eat it! So stop putting it in my mouth! I don't want to eat it! I want to come out! I want to come out!"

"That means I have to die, then," said the other voice coming out of me.

"No," Dr. Slavin said quietly but authoritatively, "you don't have to die. You can live as one, but you have to let her come out."

"Courtney and I play," said the child like first voice. "I play with Courtney."

"You can play with Courtney," Dr. Slavin reassured her.

After I became conscious again, Dr. Slavin was silent for a moment waiting for me to get my bearings. "Well, there was definitely a split off. Who's Courtney?" he inquired.

"Courtney is my sister's daughter," I said, regaining my sense of myself. "She's around five." It was true, whenever I would visit my sister Susie, Courtney and I would play.

I thought back to the child's voice that had asserted itself, "And stop putting that food in my mouth because I don't want to eat it!" I have always stuffed down fear, anxiety, you name it, with food. I have suppressed my creativity, any ability to be spontaneous and to allow myself to have fun. Feelings have been foreign. I was terrified of them—these are feelings that I lived with all of my life. There was an underlying feeling like being on the edge of a deep-seated hysteria, a feeling of wanting to scream at the top of my lungs for someone, anyone to hear: *I'm scared to death, and I'm terrified that I'll always feel this way . . . that I'll never be able to let go. I'm scared to death there won't be a way out. I'm scared to death that, if I die, my soul will stay in a state of torment.* Depression, sadness, hurt, or anger—you name it. That is what I shoved down through the years with food.

Numb it, soothe it, make it go away, so that I don't have to feel. It makes little difference what vice we choose— alcohol, food, cigarettes, sex, drugs—they all medicate the pain away. In some ways I think I have had a closer relationship with my refrigerator than with most of the men in my life.

I remember how excited I felt when I had been able to *finally* identify the feeling that I had lived with all my life. I was listening to Dr. David Viscott, a psychiatrist on the radio, and he was talking about how to identify your feelings. Anxiety, he said, is fear of loss. And there isn't a greater fear than that of losing your life. That was the fear: the strangulation, the butcher knife against my throat, the being bound and rendered helpless . . . Christ, no wonder.

What would a child do with that stuff except bury it and put it into compartments? It's called survival. But what worked then didn't work now. The prism through which I viewed life, the conclusions drawn from a child's perspective, gave me a distorted lens that colored everything with shades of fear, and shadows of falsehood formed the foundation that became my reality. I must be bad and unlovable. I'm horribly flawed. God didn't care. Life on earth was hell. I had to protect myself. I had to protect myself. I had to protect myself. People couldn't be trusted. Men would hurt me. It's better not to feel. Shove it down and make it go away. Numb the pain.

I thought about the times as a young child that I would jump off the bed so the monster that lived in my bedroom couldn't grab my feet. Most of the time, he stayed in the closet and I was terrified of him. One day, I mustered all the courage I had and opened the door to my closet. He was real. He was huge and took up all the space. I said to him, "Do you like hot dogs and hamburgers? Do you like mustard or catsup on them?" I will feed you, so you will be so full you won't eat me. That was the deal I made with him. That was the contract.

Shortly after, Dr. Slavin and I went back to revisit the closet and he no sooner put me under and asked if the monster had a name than I was instantly shouting back on top of his words. *"ED . . . ED . . . ED! HIS NAME IS ED! HIS NAME IS ED! HIS NAME IS ED!"* It wouldn't surprise me if my choice to open that closet door and confront that monster at the age of six didn't set the stage for self-exploration throughout my life.

I have so often, in reflection over the years, thought about the sensation of that ice water being poured through my soul and *feeling* that wall instantly drop down around me. Driving home, I thought about my very first session with Dr. Slavin, when he had me go to the beach, and I remembered the tiny little girl sitting in the sand who felt totally powerless as the general, the adult me circled her with such anger. "Why do you want to go back and dig all of this up now? Why? I am so damned angry at you!" That anger would resurface in another fascinating way, but not for several years, and the tapestry would grow more complex in its depth and origin.

The eighties had been a jammed packed decade of accelerated growth. It seemed as if I barely had time to catch my breath or exhale between experiences. Over the next six or seven years I watched my daughter transform from a budding teenager into a breathtaking beauty with a smile that could stop traffic. She had an innate sense of wisdom, wise beyond her years and had this uncanny ability to assess human character, observe the struggle, and define it in a few simple sentences. More than once she left me scratching my head. "How does she know that?"

Here is a poem she wrote for me when she was seven. Not one word altered.

How it is inside
One day you are hurt
You are very hurt because he let you go.
But no matter what he is still yours inside
You fill like it is your falt
But one day you will find out that you can not depind on him
Today you are better because you found anather man
And you are old enothf to know what love is all about
And you will depind on yourself today.

Tina

I am a firm believer she carried this awareness and wisdom into this life from previous incarnations. After her move to Chico, Tina had come home for a short visit, as school was out for spring break. A friend of mine found herself confiding to my then fourteen-year-old daughter about her marital affair. I happened to be walking down the hallway and caught a glimpse of them in my peripheral vision in Tina's room. They were both lying on the bed, Annie on her stomach propped up on her elbows talking like a magpie. Tina listened intently, lying on her back, staring at the ceiling with her hands folded behind her head; one leg crossed at the knee swung back and forth as if the motion helped her summarize Annie's situation. She paused. "You know, I just love how you grown-ups screw up your lives." I shook my head laughing while Annie erupted in a giggle. That's what I mean.

Tina and Olive

For the next four or five years, she vacillated between Chico and Los Angeles; it felt to me as if she was trying to find where she belonged. After high school she moved home for a brief period but within a short time she was ready to stretch her wings further. She moved to Malibu and surrounded herself with horses. Animals feed her soul. If it walks, trots, squeaks, or waddles, she's got it. Dr. Peebles told her once, "Tina my darling, if you can transform the love you feel with animals into a personal relationship with human beings, you will know complete fulfillment in this lifetime."

I don't think there will ever be a time when I won't have a wistful desire to have those early years back. It was what it was, and it is what it is. Period. Our relationship is evolving, and I like the kind of person she is growing into. I am proud of her. I love her. In this lifetime, Dr. Peebles commented, I volunteered to be a vehicle for her to come forward into this incarnation. "Her greatest love for you Athena will happen as maturity comes upon her in life."

Mark had now been released from prison along with dreams and aspirations of a new start. Although my family had reservations, once they got to know him, they accepted him into the fold. When Mom met him, she said, "I have my three sons and I guess I have room for one more." Dr. Peebles called him a beautiful and unusual opportunity and gift. Dr. Slavin called him one of the most sensitive men he had met. I couldn't call it like it was—a mistake.

PART THREE

THE MOTHERLODE

29
A Bitter Pill To Swallow

Even Popeye didn't eat his spinach
until he absolutely had to.
—Anonymous

I stood by the window and found myself "trancing," staring off in space. I was aware that I was daydreaming, suspended somewhere else with my eyes transfixed on nothing. A vision flooded my conscious mind, and I saw a multitude of police cars around the house. "That's weird," I thought to myself as I let the curtain drop back into place. Had I known then that I was being shown a premonition as a warning, I would have scurried off to the hills like a hermit crab.

We hadn't been in this house long and, although I was happy to be closer to my sister, it never felt right, nor did the housing development, or the cul-de-sac scattered with toys, or the barking dogs nipping at the heels of teenagers whizzing by on their bikes.

Perhaps a new town and a change of scenery would prove to be the right kind of distraction to help ward off the growing feeling of discontent. I was feeling trapped. It isn't easy telling someone you aren't in love with them, and it wasn't easy living in a situation that I wanted out of. It's hell saying, "I don't want you to make love to me." Or to wonder What am I going to have to think about to not be present? This was the second time I had married someone I wasn't in love with, and what was that all about? The first time, I married for security, because I thought he would be a good father for my daughter. I had already tuned out and turned off, so my attitude was, why not? What was the difference? That backfired in my face, and I found myself slipping into la-la land. Talk about a mismatch.

This time, I married because I wasn't strong enough to say, "I made a mistake. I can be your friend but nothing more." Or perhaps I married to prove how good I was. After all, wasn't I something? Look at how this man had changed, and it was all because I saw something good in him. Oh, the arrogance of it all.

Inside, however, I was miserable, and I knew he felt it, I knew he could sense it. You can't fake it all day, every day. He told me once that it was torture being married to someone who isn't in love with you. So, on top of trying to make it in the real world, he had to watch his "savior" detach. I went into full-blown denial. I can make myself love him; I can make myself feel all the passion I'm supposed to have for my husband. But I couldn't. If it ain't there, it ain't there.

Desert terrain has never been my favorite. It is hauntingly depressing. It's as if there is an origin so deep and old, it makes my heart hurt and fills me with a melancholy that is hard to describe. So here I was, in an environment that seemed only to stimulate that which I was already feeling. But I have learned that my style of growth has been to jump into the fire, and without a shadow of a doubt, growth was accelerating, and a series of experiences was about to unfold. They were being stimulated into manifestation, and my denial and his desperation were not going to be shown any mercy.

In my discontent, I sought counsel with Dr. Peebles, my spirit guide. This was something I did about every six months, and his opening statement was always a confirmation that he was aware of what was going on in my life at that time. I was always fascinated by that and wondered how his opening statement answered questions before I asked them. At some point, he asked me, "Have you considered taking another Journey to the Heart class with my channel?"

"Uhhh, . . . yes," I stammered. "I have."

"Well," he said in his sing-song voice, "let's put it this way: We won't stop you!" It was true that I had been thinking about taking another of Thomas's classes, and although it had been only a fleeting thought, it had entered my mind. As painful as that last experience with Thomas had been, I grew in leaps and bounds and found a key to a missing part of my psyche.

Fuck Me! I thought to myself. *Another delightful opportunity for growth!*

He blatantly threw me the bait, and I knew the nature of "who I am" would make me reel it in hook, line, and sinker. I also knew that if Thomas had his way, he would want to "sink her," as I always rubbed him the wrong way. But somewhere in the murky water of my life, among the rusted garbage at the bottom, there was a treasure chest filled with jewels for me, if I could only muster the courage to dive in.

Whether we are individually aware of it or not, we are all being guided by spirit, and the choice to listen or turn away is entirely ours by free will. I have come to recognize in my own life that, for example, people may be moved to say a certain phrase at an exact moment that may be exactly what I needed to hear. And they, as a messenger, can be completely oblivious as to the impact that their words have upon me. That is what I call *life's disguise.* On one level, Thomas was offering another workshop series to his clientele of mystics, and of course it also helped to pay his bills. I knew, however, that beneath the veil, on another level, spirit was at work and what was to unfold would have to be experienced through participation. Thomas was equally led by spirit. For me, outwardly, at times his demeanor left something to be desired. However, on the inner realms, there was a grander purpose to the workshop that he wasn't even aware of. Nothing happens by chance or accident, as the following vision suggested.

That night I had a lucid dream in which I saw Thomas's face, bigger than life, directly in front of me, and upon awakening, I knew we had met in spirit to set the stage. Ain't my first barbecue. The following day I received a flier, outlining the upcoming ten-week series, and after I read about the workshop, my phone rang.

"Hello?"

"Hi, Athena, it's Thomas. How are you?"

"I'm fine, Thomas. How are you?"

"Okay, thank you. Listen, I just wanted to let you know that I am starting another Journey to the Heart class, and I thought you might be interested."

Oh yeah, I thought to myself. *The last time you completely humiliated me, you fucker.*

"Thomas, this just isn't a good time. I've got too many financial obligations to take care of. If I had the extra money I would." (*Liar,* I thought to myself.)

"You sure you can't swing it?"

"I'm sure. If something changes, I'll let you know."

I felt a sense of relief when I hung up the phone, and at the same time, I couldn't shake the nagging feeling that this was being orchestrated on a higher level. I knew my fear was getting the best of me. "Athena, you big weenie." I hated this, now that I knew I was backing out of something consciously. "Oh, alright!" I said in haste and disgust. "Okay, God, if I get a call for a five-day commercial in the next two minutes, I'll take the class. That's the deal!" Just then the phone rang.

"Hello? Hi Athena, this is Wright Banks Films we'd like to book you for a five-day job the fifth through the tenth. Are you available?"

FUCK!!!

It seemed to me that there was hardly an area of my life where I wasn't being confronted with having to address honesty: how I really felt about my marriage, how I felt about my mother, how I felt about myself. I had this underlying fuel of anger that I didn't know what to do with or how to release.

I had the feeling that Thomas was somewhat guarded in his communication with me during class this time, as if he knew how hard he had clobbered me in the last class. Because of that, I began to relax and looked forward to my Saturdays and the drive into LA. I enjoyed the people in the class and, selfishly, I enjoyed not being with my husband. This was something I was doing for me. There was a man in the class whose daughter had died tragically in a car accident some years prior, and as an exercise once, he was to stand in the middle of the circle and allow whatever communication came from spirit side to flow through him, writing down what he received, his intent being to contact his daughter.

There he stood, with tears flowing down his cheeks, and I, like the rest of the group, felt great compassion for him. My eyes were drawn up to the ceiling, and I saw a ball of white light floating towards him. I watched in fascination as it hovered some inches from his head. Greg began to write fast and furiously; then the orb floated towards me and positioned itself to my right by the window. Thomas encouraged Greg to share what he had received from his daughter with the class. He was wiping away the tears with one hand while his other, shaking, held the paper. It was obvious how difficult it was for him. "I am with you, Daddy. I am right here with you. I am right above you. You can do it, Daddy. You can go into those dark places in yourself. I'm with you. Now I am over by Athena, by the window."

And just when I thought it was safe, we were given an assignment to bring to class the following week. Each of us had written our names down on pieces of paper and placed them in a basket, which Thomas passed around at the end of the class. We were not to look at the name hidden in the folded square, but were to write down the impressions we received or any other symbols or messages pertaining to the individual and were to bring it back to class to be shared. That night I had another lucid spirit dream bigger than life, in which I saw Greg, myself, Roger, and Thomas's face. In the dream we were standing in a bathroom, and I remember seeing a lion's face.

I felt anxious driving to class that day, edgy and pissy. I have since then learned that my personality is "picking up" that my ego is about to go into the dumpster and it doesn't give up willingly. The three of us set the stage on the etheric realm, and that melodic sing-song voice of Dr. Peebles'—"We won't stop you"—should have been my first clue I would have been better off staying in bed that day.

I stood in the circle and took the "hot seat," as I called it, unfolded my paper, and saw that the name that I had drawn was Roger. I read the impressions I received and was immediately cut off by Thomas. "You just had to impress us with your psychic ability didn't you? You just had to show off."

"What are you talking about?" I replied, perplexed. "I did the assignment—what we were supposed to do. This is what I received."

"You just had to show off," he said with a smirk on his face. "If you would have asked spirit when you received this symbol, 'What does this mean, spirit?' it would have taken you in another direction, but no, you had to show us how 'psychic' you are. Okay everyone, follow me into the bathroom."

The bathroom—the dream from the night before flashed again in my conscious mind. What the hell is he going to do? Shove my head in the toilet? My heart was pounding hard now, but I was not going to let this fucker win.

Everybody squeezed in, forming a circle behind Thomas, and he shoved me in front of the mirror. "Tell yourself how much you hate yourself," he insisted. "Go on . . . tell yourself how much you hate yourself."

I stared at my own reflection, and it was true. I did hate myself. "I hate you," I said.

"Louder," he said.

"I hate you. I hate you. I hate you. I HATE YOU! I HATE YOU! I HATE YOU!" The people in the mirror lost their faces and all I was aware of was this person screaming back at me. I could feel myself begin to get small, and I began to stutter. I felt myself slipping away, and I became a young, terrified child of six, stuttering. I could feel myself begin to lose consciousness and droop to the floor like a rag doll. I could hear Thomas's voice far off in the distance, like an echo in the darkness, saying, "Help me get her into the front room on the floor."

Wherever I was, *I wasn't present,* for I had slipped into another state of consciousness, and I could feel myself stuttering, back in the basement as a young child. I was being raped. Mother was there. She was drunk. I tried to push the words out of my mouth, to call for help, but they only came in broken sounds. I could hear a voice through a far-away tunnel telling me to slip into the consciousness of my mother. I dropped through another veil and everything became woozy and blurry, and I felt sick to my stomach. Nothing had boundaries—it was all a blur, like slow motion, and I couldn't focus on what was transpiring in front of me. I was drunk. Something was happening in the same room I was in, but it was a blur. I couldn't focus on it. I was drunk and sick. I left the scene and followed the distant voice. I was aware of being inside a film strip. Scenes became blurred images, like looking through the window of a train speeding down the track, speeding, speeding—and then it stopped.

I was in Athens, Greece, at the Parthenon. A soldier had just reported to me that my husband had been killed in battle. I had began to cry, to wail, and to scream . . . and then I sped to another life in Greece. I had been stabbed and was dying, my husband crying at my side as the life force ebbed from my body.

In the distance I heard a far-away voice. "What's the judgment? What's the judgment?"

"It hurts too much to love," I replied through the sobs. "It hurts too much to love."

I struggled to regain consciousness as somebody was trying to wipe the snot and tears off my face. I was aware of grabbing on to the front of Thomas's shirt trying to gain the strength to lift myself up. I felt as if my guts had just been blown apart and there was no energy left in my body. Everybody around me was crying. To have witnessed the depth of my vulnerability left people touched to their core. Once I was able to focus, I could see the compassion and tears on their faces, and it was as if I were surrounded in acceptance and love. I had not been aware of any of them since we all went into the bathroom. The class came to a close and people reached out and touched me, hugged me and whispered in my ear heartfelt messages.

Driving home, I reflected on something Dr. Peebles had said once: that when you allow yourself to be totally vulnerable, that's when magic happens. I know that on a conscious level, Thomas was unaware that he was being guided by spirit to bring something up from my subconscious for healing. He was psychically stirring up within me a root belief that I would never acknowledge on a conscious level to myself, let alone to anyone else. I tried too hard to be perfect to hide what felt like such gross imperfection. With spirit and Dr. Peebles leading the way, our souls orchestrated that which would promote healing. I think it was this event that created the platform from which Thomas began to view me with respect as a spiritual warrior.

I crawled into bed and slept for hours.

The next afternoon, Thomas called to see how I was doing. "What you did took a lot of courage," he said. I thought back to the same statement made by Dr. Slavin after a session of equal intensity. To each of them, to myself, and to the universe, I reply, "The courage comes from the desire to be free."

30

Jeepers Creepers Where'd Ya Get Those Peepers?

If it is true that our species is alone in the universe, then
I'd have to say the universe aimed rather low
and settled for very little.
—George Carlin

It was November of 1988. I had just finished Thomas's class a month or so before, and all of the new insights were settling in. Although it had been hard, I knew I would extract a few gems. I had a deeper understanding now of my fear of love, the origin of the loss, and the judgment I had made around the pain. It hurts too much to love. Such a strange paradox: What I desired the most, I feared the most—love and intimacy.

I thought back to the sensation of being on that time track, viewing events of my life speeding by like blurry frames of film and moving into the consciousness of my mother, and how sick from the alcohol I felt. I thought of my hatred for her and the guilt, the guilt of feeling the emotions I did. I had extracted gems all right, and this much I knew: I was feeling more connected now. That feeling of wanting to isolate was not as pronounced. It was a time of quiet reflection, late at night, when Mark was asleep, the house was still and quiet, and I was sitting on the couch staring at the vastness of the universe.

The stars were magnificent, clear and bright; the silent questions, endless, and I felt that all-too-familiar feeling of homesickness tug at my heart. "If any of you are out there and can hear my thoughts," I said silently, "I'd love to communicate with you." More than a thought, it was a statement, a feeling, a resonance, and it came straight from my heart. I never gave it much thought after that; however, contact began almost immediately and unfolded in a variety of bold encounters that varied in species and experience.

We had made plans with other family members to have an old-fashioned Christmas, and we were heading up to the mountains to a cabin we had rented in Big Bear. I was so hoping that it would snow. I couldn't wait to be inside with a fire, where it was toasty and warm, watching big, fluffy snowflakes drift past the window, transforming everything into magic and wonder.

I had picked up a book of Whitley Strieber's, *Communion,* for my brother Paul, who was intrigued by UFOs, and certainly believed in them and found the whole subject fascinating. I knew Paul would like the book, and I found the face of the alien on the cover almost magnetizing. I have always known UFOs exist; however, I have never studied anything on the subject nor has it been a subject of great interest to me. I accept them like I accept breathing. They are part of life—more life, that's all. Listening to theories of government cover-ups, or any kind of lectures proving their existence bores me to tears. It is so elementary. How could anyone look at the stars and feel that this is the only planet with life? I don't get it, but on the other hand, I don't have to; non-belief is their reality, not mine.

Mark sat in the passenger seat reading the paper as I drove. I glanced out the window to my left and saw the strangest darned thing: three disc-shaped clouds, hovering low, moving at the same speed as my car. I kept getting the distinct feeling telepathically that there were UFOs hidden inside them.

"Mark! Look at that. Look at those clouds, out my window. Look at them! Don't you think they're weird?" He barely glanced up from the paper and gave an automatic "uh-huh" kind of a response and continued reading. *So much for that,* I thought to myself. Still, I couldn't shake this feeling that we were being followed. At the same time, however, I found a growing sense of excitement stirring in my feelings. Perhaps it was simply because of being in the mountains for Christmas.

Christmas memories had been flooding my mind as I drove. One Christmas stood out.

It had been a wonderful day. We had gone up to the mountains above Klamath Falls, Oregon, the day before and cut down our Christmas tree. We had had a snowball fight, drank hot chocolate from a thermos. I remember hearing the snow crunch under my feet, gathering up the fine white powder and eating it by the mouthfuls, and smelling the wet wool from my mittens.

"Deck the Halls!"

Santa Claus was coming tonight! I, along with my brothers and sisters, had been sent off to the matinee that day. My sister Judy told us it was okay to watch the movie more than once, so we did. High Ho, Silver— Away! That was the message. Stay away, play outside. Mom and Judy had lots to do.

We had plenty of steep hills in the neighborhood for sledding. The boys took every opportunity to pummel us in the head or back with snowballs, and eventually we came in soaked and frozen, with chattering teeth, red toes, and fingers that stung when we held them under warm water. We were going to decorate the tree after we ate dinner and had our baths. Judy gave us new flannel pajamas to put on. Mine were pink, Connie's were blue; and Susie's were yellow. They each came with matching slippers with white plastic feet on the bottom. I liked the way mine smelled, all brand new with creases down the front where they had been neatly folded. They felt soft, and I felt special.

Santa Claus was coming tonight!

The fire crackled and sizzled. Judy said that it would be out by the time Santa came. She strung the lights around the tree, gave us shiny bright bulbs to hang, and laid silver tinsel across our fingers with instructions on how to lay it across the branch so that it would hang straight and pretty. That was good for only a few strands. I, like the rest of the kids, got impatient and started to fling it on, which seemed like a sure-fire method of speeding things up. Our stockings were hung on the chimney with care, and the cookies and milk were put out for Santa. With a few embers still glowing among the charred logs, and nothing under the tree, we went to bed to dream.

Judy said I could sleep with her. I scooted next to the wall, so that I could look for Santa through the frozen windowpane. Icicles hung from the edge of the roof, and I watched as cotton-ball snowflakes drifted by my window, lit by the golden light of the street lamp. Everything was white and beautiful, and I swore I saw the shadow of Santa Claus and the reindeer as they crossed the full moon.

I woke up in the middle of the night, threw back the covers, and scrambled over top of Judy. She moaned in her sleep as my knee sunk into the softness of her tummy. The scratched hardwood floor in the hallway was alive with colors, flashing with hues of red, blue, and green, signaling something magical lay hidden beyond the archway that led into the front room. "Santa Claus came! Wake up everybody! Santa Claus has been here!" I peeked around the corner and ran into the other bedroom, screaming like the town crier. "Wake up! It's Christmas! Santa Claus came!"

It was still dark outside, and the Christmas tree lights were flashing off and on, turning the walls and the toys different colors, and if ever the spirit of magic graced our hearts, it was then. Santa Claus brought me a dolly that looked like a real live baby, with little eyes that opened and shut.

It was such a wonderful time.

Not long before my sister Judy died, I was visiting her, and I sat on the hearth enjoying the warmth of the fire, drinking coffee, talking about life, smelling the wonderful aromas coming out of the kitchen. Somehow, we got on the subject of Christmas, and I shared with her how that memory will always stand out in my life and that nobody could convince me I didn't see Santa Claus as I lay in bed that Christmas Eve and looked out the bedroom window. It was pure magic.

Judy stooped over in the process of picking up a log to put in the fire. I could see her hesitating, thinking, and for a moment she said nothing. She stood up, and I watched her exhale with a kind of "oh, God" feeling. I wondered why she responded in the manner she did. She turned her head slowly, looked at me, and said dryly, "I shoplifted those toys. Mom had given me twenty dollars to buy presents for you kids. Christ, that wasn't enough money. You all had written your lists, and you were so excited. I couldn't bear to see your disappointed faces. Remember that dime store on Main Street? I went in and took what I could and went out in the alley behind the store and hid them. I was so afraid of getting caught. I had never done anything like that before."

I think about that a lot now. I think of the sharp contrast of her fear back then and the pure joy and enchantment that enveloped my spirit that Christmas, for I would need something that I could draw upon, some special memory that showed me the promise of a different world through the innocence and wonderment of a child's heart. I would come to need the memory of joy.

I think of Judy, clandestinely stowing stolen toys in a back alleyway, her heart pounding. And I hope that whatever grey film of guilt that has ever clung to her soul can be washed away by the pristine purity of the white light of that winter's love.

We arrived at the cabin mid-afternoon, and after we unpacked and built a fire, I suddenly felt tired and went into our room to take a nap. What happened next is still, to this day, one of the strangest sensations I have ever experienced—and that's saying a lot, as my life has been filled with weird experiences. I had almost drifted off to sleep, and I was caught in that place where I was still conscious but not enough to open my eyes. My body was being touched, and it was the most electrifying feeling that I had ever experienced. It was highly charged with electricity, and I could feel every atom and molecule moving within the sheets. I don't know if my body was actually being touched, but whatever was in the room, just by its presence alone, had charged the surrounding atmosphere by its frequency and vibration.

The next thing I knew, I was out of my body in a large, gray room, round—almost an amphitheater of sorts. I was fully conscious. There, across from me, seven or eight feet away, was a form of pure white light—formed but somewhat formless at the same time. Somehow I could tell it was very intelligent, and it said to me telepathically "I am ---------, from the star system of ----------." Then it came towards me and entered me, and I began speaking on creation and fertilization. I knew in that state of awareness that I was being used as a conduit or a channel. My sister Susie was there with me. Then I saw an extraterrestrial that had a more solidified form, and he felt familiar to me somehow. He had a child with him that I knew. I was excited to see her, and I got on my knees, and as I took her face in my hands, the alien said to me, "She's been sick."

"I don't care," I replied, as I cupped her little face in my hands and kissed all of the little pockmarks on her face. I knew her, and I felt as if she was brought specifically for me to see.

I opened my eyes and became fully conscious, my body still feeling highly charged by electricity. *My God*, I thought to myself. *How strange was that!* I knew it had happened—on some level, it had happened. I could still see that white light floating towards me . . . what was its name? It started with an A and so did the name of the star system, they both started with an A. It was twilight now, and Mother Nature had responded to my prayer for snow. I lay in bed, thinking about all that had transpired, watching the snow begin to rest upon the tree limbs. Icicles were already forming on the overhang of the roof, and it was guaranteed to be a winter wonderland of glistening white upon awakening the next morning.

Some three hours had passed since I had lain down to take my nap, and although I never mentioned it to any of the other family members there, I couldn't help but wonder if my sister Susie brought back any kind of memory from the experience. Come to think of it, Susie had lain down in the other room to take a nap at the same time I did. I rejoined the family but never mentioned what had transpired with any of them. I never mentioned the event to Susie, as aliens freaked her out, and I didn't want to instill fear in her.

That night, after we had gone to bed, I felt the very same sensation: the heightening of the electrical sensation once again made my skin feel as if every hair on my body was standing on end. What happened next was most bizarre. I was compelled to go look outside the living room window, and I saw three UFOs. More than fear, I felt excitement. "Look! Look!" I exclaimed excitedly to family members sitting in the same room, but they were engaged in conversation and were completely unaware of what was transpiring. I was trying to get them on the bandwagon. "Aren't you excited? Don't you want to see them?"

My family wasn't even aware of me. I walked outside and looked at the alien walking towards me. I was feeling intense excitement. Again, I had this familiar feeling that I knew him. He was more human-looking than not, a humanoid, milky white, large eyes, around 5 feet, 3 inches tall. In the state of consciousness I was currently in and perhaps because of the earlier contact, I had no fear.

He held his hands straight out in front of himself and I knew that I was to do the same. As his fingers touched mine, electricity shot through my body. I stood there, shaking, connected to him by the voltage that surged through my being. That seemed to go on for some time, and that was all I remember. "Strap on your seat belt" took on a whole new meaning.

Was it a dream? I don't believe so. It happened in my reality. Could I prove it to you? No. Would I try to prove it? No. I am simply sharing my experience as it happened. Something I read once that made sense to me is that what we experience in a lucid dream state is closer to the realm in which they exist; it is like the in-between plane where the meeting and exchange takes place because of a closer match in vibrational frequency. In other words, we have a spirit counterpart that is conscious and real and that vibrates at a higher frequency than our dense physical body. Perhaps that is why people always say of lucid dreaming, "It was so real." Lucid. I am not a scientist, but this made sense to me.

There seemed to be a strange acceleration that was taking place in my life, almost as a quickening of events. I was getting a feeling of something I couldn't quite put my finger on, but I felt as if some kind of communication was taking place on inner levels that had not manifested itself to me in a conscious, everyday, waking state. I had given a lot of thought to what had transpired at Christmas—how crystal clear and lucid those experiences had been. I knew I was highly telepathic, but it seemed that, along with meditation, my recent experiences were like the peeling of an onion. There was no denying that certain finer faculties of my senses were becoming sharpened and "waking up."

I have always felt as if I belonged out there somewhere among the stars. Feelings have an origin. Stargazing makes me homesick. It is what it is. Certainly, if the soul is immortal and the earth is simply a schoolroom, we would limit ourselves to think this is the only one we could explore on our journey.

31
Another Perspective

Let your soul stand cool and composed
before a million universes.
—Walt Whitman

I made an appointment upon my return from Big Bear
to see Dr. Peebles. I never discussed the experiences
there with anyone, including Mark. Something was
different. I couldn't dismiss what had transpired during Christmas, nor would I want too. I felt like Alice in
Wonderland chasing after the rabbit. I was off and running, down the path and into the hole—which may well
have been a black hole—and a universe different from
my own had pierced the membrane of my conscious life,
my world as I knew it.

Dr. Peebles, in his opening statement, nailed, as
usual, exactly what had been happening on levels that
I couldn't find explanation for or put my finger on. It
never failed to fascinate me exactly how he was able to
confirm and identify what had been stirring on levels
within my subconscious that I couldn't articulate,
concepts without a voice.

"God bless you. Dr. Peebles here. It is a joy and
blessing when man and spirit join together in search to

increase our awareness. Might I offer encouragement, my dear friend, as you understand your right to receive and to give inspiration in this your current and chosen lifetime, for you are upon the school called Earth of your own free will, hand in hand with all humanity, each and every one a student, a student of the divine. Certainly it is a quest for love that you and life are embarked upon, and in that journey to the heart, you will discover temporary illusions of separation between self and life. It is your own labor of love to diminish and to dissolve those very same illusions; therein you will discover fulfillment beyond even your wildest dreams and imaginations. We offer to you the principles of loving allowance, increased communication, and self-responsibility as tools to be used in tandem to understand your divine nature, your permission for prosperity.

"Athena, you are a beautiful spirit and you continue to accelerate your consciousness as you welcome the rising sun as an eternal opportunity to understand your relationship with all life everywhere, and in that pursuit, you will know freedom as the flight of an eagle in the sky, and indeed it is at hand. We have worked with you more closely of late, to help you understand the various illusions of separation within your past, now being bridged. To help you understand the great wonder, the great resources, the great abundance therein of diversity, including within species, form, intelligence, culture, source, and history. We have worked with you to help you understand a greater geography of your own total self therein and in that greater geography, wonderful permission to roam, to wander, and to seek, and in that energy you have created a platform, you have created a foundation for spirit as well as others to come forward through your being.

"You have been counseled by your brothers and sisters of space to reconsider your local region, to

reconsider your place of living, for you have already made a decision, my dear, in the weeks past. This decision was of commitment, commitment to serve the transformation of the planet Earth—to be of service to those who are seeking to reconcile their own collective karma to the planet Earth as a society and as a race of human beings from another place in the universe. You have made yourself available as a conduit for the energy from the higher realms of wisdom to come forward to the planet Earth to help understand its place in the scheme of things, that never, ever is it isolated but always as part of a community; and it is high time that human beings, come to this awareness, as some species of the planet Earth are already aware, and so you are in a time of preparation. We are here to confirm this for you.

"Because of your courage and perseverance in life, you have created a platform for communication. There is one known as Almak who will come into your being and speak through you. There is another voice who will come through you as one with no name, will present not only words of wisdom but energy of form, function, and for-mula. This energy will come forward through you in some diversity, never to be the same, never to be confined by design, instead to be discovered and rediscovered each and every time. This is part of your family that is going to help you understand the wonder of you—to help you un-derstand the delightful and beautiful being that you are. You, of course, will continue to work hard to understand movement within you as the foundation of your own re-sponsibility, as a vehicle that allows others to steer, to drive, and to acclimate their own locomotion and in that form, surrender. You will confront your greatest fears of all, my dear, and thereby recover your greater powers, and all of it is at hand.

"Remember always, this is not only a service to the world, but to yourself as well. Remember always, this *is not intended to change the world or to change people, but merely to offer yet another piece of the tree of life, for others to take what fruit they will thereof. We love you very much, my dear, and we are proud of you. God bless you and welcome, and would you have question or comment?"*

I asked Dr. Peebles about the experience at Big Bear, about the jolt of energy that I felt. His comment was as follows: *"You will find that your body will become lighter; you'll feel lighter. Your metabolism is already 60% beyond what it was from this jolt . . . ahhh—it's an acceleration of your frequency, so as to allow them to comfortably sit in your body without you being burned—also to quicken your metabolism . . . your physical metabolism and your non-physical metabolism."*

"Can you tell me more about Almak and the planet that he is from?"

"Ahhh—yah, let's see here . . . Almak is part of a group who come from a region called on Earth Alpha Centauri, a star system, and Almak is part of this group who do have feelings, who do have a sense of care. There are other visitors where this is less true. And this is a community that feels a very deep relationship with Earth; they are teachers, counselors. They have a wee bit of karma that they are reconciling from thousands of years ago, where they did not see Earth as kin but rather as an experiment, and now they work to be of kin, in kinship.

"Almak likes to teach people through history—not only history in literal terms of your planet but of the universe as a system, as a process for inspiration and education, to help people look at yesterday without fear, and with increasing good cheer, to help people understand tomorrow. And so Almak is also a teacher of community and family, commitment, loyalty, friendship therein, that no man is an island, all people are part of people and all people are part of life.

"He says that he has been able to affect the muscles in the lower part of your neck, a little bit in your lungs. He will have friends stand on either side of your body, helping to move your body side to side, and in that rhythm of side to side, it will help to create space. You will feel him as a force, that despite your best intentions you will find yourself resisting, my dear. Do not see that as failure, but simply as signal of new success at hand, . . . and it is going to take practice and practice . . . surrender. Do you understand me?"

"Yes, I do. Have I known him before?

"Well, I am not sure that you knew him, but he knew of you in two previous visits to Earth, yourself in different personalities. Once as a man, long ago, you were seen as a wizard by some humans, and in part, because he, as a non-earthly being, spoke to you of visions in dreams which tended to be validated on Earth, people attributed this to God speaking through you. So he has already worked through you. You have a close camaraderie there. Ahhh, yes, he has known you."

"Can you tell me what he looks like? His physical? Or is he beyond physicality? How tall he is?"

"His self-image relative to his environment and his own experience is rather tall . . . quite tall. However, rather to earthly humans, he is a little short. He is very slim; his face does not hold great expression, but his eyes do. His expression is one of great compassion through understanding. His eyes and his being are very, very soft—extraordinarily telepathic—and you can become more confident and aware of his telepathic communications because you are exceptionally telepathic as a receiver. And they will reveal more as time goes on, they want to have this revealed through you. He will come through you physically."

"And what is the name of the system again?"

"Alpha Centauri."

Well there you have it. The name and the star system that both started with the letter A that I couldn't remember. I thought back to the experience of seeing that light and hearing it telepathically communicate to me: "I am Almak from the star system of Alpha Centauri." No one knew of the experience, and I had not mentioned it to Thomas, Dr. Peebles' channel.

He continued, telling me there was another group that would come forward and identify themselves in time, that would communicate foundation and formula. Not that I understood that then, but like all else, it would unfold. Like I said, strap on my seat belt.

Dr. Peebles had also asked to come through me, with my permission, of course. "By all means," I replied. I loved the Doc. He gave me guidance and inspired me in ways that made sense out of my journey. Half the time when I felt like ending it all, he sang my praises for staying present, and who in God's name doesn't need that hope? The earth is not an easy place to be. I drove home excited, feeling emotionally full and happy. What a concept!

32

Strangers In The Night

*The most beautiful thing we can experience
is the mysterious.*
—Albert Einstein

It was the middle of the night when the phone rang. I picked up the receiver and listened as my sister Judy described Mom's passing. I wasn't shocked; I didn't feel much of anything— sad, but relieved. Relieved that it was over. Over for her, over for me. "Who's that?" Mark inquired.

"Judy," I said, "Mom died." I lay back down and shut my eyes. I had to be on the set to film a commercial at 7:00 a.m.

I never cried about it. I had cried enough to overspill a dam where Mom was concerned, around the events of my childhood that I had explored with Dr. Slavin. Things needed to settle, and I knew any unresolved issues that I still harbored towards her would eventually surface again in their own time. Right now, I had enough on my plate just struggling with my feelings of anger and guilt. I found it amazing that the woman I had said as a child that I wanted to be like was now everything I feared becoming. We had one thing in common though: denial.

We were both queens of denial. There was, however, no denial of the relief that I felt at her death.

The year had already started out with change, but isn't that what we always look forward to with the New Year? The promise of change? It was a good thing I didn't know what was going to unfold, or I would have said, "Hang on, Mom, let me pack a bag. I think I'll go with you! Let's see if we can't work this thing out."

If Mother would have known about my recent UFO encounters, she would have probably hung around for at least another month or so. Her face could become completely animated and alive if she were discussing anything paranormal that caught her attention on a late-night radio show. George Noory, the host of the popular *Coast-to-Coast* radio show, would have been her dream man. She was a firm believer in Bigfoot and Nessie, the Loch Ness Monster. She always had a stack of *Fate* magazines piled by her bed, and I can't count the times I would go into her bedroom and would find her lying on her side, propped up on one elbow, a *Fate* magazine opened to some article she was completely engrossed in. "Listen to this!" she would say and proceed to read a quote or a paragraph about a sighting, a ghost, or something that had gotten her full undivided attention. I would be able to feel my growing impatience and irritation. I didn't have time for it. Truth be known, I didn't have time for her. I wanted to get out of the house, where I could breathe.

One of Tina's favorite memories of her grandmother, "Nanni," as she affectionately called her, was spending the night when they would burrow in on the couch, Tina curled up in the crook of Mom's leg, and watch late-night creature features on television. Mom would wake her in the middle of the night with a cup of hot chocolate and a stack of cinnamon toast. "Come on, Teener, wake up! Let's go outside and see if we can spot some UFOs!" Wrapped Indian fashion in blankets to ward off the chill, they would sit on the back porch steps, watching for UFOs and shooting stars, Tina with her tiny hands cupped around the warmth of her hot chocolate, and Mom with her panther-piss coffee and Pall Mall cigarettes, giving a convincing lecture as to the reality of their existence to her captive six-year-old audience.

Mother would have given her eyeteeth to wave good-bye to planet Earth as she sped off in a craft towards another dimension. My brother Paul once drew a cartoon of Mom, sitting in a UFO, a cup of coffee in one hand, a cigarette in another, smiling at two confused aliens who were engaged in telepathic communication. "This earthling," Zoltare said, "calls herself 'Nanni,' and states that the black holes are comprised of hair net puzzles, coffee grounds and bobby pins."

In the late 1960s, I remembered driving her to a little church in which a documentary was being shown on the psychic surgeon from the Philippines and the now-famous UFO Roswell case. Mom and I sat with a small group of people and listened to the man who excitedly spoke of the government's conspiracy to cover up the event, while a picture was projected on a screen of a strange little creature that two bewildered farmers held up by its arms. The two farmers were completely perplexed and dumbfounded. I will never forget the look on their tanned, weather-beaten faces as they posed the alien for the camera with its limp little body and drooping head. I felt sorry for the little creature. I was around nineteen at that time, and the Roswell Crash happened in 1947, almost twenty years prior. In recent years, I have often wondered what ever happened to that picture and whether it was confiscated by the government.

The year 1989 presented itself to me in ways that enabled me to piece together a sequence of events that began for me as a child of eight, when a large craft hovered over our car in broad daylight. I was with my sister Judy and her friend, and we were going to the beach that day. I was sitting in the back seat, hanging my head out the window, like any kid will do, feeling the wind on my face. A dull, gunmetal gray disc was hovering low, directly above the car. I remember getting out of the car, and seeing my sister Judy standing by the hood of the car. Judy remembered nothing. The following year, I woke up almost nightly soaked in blood from nosebleeds, which progressed to very lucid dreams in my 20s and 30s, in which I witnessed UFOs at night flying in formation. Without fail, their presence would ignite excitement and fear within me. This was a prerequisite of all that was to follow, upon my invitation.

It was late at night. I sat up in bed and stared at the two intruders in my bedroom. Their milky white skin and black luminous eyes caused the adrenaline to pump through my veins. The fear was paralyzing, and it felt as if my heart was going to pound out of my chest. "You have nothing to fear," I heard telepathically as one walked towards me.

As I swung my legs around to get out of bed, I heard the words of my spirit guide, Dr. Peebles, in my head: "You *must* meet them with equality," the voice said. "You *must* see yourself as every bit as wonderful as they see you." At that moment, *I made a very conscious decision to go with the wonder, the mystery, and the awe of the experience.*

We walked down the hallway with Norman, my basset hound, leading the way. "Norman likes them," I thought to myself, as I observed his little tail wagging back and forth. We entered the living room and I caught a glimpse in my peripheral view of another alien, slightly shorter than the others, standing by the doorway on my left. I felt a growing sense of wonderment, and as I turned my head to get a better look at him, I felt a grin emerge on my face.

"Greetings," he said telepathically. I felt like Richard Dreyfuss in the movie *Close Encounters*, enveloped in that same sense of awe and fascination. Two more ETs stood by the French doors that led to the backyard, a total of five extraterrestrials in my home. We walked outside.

The house shook with a jolt, the windows rattled, and instantly I was jarred awake with my heart pounding. Either we just had an earthquake, I thought to myself, or a craft took off. That exact sensation was one that I would encounter over and over again as the experiences increased with rapid frequency.

33

In The Jaws Of The Dragon

If you're going through hell, keep going.
—Winston Churchill

The car was packed. I started the engine and flipped on the heater. Desert mornings were nippy. Tina had just pulled up and was waiting for me to back the car out of the garage so that she could park her pickup in my space. "Honey, put your stuff in the car. Give me one minute." I left the motor running and walked back into the house to say goodbye to Mark. He seemed a little ambivalent—I couldn't quite put my finger on it. After all, he had been asleep. Still, it was something that I sensed, and I felt a certain tenderness towards him as I sat on the edge of the bed and kissed him goodbye. I had such a strange feeling. Walking towards the garage door, I stopped in my tracks. I turned around, walked back to the bedroom, stood in the doorway, and told him goodbye again. I did that three or four times. I couldn't explain the sensation; I just had the strangest feeling that I wasn't going to see him again. Something felt off. I could feel it in the air.

It was early morning as I backed the car out of the garage. The neighborhood was still and quiet. This place just never felt right to me. I liked the guy across the street. We spoke on occasion, usually when I was I was hosing off the driveway or puttering in the yard. He was friendly enough, and oddly, he was a Vietnam Vet like Mark. I would have expected that the experience of Vietnam would have provided some kind of bridge between the two of them for a deepening friendship, but I noticed that Mark was more reserved around him.

Strange . . . who am I to brand anything strange? Christ, my life is what's strange. There was always the activity of the paranormal manifesting around me—not that I saw my recent experiences with aliens as negative; on the contrary, I was delighted by them.

But forces were gathering, all right. The light and the dark. Little did I know then of the protection that was being given from the spirit side that created the façade of a family reunion, one in which my daughter, my sister, and I would all be removed from the locality in which a series of events would transpire and change some lives forever. *There but for the grace of God go I*, my daughter, and my sister, off to northern California to be well out of reach. No wonder I felt so strange and unsettled. *Ignorance is not bliss*! It can be downright dangerous. Blindly believing the best in people, coupled with naiveté, can create an open invitation for disaster. My weakest muscle, I have come to learn, is discernment.

We pulled into Chico some time in the late afternoon. Judy, my oldest sister, was coming by bus from Eugene, Oregon, and was due to arrive the next day. Susie and I dropped Tina off in Sacramento, as she was meeting her boyfriend there to look at property outside of the city, and I couldn't help but think how unusual it was that we would all be together at the same time. What a rare occurrence. It had been some ten years since Judy had been home, as her bedridden husband, Ted, took all of her attention and focus, and she was so looking forward to a break in her routine. What a caregiver she was. My survival alone was living proof of that, and once again our pillar of strength would find a center in the midst of chaos. Judy was a solid six feet of stability in stocking feet. When I was little, I called her my "king-sized Tinkerbell." Ted's doctor said to her once, "Christ! Do you walk on water?" In my opinion, she did. She was a lighthouse of sorts. She was strong, and I adored her. I am convinced that a call must have gone out on the spirit side: "SOS . . . Shit hitting the fan . . . SOS . . . SHTF . . . family support needed," and *everybody* followed the *inner impulse* from their God-self and showed up.

The family had plans of meeting up at my sister Connie's cabin in the mountains, some thirty miles north of Chico. I know I sure was looking forward to it. Mom had died in January that year, and we were going to do a memorial "our way." We knew that it was going to be full of stories and laughing about her weird "isms" and quirks, like how she cut the end out of tennis shoes so that her toes wouldn't be cramped. It was that kind of thing that could bring us to tears, and for her, the setting could not be more perfect, as Mom was never happier than when she was amongst nature. She was a master at cooking over an open flame; however, her "hobo coffee," as she called it, was too damned strong: "panther piss" is what we called it. "Nectar of the Gods," she corrected. Paul called it "rocket fuel" and Charlie, an outspoken friend considered part of our family once said, "I could drink one cup of that shit and stay up till four a.m. cramming for my finals." All in all, who could complain? We were going to be together. Mom and those on spirit side would have a good laugh as they eavesdropped around the campfire.

There is nothing like cool mountain air, the smell of pine needles and the sizzle of popping pitch that sends orange embers up in a billow of smoke only to be extinguished against a star-studded night. It doesn't get better than that.

When you gathered all of the misfits around the campfire, there is a camaraderie of experience, a foundation based on absurdity and humor, frightening events, hidden despair, and a mutual questioning about life and the *whys?* and *how comes?* And in the middle of it all, we found our common bond through laughter. I still get tickled as hell at my brother's description when a therapist once asked him, in his own words, to describe our family. In his dry Robert Mitchum kind of voice he replied, "Well, to the best of my recollection, we were kinda like a pack of fuckin' wild dingoes." Still, all of us dingoes or dingbats never had a feud that stained our relationship with each other. Mom would boast that none of her children ever had a broken bone or wound up in jail. She really couldn't brag about our grades because I think most of them were piss poor. But either through luck or pluck, we were all still free and in one piece.

Susie and I got a motel that night, as the next day, after picking Judy up at the bus station, we were going to head up to the mountains. I woke up pissed. I was pissed, and I didn't know why. I was agitated, irritable, and angry—the same feeling I had prior to my bathroom episode at Thomas's class. I know now that this feeling means I had met in spirit with my guides and I was shown what was about to be my next major growth experience. But I also know I came back into the waking reality of the physical dimension that morning kicking and screaming and shouting, "THIS SUCKS AND I DON'T WANT TO DO IT. NO!!!" That fell on deaf ears. Amazing how something can flip on a dime.

I listened as the phone rang, waiting for my own voice to come on so that I could activate the answering

machine to pick up my messages. "Hello?" I was taken
aback by a voice I didn't recognize.

"Who is this?" I inquired.

"Who's this?" The voice repeated back with deliber-
ate alertness.

"*Who is this?*" I was getting pissed now.

"This is the police department."

"He didn't do it!" I blurted out.

"Didn't do *what?*"

"Whatever it was . . . he didn't do it!" *Talk about denial.* It had all begun. My premonition was no longer a
premonition but a reality. "What's going on? Why are
you there?"

"Who are you?"

"I am his wife."

"Do you know where he is?"

"No. . . . What happened?"

"We got a phone call from the Los Angeles Police
Department that a crime had been committed and that
he was threatening suicide."

Drugs, rape, and kidnapping.

Mark had called Dr. Slavin crying, saying that he
had done drugs and had committed a crime. He wanted
to get a message to me. Dr. Slavin called me in Chico—I
am not sure how he got the number, but I know that we
didn't have cell phones then, just pagers.

He shot up crystal meth, in his fuckin' jugular. That
makes me shudder from the inside out. I can't comprehend
that. It's bigger than life in a most frightening way. I
simply can't comprehend it. But there is so much about
all of this I can't comprehend. I still have great difficulty
thinking about this in any kind of a linear fashion. I
think they call it "selective memory." It is one of those
events that is overwhelmingly surreal, like something
that only happens in the movies or something you watch
on television, but *not* something that transpired in my

own home, not to someone I know. It's too surreal. That I was married to someone who was capable of such an act astounds me.

It's like one of those stories that grabs your attention when you are flipping through the channels trying to find something to watch that's not graphically violent or full of blood and guts, and there it is—it grabs your attention by the very nature of it. Truth. It was real. It happened. Humpty Dumpty sat on the wall, Humpty Dumpty had a great fall, and all the king's horses and all the king's men were after Mark, and he was on the run.

It became a blur of phone calls, first to Tina.

"Mom, what's the matter?"

"Come home *now*. Something awful has happened."

"Is the family okay? Did someone die? Tell me!"

"They're okay. . . . I don't want to get into it over the phone. Not over the phone. Get up here as fast as you can."

I sat in the car crying. The bus pulled into the station, and Judy was all smiles as she stepped off the bus; she was so excited to be home. As soon as she saw Susie, she knew something was terribly wrong. I watched the look on her face become instantly somber. "Oh God." Her shoulders slumped, and all joy left her body as she looked in my direction and back at Susie, who walked over, hugged her, and proceeded to describe the sequence of events.

Something about this felt vaguely familiar: the chaos, the police, the hysteria of terror and violence. *The shock.* It was the night my mother's boyfriend had tried to strangle her after the police took him away. I never remembered the actual event, but I was told years later that I, along with the rest of the kids, was screaming; we were all on him beating him on his back, trying to pull him off of Mom. Like I said, selective memory. I remember everything immediately after the police arrested him— clinging to Judy's friend who came over to help settle things down, plastering myself to his leg. I was afraid. The world was overwhelmingly large and frightening, and the inside of me felt that same kind of powerlessness toward terrifying events over which I had no control. I felt like a six-year-old child again, scared to death. And there was Judy, like she had always been— *there*—and now she was *here,* again. Thank you, God.

As near as we could piece together, Mark had driven to a friend's house—Janice's—knocked on her door, and when she opened it, said that he had something in his eye. She let him in, and there, at knifepoint, he handcuffed her, took her back to his car, and forced her to get on the floor of his pickup. He took her to her ATM, made her withdraw money, and then drove her back to our house, where he proceeded to shackle her to the bed, and forced her, at knifepoint, into oral copulation for hours—literally hours—while he hit the rewind button on a porno flick, over and over again . . . rewind . . . stop . . . play . . . rewind . . . stop . . . play . . . rewind . . . stop . . . play.

Dan Slavin had paged me, and once contact was made, the story began to unfold. We headed up to the mountains, and although I personally never spoke to the police again, Dr. Slavin was in constant communication with them, as Mark, now suicidal and on the run, was stopping at different locations and calling Dr. Slavin, but not staying on the phone long enough to get traced. He was irrational, a Special Forces vet with a record, suicidal, an addict—and he wasn't going back to prison. They had wanted to have Dr. Slavin set a meeting up in the graveyard in Santa Monica, away from people, I suppose, for obvious reasons: that way they could position a SWAT team on the surrounding buildings and take him out if need be.

I talked to Mark once. He was crying on the phone,

and I just kept telling him, "Mark, you've got to turn yourself in."

"I didn't love myself," he kept saying through his sobs. "I can't go back. . . . I'm so sorry. . . . I'm so sorry." He was crying so hard. They were going to take him in, dead if necessary, and part of the fear was that he would get hold of a weapon and raise the gun, knowing that they would be forced to kill him.

"Don't let your mom come home," the police told Tina. Tina and Susie headed back for Los Angeles, and I drove Judy back to Oregon. I don't recall much about that time, but Judy kept saying to me he wasn't who he said he was. They finally apprehended him at a phone booth in Topanga Canyon. What transpired in the next week was a blur, for I went into a state of shock, for lack of a better term, and my daughter stepped up to the plate like nothing I had ever experienced before. I had been the mother; now, it was as if, for the time being, a role reversal was taking place.

34
This Too Shall Pass

But in the mud and scum of things,
there always, always something sings.
—Ralph Waldo Emerson

This too shall pass . . . .

Somewhere in there I began to detach. It was like every emotional circuit in my nervous system went haywire and ran amuck. I was on overload. The air was charged with hysteria, and I couldn't stop crying, I couldn't stop shaking. I felt as if someone had skinned me alive, soaked me in acid, and with all my nerve endings raw and exposed, strapped me in an electric chair and pulled the switch as they walked out of the room, leaving me to twitch and spasm in the dark. That feeling would stay with me for months.

I was with the only person who ever provided any kind of safety for me. I was with Judy. I was glad to be with her, although she was relentless in trying to get me to insights that I couldn't begin to comprehend at that time. It was too much, too huge, too overwhelming. Everything lacked clarity, and it would be months before anything surfaced that I could look at with any kind of objectivity. It was all too surreal.

Somewhere in the middle of that mess, I received a phone call from Janice, describing the events more fully, what he had done. I remember answering the phone and hearing her voice and hearing her concern *for me*—it was the way she said "Athena." After all, this took place in my home with my husband. She sounded fragile, unsure of her wording, and I felt so ashamed and horrified for her, not knowing *what* to say, *how* to respond, or what to *do*, because I could never erase the event. I couldn't make it go away. She had to live with the memory, and I had to live with the fact that I had brought him into her life.

"Why didn't you tell me he was a registered offender?" There was no anger in her question, just wanting to know. I didn't have an answer for her. I remember when he had to go down and register after he was released, but I never put it together with a sex offense. I assumed that it was because that was part of the system, because he was in another state and on parole. That's what I mean—the shame of it all, and the blatant naiveté. I hung up the phone and lay in the darkness, trying to take it all in. *Dear God, how I would give anything to have it be six months from now, a year from now, five years from now, anything to speed up time so I don't have to be where I am.* How would any kind of "normalcy" ever transpire and take hold in my life again?

"Hey Hon?" Judy's husband's voice carried from the next room. He probably needs to be turned on his side. I lay in bed, half listening, hoping she would respond so I could just fall into a deep sleep to escape.

"Hey Hon . . . Hon?"

"I'll find her, Ted." I threw back the covers and swung my legs over the side of the bed.

"Jude? Judy, Ted's calling you," I said, as I walked into the living room. I noticed the front door was open, and Judy was standing on the front lawn with her neighbor, both standing motionless, staring at the stars.

"Judy, Ted's calling you."

Her friend glanced in my direction and placed her finger up against her lips, giving me the signal to be quiet, then pointed to the sky with her index finger, almost like, "Don't move, don't make noise—just look." There they were: three UFOs flying in formation, speeding up then slowing down. We watched them for a few minutes, and then after an erratic pattern, one sped off and disappeared; the other two continued for another moment and then simply vanished in the night. After tending to Ted, we talked about the sighting over coffee, and it was good to have something else to occupy my mind for a while. Although my experiences with aliens had been increasing over the last six months, it was almost like, "Ya know, I have too much on my plate to deal with aliens right now. Can't we put this contact stuff on hold?" What I was in the throes of could not have felt any more alien to me, and if I could have, I would have said, "*Take me to your leader!* This place sucks."

I had stayed in communication with Susie, Dr. Slavin, and Tina, and now it was time to go home and face the music. Driving back to Los Angeles, I couldn't listen to music or the radio. Instead I chanted, "*This too shall pass,*" and "The Lord is My Shepherd." I couldn't stop crying. I have said it once and I will always wonder, "*Where do all the tears come from?*"

There was virtually nothing in my house that had not been rummaged through or turned upside down. Susie said that it looked like a bomb had gone off in there. Drawers were emptied, the contents dumped on the floor, and black fingerprint dust coated all of the surfaces. Couple that with the gawking stares of neighbors. And in the middle of the mess was my picture, ripped in two. That kind of says it all.

Tina's pickup had been impounded by the police.

Both her pickup and Mark's were the same color, so it was a natural assumption. She had begun working quite closely with the detectives and, ironically enough, found the incriminating piece of evidence that linked him to the crime. It was a tag that had an SKU number on it from a sex shop—from a pair of handcuffs, I believe. Although the cops had turned the house upside down, she found it in the garage and figured that it must have blown under her pickup when they had raised the garage door, as afternoon gusts in that area were a daily occurrence.

"You know what this means, don't you?" the detective said to her. "You need to be clear on this, if you turn this over to us, that this will link him to the crime."

There was no doubt in her mind that she was doing the right thing. She loved Mark, and I know that Dr. Slavin cared about him as well. Good person, bad choices, she said once in her description of Mark.

Mark was on suicide watch and was trying to starve himself to death. They had him so pumped full of tranquilizers it was impossible for him not to feel nauseated when he turned his head, and it was difficult for him to have a conversation or comprehend any kind of communication. He was scheduled for arraignment and their concern was that he needed to have some form of clarity to know what was going on.

Tina was at the arraignment. I was not. I just couldn't. He pled no contest and was sentenced to thirty-three years. She hugged Janice, and when it was all over, Tina broke down and cried uncontrollably. She was amazing. To this day, she said that she learned then how strong she really was. The family consensus was and still remains the same. Family members speak of Mark with love and compassion. However, they know he is where he needs to be. He knew the effect speed had on him and still he made the choice to shoot up.

Sometimes I hear his parole officer's words in my head, before any of this transpired. "If this doesn't work out, don't blame yourself." Easier said than done.

Who knows what it is that each one of us came into this world to heal except the God-self, the oversoul? What stains, clouds, or colors our perceptions becomes our judgments or our joys, and those are unique unto ourselves, our karma. What is to be balanced is known only between those souls who need to balance it. Believe me, when I talk about these things, I talk to myself; we teach what we need to learn, and for me, it is self-forgiveness.

I walked into an immaculate house, fresh flowers in the vase, and although all looked as if nothing had ever transpired, I couldn't wait to get out. *I could feel it.* Norman, my basset, was a godsend, and he was as happy to see me as I was to see him. Dogs do have a sixth sense, and Norman must have sensed something terribly wrong, for he made sure he stayed close to my side. He had those big soulful eyes, like a seal pup, and at times I would bury my head in his neck and cry.

I began making plans to move up to northern California, back to Chico to be around family. I needed to heal. Many people in the film industry lived in other areas and commuted. It was an option that made sense. But most of all I needed this for my sanity. I needed to find a sense of equilibrium and balance.

Seldom since my return did I leave the garage door open, for I didn't want to be prey to the stares and whispers of the neighbors. I just wanted out of the house. I couldn't wait. The furnishings and household goods were in the moving van *en route* to northern California, and I raised the garage door for additional light as I began to hose off the cement floor. I glanced up and saw my neighbor, the Vietnam vet, walking across the street towards me with a long-stemmed rose in his hand. He just looked at me with such compassion in his eyes as he held it out to me, not saying a word. I was so overwhelmed with emotion, and so taken aback that I could barely whisper "thank you," and the tears just spilled down my cheeks. To this day, I have never received a flower from anyone that has touched my heart more deeply, and it is literally impossible for me to write about it, talk about it, or think about that rose without it bringing me to tears.

Pure unconditional love. . . . That's what that crimson beauty was.

Strangely enough, in blatant contrast, though in a somewhat apologetic demeanor, my other neighbor came into the kitchen holding something else in his hand. I was rinsing the grit from the Comet out of the sink. "Hi, David," I said as I finished the final rinse.

I grabbed the dishrag and was wiping my hands when he said, "I found these under the tool chest that you gave me." I looked, blinked, and stared at the pile of S and M magazines in his hand. It took a minute for it to register. I was flabbergasted and bewildered, if you could wrap all of those emotions into one.

"Oh my God!" I stammered.

Get me the fuck out of this place! I couldn't get in the car fast enough, I couldn't get the key in the ignition fast enough, and I couldn't get out of there fast enough. I started counting the cars on the freeway as they sped by. Ten. That's how many police cars were at my house. Ten. I thought back to the premonition of looking out the window and seeing police cars surrounding the house.

Ten.

I thought back to something a director told me. I liked him a lot. He was from New York. I loved his sense of humor, his big heart, and how wonderful he was to his crew. He had befriended someone in prison, took him under his wing, and got stung. I will never forget the way I caught him looking at me once, and he said, "That was really a stupid thing that you did."

"Yeah, it was," I said. "We both tried to see the best in them." I think he felt angry at himself, and somehow I was a projection of his own self-judgment.

Now, I wanted to go home. I drove out of town feeling like the biggest loser in the world.

35

You Implanted *What?*

*In certain circumstances, urgent circumstances,
desperate circumstances, profanity furnishes a relief
denied even to prayer.*
—Mark Twain

I had only been in Chico for a few months—barely had
gotten myself unpacked—but I knew I was where I needed to be. So much had already transpired, and that was
putting it mildly. Mark was now in prison. Everything
still felt as a shock, and I cried continuously. I couldn't
understand anything anymore. Shame can burn from
the inside out. It downright scorches a soul, and I wondered if I would ever find a sense of equilibrium again. I
felt such a mess, and I was in a place for the first time in
my life where I had no control or where I couldn't control the events that transpired around me. They were
bigger than I was, and perhaps that is exactly what I
needed—to be out of control.

I wonder if I could have learned any other way. I
suppose the magnitude of what transpired was the only
way for me to drive the lesson home and hit me hard
enough to get it—and hit hard it did.

Thinking about the enormity of what transpired is

still almost impossible for me. I find that I cannot even think about it in a linear fashion. I still have to compartmentalize the magnitude of it all. One phone call, one second, one phrase can completely redirect one's life, and nothing remains the same.

There have been a few times in my life when I have been awakened from sleep by my own sobs and am gasping to catch my breath. This was the first of three dreams that happened in nightly sequence. In the first dream I watched as a bubble burst and vanished in mid-air. That's what woke me up. Could I say exactly what was held within the crystal-clear globe of that bubble? No, but I could see it was full with something. When it burst, whatever went with it felt like loss enough to wake me up crying. I felt exposed and vulnerable to attack, vulnerable to forces I couldn't protect myself from. My ego? My hopes? I could speculate, but why? It was gone, and it hurt.

The second night I dreamt I was walking through a house that had burnt to the ground. There were no walls; only a fireplace stood in the blackened ash.

The following night, in my third dream, I was pouring a new foundation on the dirt. Nothing made sense to me. It seemed as if all my hard work on myself was meaningless, and I was angry at God. I was angry at Mark. I was angry at myself, angry at life. *I had control over nothing.*

And to top it off, it didn't seem to matter if I was in Chico or Los Angeles; I was having regular visitations from aliens. I was still in a state of anxiety trying to digest all that had transpired and if anything, the timing of these encounters left something to be desired. I felt like screaming "Back off, Casper! Give me a friggin' chance to catch my breath!"

It was 2:45 in the morning. "Norman! Sh-h-h! Stop barking!" Stop it!" I commanded. He continued. *I may as well take him outside to pee*, I thought to myself, as I grabbed for my robe. I walked past my brother's room and down the hallway that led to the back door. Norman, that fat little toad, had already bolted past me, darn near knocking me over. He was waiting at the back door, squirming and whining, excited to get outdoors to mark his territory. We did what we always do. He looked for the nearest bush; I looked at the stars. In a split second, I had a realization that we weren't alone. *They're here!* I could *feel* them, and I halfway ran back into the house, jumped into bed, curled up in the fetal position, pulled a pillow close to my body, and burrowed myself into a ball. "I don't think I want to see them tonight," I said, as I shut my eyes tightly.

I opened my eyes. I wasn't asleep; I wasn't dreaming. I was on my back looking at the large hand and bony fingers inches above my forehead. They were physically in my room. There was a blue ray penetrating my skull that was being projected out of the palm of the alien's hand, into the region of my third eye. I could feel it penetrate to an inch below my skin. It was so cold, it was like dry ice, and it felt strange against the warmth of my skin. I could see the shapes of more than one body in the room, all standing close. "Remember this," I commanded to myself. "Remember this. This is very important. . . . Remember this!"

In my travels back and forth to Los Angeles, as work dictated, it seemed not to matter where I was; my contacts were continuing with great frequency. It didn't appear to me that they were all from the same planets or star systems, as upon more than one occasion, I was able to physically see them in my waking state of consciousness. I remember a session with Dr. Peebles when he had commented that there were many visitors coming to the planet Earth, and he stated that I was determined in my soul to understand the larger universal family.

I drove to Los Angeles to shoot a commercial, and after the job wrapped, I made an appointment with Dr. Peebles, as I wanted to find out more about what had transpired that night. I believe that one of the reasons that I remember as much as I do was as a result of my work with Dr. Slavin concerning my childhood rapes. He always gave me the choice of remembering or taking back with me into my full waking consciousness whatever I felt comfortable with. I chose to bring back all of my memory of those events. It seems to me that I have spent my whole life trying to "wake-up," to become more conscious. I had a good amount of cognitive memory; however, I wanted the input and insight of the Doc.

"This is one of the final steps in the long view, the overview of the opening of an implant inside of you," he said. "This implant is from your friends in space, and I am not able to be precise with their intentions, for they are of their own life and world. Perhaps it is seven steps, and if it were, it would be the fifth or sixth step of the initiation of this implant and of you. This implant is becoming active with one or two more steps to follow. I am not precisely aware of what they are, but there seems to be another step or two.

"You will become a spokesperson in the near and coming years, and this would only happen with your own cognitive and free will choice. This is part and will be part of your free spiritual pursuit, fulfillment, and study, and so you are encouraged to feel permission to respond within you. The precise level of operation on your part and representation will become clear through some new relationships you will be developing—new relationships of a semi-professional nature, of a spiritual nature as a seeker—and you will be directly and indirectly led to encounters within the next three years. Somewhere down the road—I am not able to say when—you will find yourself speaking from a platform, participating in the production of events and perhaps media activity, and it will all make sense at the time. You will be receiving pictures; simply draw what you receive. We encourage you to keep a tablet close at hand. It won't make sense at the time, simply draw what you receive, and in time, you will come to understand them and to translate their meaning. You are extraordinarily telepathic."

"Is this part of the channeling process with Almak or something in tandem with it?"

"Yes and no. Yes, it is in tandem with the channeling process. You might see it as the backside of the chan-neling process, where you will speak from a platform as yourself, but you will feel more confidence because of the pictures in your mind, their source, and your trans-lation of them as well. You will be all the more aware of your friends in spirit and your friends in another di-mension of space."

"So then that was not Almak?"

"Oh, I did not look at that; let's see here . . . ah-h-h, no . . . Almak is aware of this. He was not of the party that transferred that energy. This was what Earth calls aliens in their other dimensional form affecting your non-physical state through your non-physical implant."

36
Something Quarky's Happening

I've discovered that I have this preoccupation with ordinary people pursued by large forces.
—*Steven Spielberg*

Doctor Peebles told me in a session that I had "entered into the jaws of the dragon," and yet I found myself still whole. He said that this experience held more value for me as I was "getting down to the proverbial brass tacks in life." I re-evaluated everything. The nature of the experiences demanded it. They call it "the dark night of the soul," an encounter with the shadow self. I will name it the "asshole of the rhino." Why not, it's my story, my life—and it has felt that way at times.

I returned to Los Angeles a year later. I was able to show my face, at least to myself in the mirror. I hadn't had contact with Mark, and I was finally writing him a letter. Twice I typed it out, twice I read it, and twice I said, "I can't send that. It's too blunt." I wrote it a third time, and it came out identical to the first two drafts. When I put the last period on the final sentence, the typewriter broke. What else should I expect in my life? It felt to me as if spirit was taking me by the shoulders and saying, "Let's try this again. You see that hole over there? Why not try walking *around* it?" Now that's a concept.

The truth was I wanted everything in my life that was connected to him to be over, and the feelings that colored my waking thoughts to end. I wanted completion; I wanted to move on and not ever have contact with him again. I wanted closure. I felt saddened by how he chose to live out his life and saddened that he chose to shoot up again and the effect that had.

I took responsibility for marrying him when I knew it was a mistake. I hadn't been strong enough or had the guts to say, "I can be your friend and nothing more." Those events, as horrific as they were, magnified how dysfunctional I was, and that lesson changed me forever. I knew that, in its own right, it was a blessing. I shared all that with him in the letter, and more.

I wanted him to know that I forgave him and that I was hoping that someday he would be able to forgive himself. I knew how deeply he was suffering, and I remembered that Dr. Peebles had said that his pain was so great that it was literally changing the DNA in his cells. Let the scientific community balk at that statement; I don't care. I believe there is great truth in it. Thought impacts matter.

I did tell him what Dr. Peebles had said, and had wanted me to share with him, "This was death to the Universe as you know it, Mark. You will begin life anew. There is great probability to still create a life with nobility but you must see yourself coming out of the womb as a baby, and not view the world as a threat."

I stood in front of the mailbox and dropped in the letter with a sigh of relief that rose from my toes.

I was feeling a sense of peace and an enthusiasm for life beginning to emerge unlike anything I had ever experienced before. It was new, but it felt good. I think they call it resurrecting from ash.

It was a time for me that was rich in discovery. Lo and behold, I was letting people in! And they accepted me with all of my failures and my flaws. I don't know whether they pitied me or were amazed that I had actually survived the kinds of experiences I described to those close to me. I know, looking back, that I have had some grand teachers where unconditional love is concerned. I wasn't "in the closet" about my experiences of a mystical nature, and I was beginning to own them in a way that intrigued others and fascinated them. I was still in the throes of exploring the larger universe through contact—or I should say some of them were exploring me. I think it was a joint venture.

I stumbled out of bed from a sound sleep and fumbled around for paper and pen. "Gateways into dimensions begin with the understanding of the mathematical equation *pi* equals 3.14 . . . ." I glanced at the clock; it was 3:30 a.m.

What in God's name was that all about? I stared at the message in the morning and at the strange symbol that looked like algebra of some sort. Beats me. Math was my worst subject. I had the strangest feeling that communication had begun in a more blatant way. I didn't understand it, but on the other hand, I don't have to. The next night the same thing happened; once again, out of sound sleep, I staggered from my bed and grabbed a pen. I had no idea what it was that I was writing; I was simply struggling to focus my eyes on the paper: "There currently exists within your government files pertaining to the technology of inter-dimensional space travel."

Now that's a hell of a thing to be writing about at 3:30 in the morning. I recalled what Doctor Peebles had told me about the activation of the implant. "You will receive drawings. You won't understand them; simply draw what you receive. The drawings will eventually begin to make sense to you."

The next morning I went to an art store and purchased a large drawing pad and a few pencils, and shortly after, I was compelled one evening to grab a pencil and pad and began drawing so quickly that it hurt my wrist; that's how automatic writing is for me–the pen has a life of its own. It seemed to take only a minute or two, and as I looked at the finished drawing, there was no doubt that contact had been made. I looked at the large eyes and the hand over the head that showed a ray coming out of the center of the hand going into the forehead. They were showing themselves to me and letting me know that it was them that had made contact with me in northern California.

At first the drawings made little sense to me; however, I received a series of them quickly, and always as a precursor to any communication, whether in the form of a written message or pictures, I experienced a muscle contraction at the base of my skull. The symbols became more defined as time progressed, and still their meaning was unclear. But I began drawing crop circles before I knew of their existence.

Finally, they began to make sense, and I saw that they were showing me a series of drawings of how they entered into one dimension from another. I was drawing time-frames and symbols that became very precise, and one day, while at a friend's house, I picked up a book and it fell open to one of the symbols that I had drawn. The book was Stephen Hawking's *A Brief History Of Time*. I was told around that same time by my channeling teacher Torah that my naivety is a treasure. I don't read books on the subject of ufology because I don't want to. I have been too busy experiencing it.

There is a wonderful consciousness, an alien called Bashar who is channeled by Darryl Anka. It is fascinating to witness: When Bashar enters his energy field, Darryl looks almost alien. The information shared by the consciousness of this alien presence through his channel is incredible and inspiring. Bashar commented once that he was Darryl's future self. One evening I attended an event in which Darryl channeled Bashar. This, I decided, was the perfect opportunity to receive some feedback concerning my telepathic communications. "Describe one of your drawings to me," Bashar said. After I gave him a detailed description, he said, "Ahhhhh, you're understanding the theory of bending light." Who would have thunk!

And speaking of aliens . . . we think *they* are strange? Think of what we must look like to them. Spiked hair like a Tyrannosaurus rex in hot pink or purple so stiff it could be interpreted as a weapon. Massive colored markings on our bodies with metal rings attached to our ears and mammary glands and studs in our tongues, not to mention paint on our lips, cheeks, and eyelids and black gook on our eyelashes. Hairy little critters we are too—beards on our faces, little tufts coming out of our armpits. And we certainly come in every size, shape, and color. *Why wouldn't they find us a study?* I don't know about physics or mathematical equations, but I have understood this: that all life is made up of energy that vibrates at different frequencies. The slower the vibration, the denser the matter. And we are dense in more ways than one.

If you buy a can of paint, they secure it in a machine that shakes it up; you see it, it's real, and it's there. When they flip the switch and it begins to shake, you still can see it, but when it begins to shake really fast, it becomes almost invisible to the naked eye. Doesn't mean it's not real or that it's not there. It's just vibrating at a frequency that is out of the scope of our normal visual range.

It is like walking from one room to another. Their

worlds are just as real as ours, just in a different state of frequency. As I enter what feels to me as a winding down in my life, at the same time I am experiencing a strange acceleration. Events are coming full circle and I have found myself piercing veils of dimension and magic—falling in love with spirit—and my life could not be any more diverse or colorful. In this last decade, I have worked with spirit as a channel, a conduit, in a myriad of ways, and I find myself in absolute awe of the spirit of humankind, whose journey is arduous and trying—at times beyond what we think we can endure—and yet still we seek to embrace the mysteries of the universe. The UFO is the *Unidentified Foreign Object* within ourselves, as Doctor Peebles says.

To a greater than lesser degree, my experiences have been positive—not all, but most of them. I am highly telepathic by nature; however, I cannot help but feel as if my conscious decision to redirect the energy from fear to fascination created the platform for greater communication to take place. Planet Earth, I believe, is a school—the path not always easy, the lessons often hard. The more I have been able to shift my perspective from that of victim-hood to that of creator, the more things in my personal universe begin to shift as well, even the way I engage other forms of life. I see things less from threat.

As a spiritual seeker, in my pursuit of illumination and understanding, I have come to know that that "no man is an island entire of itself." All life is part of life. Perhaps our mutual curiosity about how life expresses itself in its multi-dimensionality is seeded by the same driving need to feel that greater connection with all there is. There is a lot of magic in wonderment.

I stood outside a few nights ago and looked to the heavens; those stars so bright and clear that speak to my heart for the first time in my life didn't look so far away. It was the feeling I had that "I AM" indeed a greater part of the All.

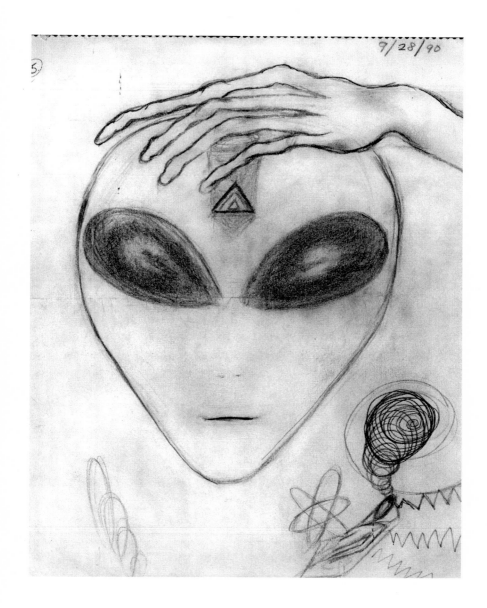

2/8/91
6:30

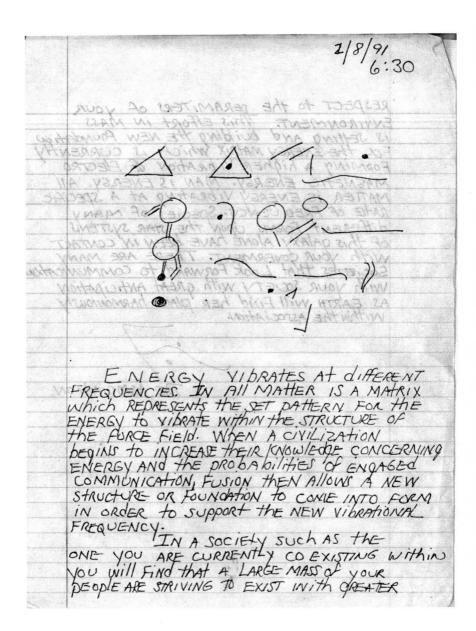

ENERGY VIBRATES AT different FREQUENCIES. IN All MATTER IS A MATRIX which REPRESENTS the SET PATTERN FOR the ENERGY to VIBRATE within the STRUCTURE of the FORCE FIELD. WHEN A CIVILIZATION begins to INCREASE their knowledge CONCERNING ENERGY AND the PROBABILITIES of ENGAGED COMMUNICATION, FUSION then Allows A NEW STRUCTURE OR FOUNDATION to COME INTO FORM IN ORDER to support the NEW VIBRATIONAL FREQUENCY.

IN A SOCIETY such AS the ONE YOU ARE CURRENTLY CO EXISTING within YOU will FIND that A LARGE MASS of YOUR PEOPLE ARE STRIVING TO EXIST with GREATER

RESPECT to the PERAMITERS of YOUR
ENVIRONMENT. This EFFORT IN MASS
IS SETTING AND building the NEW FOUNDATION
FOR the ENERGY MATRIX which is CURRENTLY
FORMING A higher VIBRATION OF ELECTRO
MAGNETIC ENERGY. MAN IS ENERGY. All
MATTER IS ENERGY VIBRATING AT A SPECIFIC
RATE OF FREQUENCY. SPECIES OF MANY
different FORMS UPON the STAR SYSTEMS
OF this GALAXY ALONE HAVE BEEN IN CONTACT
WITH YOUR GOVERMENT. THERE ARE MANY
SOCIETIES THAT LOOK FORWARD TO COMMUNICATON
WITH YOUR SOCIETY WITH GREAT ANTICIPATION
AS EARTH WILL FIND HER PLACE HARMONIOUSLY
WITHIN THE ASSOCIATION.

THE ASSOCIATION

37

Ooooh, Scawie!

Not only is the universe stranger than we imagine,
it is stranger than we can imagine.
—Arthur Eddington

Dr. Slavin: You're in full trance at this point. I'd like your throat and your voice chakras to be engaged, to be able to speak without disturbing your current state. Do you perceive anything? . . . Is it all right at this point if another member in the room asks you some questions?

Athena: Um-hum.

Dr. Slavin: She's going to identify herself and then ask you some questions, and at the end of this session, I will bring you out of the trance. You are safe and comfortable and able to access anything that you need to during the trance state. Okay?

Athena: Um-hum.

Beth: This is Beth, and we're going to go back to the night in Marina Del Rey, about three years ago, when you had an interaction with some extraterrestrials. We're going to go back to the point in the evening where you first realize something out of the ordinary was happening. . . . Where are you?

Athena, *agitated*: There's a white light outside! Oh it's so bright! PAUL! LYNN!

Beth: What are you seeing?

Athena, *breathing heavily*: They can't hear me!

Beth: Where are you?

Athena: I'm going up a shaft of white light. It's SO bright. It's so *bright*. My heart's pounding.

Beth: Is there anyone with you in the light or is it just you?

Athena, *voice shaking:* Just me. Just me. They can't hear me. They are like they're sleeping. They're all sleeping.

Beth: Did the white light come into the house?

Athena: It came into the bedroom, and it's outside the alley, outside the house. It's so bright. Everything in the whole neighborhood is covered with this real bright light; it's like this big shaft . . . big shaft.

Beth: Can you hear anything in the light?

Athena: Humming. There's a funny hum . . . funny hum.

Beth: And so, you begin to go up into the light, and then what happens?

Athena: There's a doorway opening up, and I'm being carried into this doorway, and there's a whole bunch of people.

Beth: How are you moving down the corridor?

Athena, *voice tightening:* I'm being carried, I'm being carried. I'm being carried. *[Gasps.]* Oh, it's so strange! There's nobody moving. Nobody is moving. They all look like big rag dolls, . . . every one of them. Nobody's moving; this is so strange, I think I want to go back and into the bedroom again. I want to go back to sleep.

Beth: But you're being carried. Can you say who it is that's carrying you? Do you have a sensation of people lifting you?

[Long pause.]

Dr. Slavin: If at any point you would like to come back out of the trance, indicate to me by raising and lowering the index finger on your left hand. That'll be the signal.

Beth: Are you experiencing what the people in the hallway were experiencing? Are you aware at all of your surroundings? Can you feel what's around you?

Athena, *whispering:* It's really hard to talk. *[Gulps.]* Really hard to talk.

Beth: You can allow yourself to speak now about it. You can describe your experience.

Athena: They look into my eyes, and I get real sleepy. And I don't feel so great.

Beth: One of the beings looked into your eyes and that's why you fell asleep? Can you describe the being who did that?

Athena: He's got grayish skin—almost grayish brown. His eyes are huge.

Beth: What color are they?

Athena: They're like . . . black. They're huge.

Beth: How close is he when he looks in your eyes?

Athena: About eight, nine inches from my face.

Beth: Does he communicate something?

Athena: He puts a hand on my stomach.

Beth: What do you experience when he does that? *Athena breathes deeply.*

Beth: Does he communicate something to you?

Athena, *agitated, voice tightening:* I have to go now. I have to go with them now. *[Under her breath]* I have to go with them now.

Beth: Are they taking you somewhere else?

Athena: Yes! I'm going down this big hall. All those people . . . I'm going past the people. I'm being carried past the people.

Beth: So you were . . .

Athena: They all look so funny! They all look so weird! Nobody's talking.

Beth: Are they all very calm?

Athena: All the people are like limp rag dolls. None of them can talk; they're like drugged. They took someone out, and they put them in another room, and I have to go in that room where they took that person out. I don't think I want to go in there. I don't think I want to go in there.

Beth: Are you being carried?

Athena: I'm on a gurney, and there's two . . . there's one on one end and there is one at the other, and we're going down the hall into that room now. It's over on the left-hand side, and they just put somebody into a room on the right-hand side. It's all metal, and it's silver. It's all silver.

Beth: Can you see that person when you go by?

Athena: It's a woman and she's got long, dark hair. And she looks like she's asleep.

Beth: And they wheel you past that?

Athena: And there's other people in the room; I can see through that little bed. The door's open, and there's other people in there.

Beth: Other human beings?

Athena: Uh-huh. Other people. They just finished and they put her in there. She's got real long, dark hair. It's down to about her shoulders.

Beth: What does the room look like? What do the walls look like?

Athena: It's metal, and it's gray, and it has a real shiny surface to it, and there's things that look kind of like . . . they're not . . . they're not drawers. I haven't seen something quite like that before. This room is real sterile, and there's not . . . OH GOD, he is really *ugly!*

Beth: Who are you seeing?

Athena: Oh! *[Gags]*

Beth: Describe what you are seeing.

Athena, *voice straining:* He's got a head like this, and he's got big huge eyes. *[Breathes deeply.}*

Beth: How far away from you is he?

Athena, *groaning, breathing heavily, voice trembling:* He's about ummm . . . twelve feet from me, and he's very intelligent, and . . .

Beth: What is he doing?

Athena: He's getting his probe, and it . . . it's about this long, and it swirls, and it's got a blade on that, and I'm . . . I don't want to feel the pain from that, and I know it's going to hurt, and I'm asking him what it's for, and I don't talk to him because he can hear me . . . in his head, he can hear me . . . and he turns his head . . . and he's looking at me now, and he says, "It's for experimentation," and he's walking to me! *[Groans.]*

Beth: And where are you?

Athena, *shouting:* OOOH, I HATE HIS BODY! OOH, IT'S UGLY! It looks like a bug.

Beth: Is he communicating to you? Can you feel a sense of him?

Athena, *screaming:* OOOH! HE'S RIGHT ON ME! *[Groans, straining; screams, breathes heavily.]*

Beth: What's he doing?

[Long pause.]

Beth: Does he put you to sleep again?

Athena, *breathing deeply, speaking quietly:* My legs are all numb. My legs are numb.

Beth: Did he do something to make them numb?

Athena: Yes, he put a probe up me.

Beth: Do you know why?

Athena: He's taking samples of cells and tissue. *[Heavy breathing.]* Oh, I've got to tell Dr. Slavin about this . . . got to tell Dr. Slavin about this . . . got to tell somebody.

Beth: And what do you do now that that exam is over?

Athena: I'm so glad it's over. I'm in another room, and I'm lying down.

Beth: Did they do any other exams besides that one?

Athena: No. *[Heavy breathing continues.]*

Beth: Are you by yourself inside the room? Or are there other people with you?

[Long pause.]

Beth: Where are you in this room? Are you sitting, or standing, or lying down?

Athena: I'm on a gurney.

Beth: Are you lying down?

Athena: Um, yeah. I'm with about five humans.

Beth: With five other humans? Is there anyone else in your room? Besides the humans?

Athena: Um-hum.

Beth: Who else is there?

Athena, *speaking quietly*: There's one person; he's not a person. It's a human-type looking . . . he's not like the little one. He's not like the gray ones; he's got big eyes, and he's kind of whitish-looking, and he's standing by a door. He has something in his hands, and he doesn't have to . . . He's so strange looking. He doesn't write, but there's a thing of light—it looks like a little computer-type thing that . . .

Beth: With a screen you mean?

Athena: Yes, it's got a little screen on it, and it's some type of data or information.

Beth: Is it information about the people in the room?

Athena: Um-hum.

Beth: And does he talk to you? Does he say anything?

Athena: He says I can relax.

Beth: And what is his attitude like, when he says this?

Athena: He's not bad. He doesn't have any feelings. He's not bad. He's intelligent. But he's not bad; he just doesn't have feelings.

Beth: And he just wants you to relax?

Athena: Yeah, he says relax. That it's over.

Beth: And does he talk to the other people in the room, too?

Athena: He says it to all of us. We all hear him, but he doesn't move his mouth.

Beth: Uh-huh.

Athena: He doesn't even really have much of a . . . just a little kind of a slit, but he thinks the thought, and I hear it and the people hear it, too.

Beth: Have you ever met him before?

Athena: No.

Beth: The other being that did the exam on you, have you ever met him before?

Athena: No! . . . no.

Beth: Have you ever seen him again after that?

Athena: No! He's so ugly.

Beth: Okay, so you're told that you can relax and what happens then?

Athena: It's cold.

Beth: Where are you?

Athena: I'm being lowered . . . lights . . . it's so big! This ship is so big!

Beth: And is it over the house?

Athena: Uh-huh. It's over lots of houses and buildings . . . it's huge!

Beth: How big? Is it as big as football field, or bigger?

Athena: Bigger.

Beth: Is it as big as a city block?

Athena: Bigger. It's huge.

Beth: And so you're lowered down out of it?

Athena: PAUL! LYNN! DID YOU FEEL THE EARTHQUAKE?!

[Heavy breathing.]

Beth: Where are you now? Where are you? In the house? Are you in bed? Do you go to sleep then?

Athena, *quietly:* Um-hum.

Beth: Do you go to sleep naturally, or do the ETs help you go to sleep?

Athena: I go back to sleep. I think we have an earthquake or something.

Beth: So you go back to sleep and then you don't wake up until morning?

Athena: Um-hum. Paul and Lynn don't feel the earthquake.

Beth: Did they hear you talk about the quake? When you yelled?

Athena: They didn't feel it. I know it happened, though.

Dr. Slavin: Take some deep breaths. In a moment I'm going to count from one to five. When we get to five, I'd like you to open your eyes and have a sense of well being, and be able to remember whatever you would like to, and be able to leave unconscious whatever you would like to.

38
Fly-By-Nights

No man is an island.
—John Donne

January 1990

I was staying at my daughter's house in Malibu. The dogs started barking, and Tina and I went outside to check things over. We saw nothing and came back in the house and went to bed. Once I started to fall back asleep, I felt myself being lifted. The next thing I remember was standing by the bedroom window looking out. I was furious with them and was telling them off. This was the only time I remembered being angry. Why this encounter affected me like it did, I don't know. Obviously something transpired that I didn't like but whatever it was, I did not bring the memory of it into full waking consciousness.

February 1990

I'm in Chico. It's the middle of the night, and I'm outside with my brother Paul. I look towards the airport and I see a craft. It's quite large. Paul is on his knees next to me holding his stomach. He isn't bent over but is more erect, with his head back, and he is moaning, saying, "I feel sick." I'm trying to find something for us to hide under—I think the craft is headed for us. That was all I remembered.

March 1990

I woke up and glanced at the clock . . . it was 3:23 a.m. I looked outside and wondered if they were there waiting for me to go back to sleep. The pulsations in my head and at the base of my skull started again and I knew somebody was communicating with me. I felt myself being drawn into something that looked like a weird chair. I was moving—that was certain. I remember thinking, *God it's so strange. How am I going to define and explain this?*

I felt myself coming to waking consciousness when I felt the strangest thing. I felt the presence of something arrive so quickly that it felt almost like a predator that appears out of nowhere, but I felt its approach. I heard a noise in my head almost like that of a computerized piece of machinery going through different gears. I was afraid to open my eyes. My solar plexus felt weird. *They did something to it again; it hasn't felt this activated or sensitive since last year.* Interesting choice of words-activated? Where did that come from? I woke up in a strange position. I never sleep like this. They were here all right. When I came to, it was 4:59 a.m. I thought to myself, *Get up now, and write this down. It is important. I need to talk to somebody.*

I'm back in bed . . . I hear a rumble and I think to myself, *Oh, my God, a ship just took off or we just had an earthquake! They were here and they did something to my solar plexus!* It felt raw, as if someone pulled a scab off of a wound before it was healed. I felt afraid; the house felt full of electricity—just plain electrified! Mark remembered nothing.

I'm on a country road. I don't even know how I got here—am I dreaming? It is night, and I am in a group of people, but I think I was alone before this. I think to my-self, *Act like everyone else so they won't single you out.*

I drove down to Palm Springs to spend a few nights with a friend before going to Los Angeles to shoot a commercial. Cynthia got up the next morning and told me she had a dream that seemed so real to her. She said that she had a dream that she was raped by an alien and that she tried to wake up her husband but with no response. She said that she was walking down the hall-way to reach my room because she knew that I would believe her. The next morning, she said that she had the worst cramps. Now, I had no memory that night, but the following night I did. I open up the bedroom door, and a little robot-type being is standing in the hall next to the door. I bend down to get on his level. He is about three feet in height. *"This is what love feels like,"* I say to him and I try to project the feeling from my heart into his being so that he can understand the emotion.

Cynthia, upon rising, laughed about a dream she had. She dreamt that she had a six-month-old baby that she never touched. This doctor, she said, thought she was crazy for never having picked up her own baby. I didn't say much about her dream; I didn't want to scare her.

The following night, I stayed at my daughter's house in Malibu. I fell asleep on the couch, and it was the sensation of being lifted that caused me to open my eyes. There were no hands on me; I was simply rising in the air, and my body was a foot off the couch. Three sets of huge black eyes were staring at me. They stood lined up from left to right directly in front of the couch. Their milky white bodies were completely illuminated by the full moon and the outside porch light, which was flooding through the large picture window.

I'm outside with my daughter, Tina. I have my arm on her shoulder and we are looking at two light-colored ships hovering on the hillside where she keeps her horses, which is about 75 feet from the house. "Honey, they are friends," I tell her. The next morning, Tina asks me, "Mom, did you hear the dogs go crazy last night? I went outside," she said.

This either happened the same night or the following night at Tina's. I saw two little people look at me through Tina's glass door. They were waving. I let them into the house. There was a woman sitting in the chair, and she was taller than they were. We were talking about children; I asked her if she had any. She was strange-looking. Her hair was white and stringy, like cotton, and her skin was blotched and white. She had human-looking features but she looked really unhealthy, even though I knew she was healthy. It was just that she looked so strange. I remember telling her that my daughter was 25.

Sometimes I hear a long humming sound in my head, and it will either go up an octave or down one. It's different than a ringing in the ears. My first intuitive reaction is that I'm being interfered with, like some kind of mind control.

I looked at the heavens one night. All of the stars were connected with white light, as if some hand took a magic marker and connected all the stars with a line of pure, dazzling white light. Wow! If it was a dream, who would want to wake up from this!

I wake up in the middle of the night and turn on the television. I'm guessing it is about 3 a.m. I lie back down and feel that rush of electricity, and I know contact has been made. I feel my body being lifted, and I think to myself, *I want to remain conscious. I want to see.*

I'm floating through the house parallel, and I'm aware of the fact that I am being directed out of my French doors. I'm engulfed in darkness, and I feel my body rise. I'm moving fast now, and I see a planet. It looks small. I think to myself that it must be Earth.

I'm approaching another planet. Although it is night there also, it is beautiful and somewhat similar to Earth. I am greeted by two men in what seems to be a social setting. I'm quite taken by their shirts. The material is exquisite, but what is most beautiful is the design of the solar system on the material itself. The fabric has an opalescent luminosity to it that shimmers, and the colors are pale and translucent, like crushed jewels of turquoise and pink, and the planets with their rings of color are moving on the fabric.

39
Shake, Rattle And Roll

I'm glad to be feeling better. I really thought I'd be seeing Elvis soon.
—Bob Dylan

The Los Angeles earthquake hit at 4:06 a.m. I was living in Santa Monica, and we got hit hard. I was sitting up in bed, having coffee, about to go to the gym, as I had to be on the set for a 7:00 crew call. Suddenly, everything started moving. I was terrified. Instantly I got in the fetal position, put my hands over my head and began to chant non-stop, "PROTECT ME GOD! PROTECT ME GOD!" I felt like an ant in a cracker box that a giant picked up and began shaking. I didn't think my heart could pound any harder, and the adrenaline, along with the fear, was telling me to get outside. I started to jump out of bed. "PUT ON YOUR SHOES!" the voice shouted in my head. Thank God! I would have cut the soles of my feet to shreds.

I learned it wasn't dying I was afraid of; it was how my death would happen. I must have died in several earthquakes, for its effect on my psyche was like being thrown into shock. I remember vividly a dream as a young child of watching red hot lava spewing out of a volcano as it made a glowing reddish-orange river down the dark side of the mountain. I believe it was my first past-life recall. All I wanted to eat after the earthquake was comfort food. Pancakes—morning, noon, and night. "What do you want to eat?" Pancakes. Egg-white omelets and salads with nonfat dressing went out the window. That earthquake felt violent. Talk about being in the moment, in survival. I was totally in the now. Primal.

The pocket-sized book titled *God is With You* sat on top of a stack of books like the stone that brought down Goliath—the victor amongst the broken spines, crumbled pages, and overturned bookshelf.

I could relate to the guy across the street who threw all of his belongings haphazardly on the lawn with a cardboard sign that said, "I'm out of here!" I was too! I began to make plans to move to Seattle. The truth was, I was terrified of the earthquake.

A picture of an angel helping a child cross over a wooden bridge hung on my wall. The child is oblivious to the hand guiding her past the broken railing. I began praying for angels to protect me and my loved ones. A week later, a wardrobe stylist gave me an angel pendant with the words inscribed on one side, "Guarded by angels." She knew nothing of my ongoing prayer. A few days later, another friend gave me a bumper sticker that said, "Protected by Angels." That got my attention. Around that time, I had a very lucid dream of looking at a path that led into a lush green, wooded area. A golden orb of light illuminated the path with sunlight, and it held the promise of magic to be explored. It was a distinct feeling, a pull from my heart chakra, and in my dream I said, "Oh my God, I want to go there."

The next day, while browsing in a card shop, I stopped, transfixed on the card in front of me. There it was—my dream: the lush green, wooded area, the golden orb of light, identical to the vision Spirit had shown me.

I picked up the card, and the message read, "You're on your way to something wonderful."

I love the symbols the universe shows me, and I, in turn, embrace them. There is such magic and mystery that comes alive when we are open to it. I don't need to have it proven. I don't need to know *how* it happens or *why* it happens. It just does, and that's enough for me.

I had moved up to Seattle and found a great apartment in an old brick brownstone building and found myself commuting back and forth to Los Angeles, continuing to film. I figured I was on yet again another adventure. Not much time had passed since the earthquake, and I was becoming increasingly aware of the presence of angels in my life, when the following transpired.

I made arrangements with a friend of mine to stay with her while I was in Los Angeles filming. She had a wonderful Spanish home in the Hollywood Hills, and it was ideal for the both of us. One night, I was awakened from a sound sleep with a vibration *of pure love* that felt like an expansion of the light within my own heart. It was the physical vibration that woke me. I have only felt that kind of love once before. It was beyond anything human; it was purely divine, and I knew this gift was being given to me by my higher self, my God self. In that state of pure grace I was aware of only love. The following day, a friend gave me an angel snow globe.

The next night, I was shown by spirit a vision that came in a lucid dream, with bigger-than-life clarity. I knew, once again, I was being shown something divine.

I was looking at a scene on a large movie screen of two seagulls four or five feet tall pecking to death a little white dove. Drops of crimson blood flew off the dove, staining the white feathers. I turned my head to the right and observed two angels. The female was lying on her back giving birth. The male kneeled at her side by her womb with his head bowed in total prayer and reverence. He was one and equal with her. Although I didn't witness the actual birth, I knew what was transpiring. The female had short hair, and I remembering thinking to myself how beautiful she was. The wings of the male were translucent, large, and luminous, every feather perfectly visible, perfectly formed. The feeling was holy and the stillness, sacred. I heard the words "Bless you!" so loudly it woke me from a sound sleep.

A few days later, I asked my channeling teacher, Torah, about the dream. "This was not a dream but rather a vision," Torah replied. "Spirit is telling you that you have reached a milestone in your growth. Your old paradigm of growth was to transform after attack, which the seagulls, representing human consciousness, were showing you. The dove represents the innocence of spirit."

The next day, I flew back to Seattle and stopped off at the car dealership to pick up my car that I had left to have serviced while in Los Angeles.

With my key in the ignition, I watched a seagull dive-bomb toward my windshield a foot in front of me and then fly directly away from me in a straight line. I sat there, stunned, and turned to a mass of goose bumps. I instantly flashed to the seagulls in the vision. I knew Spirit was giving me, yet again, more confirmation. I started the car and drove home.

I opened the door to the lobby of my apartment building and noticed a community newspaper sitting on the table in bold view with huge headlines. "Angels Descending at Saint Demetrios." I couldn't believe my eyes. I placed the paper on my kitchen table and stared at it for the longest time. I called a friend to meet for dinner that night and was wandering around the bookstore where she worked, browsing and passing time until she finished her shift. I walked directly up to a card with an angel on the front. I turned the card over and read, "This was the angel of rebirth, resurrection and victory."

I bought the card, cut out the word Saint from the newspaper heading and glued the words, Angels Descending at Demetrios on the top of the card.

That is the kind of magic I thrive on, the synchronicity that is seamless. Thank you, God, for giving me that kind of hug, and letting me view more of the magic. I open my arms to it, I invoke it, and I embrace it. Keep it growing, keep it going, and bring it on.

40
Hope Never Dies

I pray thee, O God, that I may be beautiful within.
—Socrates

I have always said that I could never have lived without hope—hope that I could change and hope that things could get better. Hope that I could grow to understand myself and to understand the mystery of *Why am I here? What's it all about?* and *What is God?* I couldn't have made it without hope. That I know.

I took a hot bath and crawled into bed. It was the eve of my birthday. I did a short meditation and visualized myself standing beneath a waterfall of pure white light, letting this water of light flood through my body, healing it.

I fell asleep with the following prayer in my heart: "All I want for my birthday, God, is a message from you. Please give me a message for my birthday, God; that's all I want."

The next day, while browsing through a bookstore, a book almost jumped off the shelf into my hands. It fell open to the following story, reproduced here with permission from its author, Gloria D. Benish.

Once upon a time, there was a Commoner (named

Hope) who was nearing her 36th birthday. She knew that on this specified day, she was dying. As her special day neared, the pain she carried became intense, and truly, her life passed before her eyes. She mourned for days and those who loved her most felt totally helpless. Her mother asked what gift she would like to receive, and her response was, "Freedom on all levels of my being."

The eve of her birthday was spent in solitude—alone with her fears and tears. Hope was scared to die, but she was much more afraid to live. In her prayers, she said, "Father, I no longer choose to merely exist—I WANT TO TRULY LIVE," and with that final thought, she slumbered.

In her dream, she was in a beautiful garden, admiring flowers that created the spectrum of a rainbow. Lovely streams surrounded her and she was led to a waterfall. She heard the water cascading over the cliff and she felt drawn to stand in the mist. She felt healed and restored by the colors of nature.

Feeling relaxed, she chose to sit—and as if out of nowhere, a bench appeared. However, along with the seating arrangements, came multitudes of marching ants.

Hope shrieked with fright and stood upon the bench. To her amazement, they hadn't come to harm her. The ants uniformly placed themselves together to spell out the following message: "A caterpillar transforms into a colorful butterfly. NOTHING that God created 'dies'; it only changes into a more beautiful form."

As quickly as the ants had appeared, they vanished, but Hope had a realization deep within herself that would take years-upon-years to write in the physical form for others to see.

She awoke on her birthday, knowing that perhaps she had been physically born 36 years ago, but on this day, she had been born anew. She had resurrected and knew she could trust the process of life!

Hope also recognized that life is an honor—the greatest honor of all—for it is the highest gift bestowed upon us to express Divinity in the physical dimension.

Hope realized that upon acceptance of life, she had joined hands with Omnipotence. She would go forth from that day forward, with Mighty Companions, to serve the whole of humanity.

The good automatically became Hope's life, for good is ALL He knows. It was in One Holy Moment that her life was no longer her life, but His Life, which He would live through her. She no longer walked alone . . .

She was no longer afraid to die, or to truly live. She no longer walked alone . . .

She no longer worried where her steps would take her or what she would encounter. She no longer needed to experience short-term bliss in the few raises she got in her workplace, the high moments she periodically experienced in well-deserved achievements, or in new articles she could attain to better her style of living.

Through her acceptance of a greater power within herself, her life was transformed. The only ending was to the falsely taught belief that death is a cessation to existence. The new beginning is accepting that the life you seek is the life which has been seeking you. The miracle of life is yours . . . .

41

The Flower That Waved Goodbye

The universe is full of magical things
patiently waiting for our wits to grow sharper.
—Eden Phillpotts

I listened on the other end of the phone as Susan described the rebirthing retreat she had attended in Santa Barbara, California. Susan was in my channeling class, and her enthusiasm about her experience piqued my interest. "It was so strange," she said. "I could feel the cord wrapped around my neck." The more she shared of her experience, the more intrigued I became. I reflected on a statement that Dr. Peebles, my spirit guide, had once said. "Out of the two experiences of birth and death, birth is far more traumatic on the soul, as the soul fears the violence in the world and doesn't want to come forward. Death," he said, "is like walking into a warm home out of a storm."

I recalled my recent session with Dr. Slavin, the one in which I had experienced a spontaneous life preview.

I signed up for the next workshop. Not knowing what to expect, I had decided, was okay, for I was getting used to "just showing up" and letting spirit guide the rest. I had been feeling something stirring beneath the surface and I trusted whatever it was would thrust me to another level of insight. I didn't know what that would look like, however, or how it would appear.

It was a beautiful day, crisp air and clear blue skies with puffy white clouds, and I was looking forward to the two-hour drive up the coast. I had thumbed through my CD collection and chosen some light jazz and Mozart for the drive. I had plenty of time for quiet reflection and in general I felt a sense of well-being and inner peace. The nineties had been a good decade. Thank you, God.

Gratitude was a feeling that I was more aware of than ever before. I had so much that I was grateful for, and I was moving into a greater level of self-appreciation that was new for me. What a concept. I had the ocean to look at, things to ponder, I just felt good.

I drove up the winding road, did a u-turn and parked the car. I was a little early and I wanted to finish listening to a song that had caught my attention. It was titled "The Valley" from the album *Celestial Navigations*. Actually, it was poetry that was being read, and it seemed beyond appropriate. I had the distinct feeling that my higher self had made the selection earlier that day for my benefit.

It was about a man who had entered a valley to make peace with his past. How symbolic. Through reflection and new insights gained, he was able to let go of that which weighed him down in life and no longer served him. He discovered he felt a new sense of freedom. Upon leaving the valley, he turned and noticed a tiny yellow flower waving goodbye. A beautiful image indeed.

Once inside the workshop, I sat on the floor Indian fashion. Ray, the facilitator, was one of the most intuitive men I had ever met. "Alright," he said, "who wants to go first?" It was silent for a moment as it always is when people get put on the spot. I could feel the others in the group hesitate. Nobody wanted to go first; especially when we didn't know what to expect. I looked at Ray, and above his head I saw five or six beings of light—spirit guides, I was sure—poised almost as if they were going to pour insights and information down a funnel for Ray to "pick up on." "Nobody?" he said, as he started chuckling.

"I'll go," I said, as I moved off my pillow and comfort zone into the center of the room. He sat in front of me Indian fashion and for a moment or two he studied me and didn't say a word. I was beginning to feel uncomfortable with the silence, but I kept quiet.

"H-m-m-m-n" he said in a tone that was barely more that a whisper. I knew he was picking up on something that I wasn't privy to.

"How do you respond to energy work?"

"Pretty good, I think."

"I'd like to try something. I'd like you to get in the position you were inside the womb."

Okay, I thought to myself as I turned on my side. *This is a no-brainer.* I pulled my knees up to my chest and tucked myself in the fetal position, and after a few more minutes of silence, he placed his thumb between my eyebrows in the region of the third eye. I felt a rush of energy and I was gone. I was no longer aware of anyone in the room. I was nothing but consciousness. I was aware of looking through a barrier of transparent orange tissue, like I was inside of a salmon's egg. I could see cells floating in fluid—there was an inherent sense of intelligence that everything was responding to. I watched the sperm, unyielding in its focus, approach with the momentum of an arrow that had been shot from a taut bow with perfect aim. My consciousness was flooded with only one thought as the gel-like casing was penetrated by the determination of the white whale-like invader driven by the consciousness of my father. "Oh my God, I really have to do this now."

The feeling in the womb was horrible. I felt sick. The alcohol was making me sick. Everything was foreign. I felt in the womb like I did when I had a horrible bout with the flu. I don't know what was worse: the feeling of alcohol or my mother's despair at being pregnant again. The contraction squeezed my body and I felt like I had been swallowed alive by a boa constrictor and was being moved through his digestive tract. The contraction stopped. It started again.

I was being gripped by muscle and turned into position as I moved down a canal. It was such hard work. I wanted to go back and be in spirit, and I felt stuck between two worlds. The contractions stopped, and after a period of time, hit again with full force. My head turned and I felt my cheek rub deep against the pile of the carpet. I heard a voice in the distance say, "This baby worked hard to be born."

I was connected to my mother. My spirit felt chained to her psyche, and I wanted to be free. I wanted to cut my own cord. I was aware only of being in another space, another time. I heard the voice say, "Someone get a pair of scissors and give me a shoestring." Something tight was being wrapped around my fingers and pulled taut. I felt my thumb and fingers being guided into the loop, a cool metal, and the cord of connection snapped in two. I felt a psychic "whoosh" of energy as if something was being suctioned away from my center and being pulled by a force into a vortex that was stronger than it.

Once again, becoming present felt raw and vulnerable. My cheek stung as I touched the wet abrasion. I had scraped it really good against the rug. I crawled back over to my space, trying to regain my composure. We broke for lunch but I stayed behind and rested. When the group returned, one of the women bent over and held out her hand and said, "I don't know why, but I think you're supposed to have this."

There In the palm of her hand, no bigger than an inch, was a tiny yellow flower. "Look," she said, "it looks like it's waving."

On my drive back to Los Angeles after the completion of the workshop, I found myself reflecting back to an experience which was mystical and magical.

I had entered into meditation and quickly went deep into the space of inner silence and tranquility. An hour or so must have passed. I was aware of the love I felt in my heart for the soul of my unborn grandchild. I began to focus a ray of pink light from my heart going directly into the womb of my daughter. Tina was in her eighth month of pregnancy. I began to move into a state of bliss. All of a sudden my unborn grandchild showed her face to me, peaceful and angelic. It was like sitting in a theater seeing the opening image come to life on a movie screen out of the darkness. I instantly opened my eyes, jolted back into this dimension and reality—or perhaps she entered mine. "Oh, my God," I said out loud. "Consciousness knows." We truly are one.

I had wanted to be present at Ali's birth for a number of reasons. I wanted to be of support to my daughter and have her birth experience be everything that mine wasn't because of my youth, circumstance, and state of mind. I wanted that baby to be only aware of how much she was loved and wanted. The doctor was on his way to the delivery room. I was standing at the foot of the bed, and I had the strongest intuitive "hit" to tell the nurse to turn down the overhead light. "Please," I said, "please turn down that light so it isn't so bright."

"Oh, no," she replied. "The doctor needs it."

After her birth, when it was my turn to hold her, Ali was crying, and I began telling her something that my friend Dr. Wendy Anne McCarty had told me to do. "Tell her what a good job she did being born. Babies need to be acknowledged for their journey." When Ali was placed in my arms, I did just that. I started telling her softly how proud we were of her; how hard she worked to be born, and what a brave little girl she was—how much we loved her and what a beautiful spirit she was. I kept telling her that, gently rocking her back and forth. She quit crying and looked at me. I was aware the head nurse was standing close, witnessing, but I was completely into what I was communicating. "That baby is listening to you," she said, as she looked at Ali and then me with a look of awe on her face. She later requested more information concerning Dr. McCarty's work.

Two years down the road, I was giving Ali a bath and she started making movements with her head like she was banging it up against something. "When I was inside my mommy's tummy, I went like this." I knew she was telling me about her birth and the contractions. Then she said, "And when I was born *the light hurt my eyes,* Mamo."

"I know it did, Honey; I tried to get them to lower the light. I am sorry it hurt your eyes." I felt a wave of sadness at her experience, that they didn't respond to her request, and that at times the medical field can be so insensitive not to think beyond the clinical to the experience of the mother and child. I know how much it hurts my eyes when I come out of a dark space into the bright light. Can you imagine how that has to be for a baby coming out of a dark womb and staring into that monstrous light? It would be like having your lids held open while you are forced to stare at the sun seven or eight feet away. All anyone has to do is think about that for a minute to see the truth in what she said. Put the suckers on dimmers and lower it when that little head begins to emerge!

She also told me, "When I was inside my mommy's tummy, I used to kiss her from the inside a lot."

Once, my grandson said to me, "When I was inside

Mommy's tummy, I felt sad."

"Noah, why did you feel sad, Honey?"

"Because I wanted to come out and hug her so bad."

Out of the mouth of babes.

Tina with Ali

Noah riding Spam

42
Just Follow The Bouncing Ball

*My life often seemed to me like a story that has
no beginning and no end.*
—Carl Jung

I opened the door to Dr. Slavin's office this time with a
definite thought and purpose in mind. I wanted to go
back in time to a particular memory that had haunted
me for years. I was a young child watching through the
screen door as my mother lay on the hardwood floor
sobbing. It was scary. A neighbor trying to help Mother
to her feet shot me a glance to stay put on the porch
and to dare not enter. Mom had lost the house with
only a few mortgage payments left. It seemed to me that
event spiraled our family into the depths of poverty from
which there didn't seem to be any ways out.

I read once that sometimes as children, we make
psychic contracts, usually with our parents or some
other significant person. What came to mind immediately
for me was the feeling of powerlessness to change the
situation or make my mother feel better. I still remember
the exact moment I felt her grief enter into my young
psyche, as if by osmosis. Perhaps the contract was, *If
you feel bad Mom, I will feel bad with you.* Who knows,

but it made sense to me. More importantly, it felt right on. And as I write this, a memory of the "monster in my closet" just flashed through my mind. I definitely made a contract, now that I think back, by telling him I would "feed him" so he wouldn't be hungry and eat me. So there you have it; there was a contract.

It was easier for me now to look back and see how I learned to view life through the distorted lens of my childhood perceptions, colored by my early experiences. My intent was to revisit that event through hypnosis and, if possible, recreate a new belief system around that event. I remembered Dr. Peebles telling me once that as a child, I had made very firm decisions that had made an impact on my entire life. To understand and separate my beliefs from my mother's, I felt, would ultimately help me gain the insight at *how* I arrived at the conclusions that I did.

My God self and spirit guides had something else in mind, however. I had for the greater part felt good. It seemed to me that the film of deep-seated melancholy that I lived with all my life had lifted from my spirit. I had continued throughout the years with my meditations and the "I AM" teachings of Saint Germain, and to this day remain deeply committed to both. Slowly but surely I was experiencing a sense of inner-balance. My intuition was growing stronger, but the more important thing was that I was listening to it more. There seemed to be a seamless flow when I was tuned in or was able to stay in the zone of being more connected to my God self, and I was so grateful. I felt as if I was coming out of hiding. Work in the film industry was thriving, and my phone was ringing constantly from production companies calling to ask, "Are you available for work?" I remember Dr. Peebles telling me once that being a makeup artist was a very sophisticated level of art. The reason I enjoyed it so much, he said, was that it enabled me to express myself without apology. I could completely relate to that statement.

I was consciously developing my relationship with Dr. Peebles through participation in a channeling class led by Shawn Randall. I loved those classes and I admired Shawn's character and level of integrity. I enjoyed being with people of like mind; I loved the meditations, and I loved Torah, the multi-dimensional non-physical consciousness that came through Shawn. I was feeling a new level of appreciation for who I was growing into and how I was generally feeling about being alive. It seemed to me that I was able to bounce to my feet faster as long as I could let myself feel my emotions. It seemed as if everything in my life was becoming increasingly symbolic. A psychiatrist once told me, "You're one of those people who have a strange, symbolic life." That was an understatement. My life, as Dr. Peebles had recently said, was taking on a new color and different vibration.

I could feel something percolating; and when that specific memory began to bubble to the surface with greater frequency, I decided to contact Dr. Slavin. I knew myself well enough to know that if I was "feeling a tug" to explore something, I was being nudged by Spirit, and so I decided to check it out.

I had no idea what was about to happen, but I also knew that growth for me happened in layers. Perhaps I was beginning to surrender to the fact that there will always be more to explore, especially where becoming conscious is involved. I recalled Dr. Slavin once telling me, "Your soul takes you where you need to go for healing."

This is what transpired:

Dr. Slavin: In a moment, I am going to count down from ten to zero, and with each number back, I'd like you to feel more and more relaxed, comfortable, and to slowly move back in time to the time period that we were talking about last week, or any time period that comes up, to slowly layer with each number, each step, each number back . . . more comfortable and relaxed with each number. Ten . . . nine . . . eight . . . seven . . . six . . . five . . . four . . . three . . . two . . . one . . . zero. Start to get a sense of where you are, how you feel, how old you are. . . . When you feel ready to start, tell me what it is that you see, feel. . . . Where are you?

I listened to his voice, and as I floated back in time, I observed a young girl standing on a porch looking through the wire mesh of a screen door. I moved past that scene into another time and space.

I found myself on the spirit side prior to my birth again, but this time I was seeing all of my life experiences laid out before me. In that state of awareness, I knew there were going to be major growth opportunities. In spirit, they looked liked high-rise buildings made out of cement, but I knew these were symbolic of blockages in my path and there was distance between the structures—almost as if spirit was giving me time to regain my balance and give me a resting period before the next growth experience manifested in my physical world. It was as if someone threw a filmstrip and I watched it unroll for miles as the experiences came to life, taking shape and form within their specific time frames.

I felt a sharp "psychic tug" as if someone pulled hard on my forearm, and I knew it was time to go into the womb of my mother. On the spirit side, the awareness and the grandness of my soul felt as large as the United States of America. The safety and love were indescribable. As I left the world of spirit and came into the earth plane, that feeling completely diminished. In sharp contrast, it felt dense and black, like being pulled into icy, dark mud. I was aware that my consciousness had become restricted and small, relative to its previous expansiveness.

Once I was born, everything that was any sort of crisis that molded me or thrust me forward in life came up like a bouncing ball, leading spontaneously from one event to another: giving birth to my daughter, my broken engagement, my move to Los Angeles when I was 25 and so suicidal. I saw the gestalt therapist who tried unsuccessfully to coax me down the stairs into my past, and I saw that although I had been unconscious of the wiser part of me, my higher self or oversoul knew at that time I wasn't strong enough for that exploration.

Dr. S: Where are you?

Athena: *I'm not born yet. . . . I'm with people that I feel really safe with . . . that I love a lot. . . . Some of them are teachers, and they are showing me . . .*

Dr S: What are they showing you?

A: *They are showing me where I'm going to be going and what some of my opportunities are. I don't think I'm going to like being down there.*

D: What kind of things are they showing you?

A: *They are showing me that there's going to be a family and I'm going to be part of this family, and there are going to be some situations that are going to be really hard and trying.*

D: How do you feel about that?

A: *Well . . . I know . . . oh, boy . . . I just know it's going to be pretty hard, and they're showing me almost like on this big filmstrip, and I'm seeing my life, and it starts to take shape and form, and I'm seeing what can be, and I'm seeing what might be, but it is going to depend on how I perceive it to learn from it. And it's just . . . oh, boy, there's a feeling coming into my body.*

D: How does it feel?

A: *I feel kind of like this pull, and I think it's getting time to go . . .*

D: To go where?

A: *Into the body . . . into my mother and . . . it feels so different here . . . . Oh, I don't want to do this.*

D: You don't want to do what? You don't want to be in your mother's womb?

A: *I feel sick.*

D: You feel sick?

A: *Yes.*

D: Being in the intensity of your mother's world?

A: *Yes.*

D: Can you feel your mother's problem?

A: *Oh, yes. . . . What's going into my body is making me feel sick.*

D: Alcohol?

A: *Yes.*

D: You feel poisoned? Toxic?

A: *Ohhh . . . it feels different. I feel sick. . . .*

D: You are. Does it scare you about the world you're going into?

A: *Yes. . . . I don't think I like it down here at all. . . . It's going to be . . .*

D: It's going to be what? What's going on?

A: *I'm coming out.*

D: Where are you now?

A: *I'm still . . . I'm . . . I'm still inside . . . He stopped it.*

D: He stopped it? The doctor? Why?

A: *Because . . . he's someplace, and he didn't want to deliver, . . . so he . . . oh, God . . . I feel sick. It's so hard.*

D: What is?

A: *Being born . . . I'm stuck. I know I can't go back, and I want to go back, and I'm stuck. . . . It's like I'm caught between two places, and I don't want to be in this one, but I guess I have to. Oh, this is going to be so hard.*

D: What are you thinking?

A: *It's so new. . . . It's just so new . . . boy . . .*

D: What's new?

A: *Everything. . . . Everything is all new. . . . I know I've done this somewhere before.*

D: You've been born before?

A: *Oh, yes, lots of times.*

D: Did you ever feel like this?

A: *Yes—sometimes it felt happy, and sometimes I left when I was still inside, and sometimes I left right when I was born. . . . I've done that a lot.*

D: So what are you going to do this time?

A: *It's going to be hard, but I'm going to learn more about how I can change and see things differently because there are lots of things I know that I'm going to be doing here if I can make it.*

D: Is that encouraging?

A: *Yes, but . . .*

D: Does it scare you?

A: *It's . . . it just seems like so much and . . . I can see clear in front of me . . . I can see clear down to different points in my life, and I can see what can happen.*

D: Like what?

A: *Well . . . I can see that when I'm a young adolescent there is . . . is a soul that wants to come through . . . so I said that I'll be a vehicle and she can come through me, and I will give birth to her. She's really strong. . . . She's really strong, and I've known her before, and she's stronger in a lot of ways than I'm going to be at that age.*

D: In what ways is she strong?

A: *She has a perception. . . . She's very wise. . . . She's very wise, but she needs to learn about people. . . .*

D: Do you think she is capable of that?

A: *Oh, yes . . . I do, I do, and she will also have an understanding of me that is going to help me. I won't understand it at that age, but she'll understand. . . . She won't tell me that so much, but she'll know; she'll understand that, and there are going to be times when we won't be together.*

[This is reference to my state of mind as a young teenage mother and as an adult: the fragmentation I felt and the struggle with staying present on the planet.]

D: What's going on?

A: *I'm thinking about killing myself.*

D: How does that feel—the idea of killing yourself?

A: *Relief.*

D: Relief from what?

A: *Being alive, being here. It just feels like such relief. I think about this a lot.*

D: What would it relieve?

A: *Feeling dead. I know I'm alive, but I feel dead. I feel numb.*

D: Do you feel sick?

A: *Oh yes. I feel sick and I feel numb and I everything else is all foggy and sketchy, and it is like I hate God for making me be here. When I look at the stars at night I want to go home. I just want to go home.*

D: It's all right. You deserve to be loved. You deserve not to be in pain. You deserve to go home. Where are you?

A: *I'm 25. I'm thinking about killing myself again.*

D: Why?

A: *My boyfriend and I just broke up, and I'm in a place where I don't want to be, and I'm scared . . . and I can't go back, and I have to send Tina away.*

D: How come?

A: *It's just not good for her to be with me right now. Oh, boy—it just hurts so bad.*

D: Are you scared about leaving her?

A: *I'm scared . . . If it wasn't for her, I'd do it. I would do it.*

D: Does that feel like enough of a reason? Or are you pissed off that you had her and have to hang around?

A: *No . . . She'd be okay, but ultimately, I know if I did that, I'd have to come back and do it again—I'd have to do it again . . . and it would be harder next time, so*

*as hard as it is . . . as hard as it is, I need to be strong
enough to do this.*

[This was in reference to the time frame when I was
engaged and living in Sacramento with Ed. I sent Tina
to Chico for a short period of time until I could get my
act together. After the breakup, I worked for Revlon, was
promoted, and they transferred me to Los Angeles. I also
innately knew that if I took my own life, I would have
to incarnate again and the same/similar issues would
need to be confronted until I learned the proper man-
agement of the energy. Outwardly, I was ignorant of this
fact, as I was not spiritually conscious yet. However, my
higher self was revealing a truth here while I was under
hypnosis.]

A: *I don't understand.*

[Now I had bounced to my relationship with Stephen,
the doctor, and five or six years had passed. I was 32.
This relationship ended with great secrecy on his part,
and I was completely confused. I had been seeing the
gestalt therapist for four years or so. This now was the
next growth crisis, which became the catalyst for my
spiritual awakening, when all hell broke loose. All of
this happened in a period of 24 hours. What I don't
understand is why everything ended in the manner it
did. I had allowed myself to finally feel, and I wanted to
continue feeling, not to numb out again. I knew if I did,
there was no way back for me again. I didn't know if I
could hang on.]

D: What don't you understand?

A: *It felt so good to feel again. . . . I don't understand.
I was so happy. . . . God, I feel like I'm going backwards,
and I want to maintain feeling, and I don't think I've got the
strength to do it, and it's just really hard. I don't think I've
got the strength to keep feeling right now, and I have to tell
Tina the truth, and if I don't be really honest with her, then
she is going to wind up like me.*

D: Tell her the truth about what?

A: *About me . . . my life and how I really felt—if I don't do that, she is going to wind up like me, and I don't know whether I can do that. It just hurts so bad. Everything has to be from inside of me, it has to be in me. . . . The cause has to be in me. . . . I don't understand. I don't understand. . . . I want to believe in God, but I don't believe in God, but if it hurts this bad, I'm sorry for all of those people that I've hurt and pushed away. . . . Oh, God, I feel like I'm dying, and it hurts so bad, and something is going on in my life, and I . . . oh, God . . . I just told Tina . . . She wants to go away, and I have to let her . . . I have to let her do that. I don't want her to do that, but I have to let her do that . . . because it's the only right thing. . . . Oh, God, it just hurts so bad to be alive, and I . . . I took her to the airport. . . . I know that something is going on that I don't understand, and I feel that somehow that I'm being tested by God and forces that I don't understand, but I know something inside me is dying and . . . there is something that's going on, I don't understand it, but if I . . . if I give up and kill myself, then I'm failing, and it's so hard, and I've pushed away so many people because of my own hate and bitterness, and it's . . . oh, my God, I understand.*

D: What do you understand?

A: *I understand that life has had to bring to me an experience of exactly what I have created in the rest of my life to other people. . . . I have had to go through exactly what I have put people through. . . . It's the only way I understand what I'm creating in this world and God, it hurts. . . . It really hurts, but it's so exacting in its intelligence and, oh, God . . . there is a golden color that has completely filled up everything around me and this ray that has come into my front room is all around me, and it's . . . it's . . it's . . . heavenly . . . it's not of this world [sobbing]. . . . It's coming from those teachers that help me on the spirit side.*

[Here was my defining moment in life. This literally brought me to my knees. I had to face myself, tell Tina the truth. It was then that I saw a vision of a filthy pool of muddy water turn crystal clear. It was at that exact moment that I said out loud, "Oh, my God, I understand." That is when the golden ray came into my front room and dusted everything with gold.

The next day Tina shared with me that she had a dream that night and in that dream I had died. She wanted to move to Chico. I sobbed myself to sleep on the bed after I took her to the airport, and then found myself climbing into another dimension, a different reality where I saw my father. He had been dead for several years.]

A: Oh, God . . . I'm not in my body anymore. . . . I'm climbing, and it's just as real . . . It's more real. . . . We only think this is real down here, but this isn't. It's only an illusion, and I see my father, and he comes up to me, and I haven't seen him since he died, and he is looking in my eyes, and there is so much love [sobbing] and I feel that love, and he . . . he really . . . he always . . . he always loved me, and it's like that feeling . . . that feeling from him goes right through my body, and it heals me, and I know . . . I know how much he loves me, and it . . . it gives me a kind of strength, and . . . and he lets me know that I have to go back into the body, but something new is going to happen in my life—I'm going to come into my real power as a spirit, and I will come to know that, and this is what all of these experiences in my life have been leading to. This has been a test, and I am strong enough to do it and to continue to pray, even though I don't understand it, that it will be revealed to me, that I just have to have faith, and I don't have anything else to hang on to, and so I pray and I pray and I pray and I pray and I pray and then . . . it's given to me. And there is more that I will do, and there are events that I will need to look at where being little was concerned, but I will do that. This is the very beginning of a new kind of power, but it has to be from loving and it has to come from loving. I have to learn how to forgive myself and . . . oh, God . . . but if I can do that, I have so much that I have said that I want to do as a spirit here before I die and I'm going to do it. . . . I'm going to do it. . . . I'm going to do it. . . . oh, God . . .

[I repeated the psalm "The Lord is My Shepherd" over and over like a crazy person. After a period of time, a man gave me the Ascended Master Teachings by Saint Germain, and I knew I had the tools to go home. It was everything I ever felt in my heart but could not verbalize or find outwardly. This was the beginning of my spiritual awakening.]

D: I'm going to count slowly from one to five and I want you to slowly come back to your body, and when I get to five, I'd like you to open your eyes and have a sense of well-being to feel refreshed and alert and to be able to remember everything you would like to consciously and we can pick up here at a later date.

A: I need to get balanced here. . . . I know how to do that—I need to do that before I come back. . . . I need to do that. . . . Let me do that. . . . Let me do that, then bring me back. . . . One moment [sobbing]. . . . As I come back into my full and waking consciousness, all of the chakras within my body will become fully balanced, and I am asking for help from Dr. Peebles and from all of my spirit guides and teachers to take control of my emotional body, my higher mental body. . . . I am the rhythmic, balancing and energizing breath of God. . . .

Okay . . .

[Now don't ask me how I knew to do this, but the wiser self, God Self, or Higher self—whatever you want to call it—something took over and knew I was too fragmented and that I needed to find equilibrium. I indeed was being guided and watched over.]

D: One . . . two . . . three . . . four . . . five. [long pause]

A: *Oh, God . . . whoa—that was an E ticket.*

43
The Protector

The reason I talk to myself is that I'm the only one
whose answers I accept.
—George Carlin

I left Dr. Slavin's office exhausted and yet at the same time amazed at what surfaced from the depths of my consciousness. It felt like a big ball of twine that had become twisted and knotted over time was now unraveling, rolling on the ground free, gathering speed from its own momentum. *Let it roll.* This appointment followed on the heels of the other:

Dr. Slavin: When you are ready to begin, tell me where you are and what you see.

Athena: *I'm on the spirit side.*

Dr. Slavin: On the what?

A: *The spirit side. I'm in this time, and I am talking with some teachers, and there is one that I feel so much love and gratitude for. He is showing me on a big screen certain events and probabilities and how I might be able to be of service to humankind in this lifetime as I begin to acknowledge on a continuous basis "my own God Presence" within. There are certain things that he is showing me and making me aware of that are not wise to discuss, and so I honor that. This is a point where everything in my whole life has been taking me.*

I have made it to this new awareness—it all feels so brand new. There is so much gratitude and excitement, because life has purpose and meaning for me now. I am going to become more aware as I continue to grow and develop my consciousness as to my own awareness of all that "I Am" in reference to the universe. In becoming aware of that, then I might become of greater service to those people that I will be able to help in this lifetime. There will be various avenues that I will explore and develop for the betterment of my own consciousness as well as understanding that I Am part of a continuing consciousness and that consciousness is all that is, all that ever has been, and all that ever will ever be.

I Am part of that as is all humankind, and it is such a wonderful feeling to know that the blindness from my own eyes has lifted, that I am able to see that now.

D: You are able to see through the blindness?

A: *I am able to see the potential and the probabilities, for it has felt to me as if I am beginning to see through new eyes. I feel great gratitude—however, I am not always aware of this information, and it must be developed. There are certain events that will be necessary for me to heal, and these are my own illusions that keep me from knowing the God within. Those are the illusions that I must begin to understand to dissolve and to resolve and to work with that energy in a new way. And to feel a greater capacity to allow myself to experience the joy in life, and that is exciting . . . that is all new. Oh, boy . . .*

D: Where are you now?

A: *Oh, I am so sick . . . I am so sick.*

D: You're sick?

A: *I am in the body, and there is so much trauma that has affected my body. This is something that I need to look at. There is so much within my whole solar plexus,*

my uterus, and my womb—there is so much scarring that
is in there. I am in the hospital and in intensive care, and
I am very close to dying. They are operating on me, and I
am out of my body sometimes.

D: Who's operating on you?

A: I am in the hospital—I am thirty, and I am very
close to dying. The doctors don't know what is the matter with me, so they are exploring, and I am above them
right now watching these two doctors operate on me, and
I know if I want that I can leave the body because I am
so full of infection and I am so ill. They are talking. I can
hear them talk about whether or not they will be able to
save me.

D: What's happening?

A: I am still in the body, but I am in Intensive Care.
The doctor is telling me that I am going to have a scar,
and I am conscious that I am in the body, but I know that
I am going to stay. I know that this has all been created
because I have to look at all that trauma . . . Oh, God,
I don't want to go back and do that. I am having repulsive memories, and they shudder through my whole
body. I know something went on, and I see pictures,
and I . . . Oh, God, I don't want to go back and look at
all that. There are pictures in my head, and I would like
to make them go away. There is something there. I need
to do that. I need to do that. I am talking to Dr. Peebles,
and he is telling me, "You are strong enough; your teachers and I know you are strong enough. You need to look
at this—you need to look at how you have tried to heal
other people through not wanting to heal your own pain.
You need to look at this now. You are strong." I don't
want to go back and do that so I start to pray, and I ask
God, "Okay, God, if I need to do this, then you send me
the person who can help me. You bring me the person
who can help me do this. You bring them to me, God, and
you help me do this"— and I find you.

D: And what?

A: *And I find you. Then you have me go to the beach and you are saying, "Where are you now?" And I know where I am at. I'm on the beach, and I want to be able to talk to you, and she won't let me, and she's walking around me on the beach right now, and she is so strong, and she says to me, "Why do you want to go back and look at this? Haven't I been taking care of you all these years? What do you think would have happened to you? What do you think? He would have slit your throat. He would have stabbed you to death; he would have killed you! Now is this the way you thank me? Is this what you are doing? You cannot come out! I have to stay in control!"*

And I want to be able to say something but she is too strong, and you want me to go inside of a cave, and I don't like caves 'cause caves scare me and I don't like them, and they scare me, and I don't like being down here in the basement. I don't like being down here, but I don't know how to get out. And it's dark, and it's scary, and he makes me . . . I won't tell, I won't tell!

[Silence and long pause.]

D: Where are you now?

A: *I'm floating—I'm floating, and I am watching what he is doing to her, and I am not in the body. . . . I'm just floating.*

Maybe I should let him kill her, and I could be back in spirit, and I wouldn't have to go through this over and over again. Oh, boy . . . It hurts, it hurts.

D: What's going on now?

A: *I have taken over again. I just have fuller control now, and I am more prominent in her personality, and she stays away. I make her. I am going to take care of her from now on, and I can do that. I'm strong and I can do that. She has to stay under my control, because she's too vulnerable, and if she gets out then she's going to get killed, and I can't let that happen. So I'm here, and I am powerful, and I can numb her, and she won't feel it, and I'll make it easy that way. I will push my way through situations if I have to. But I'll protect her. I'll do it. . . . I'll do it.*

D: Where are you now?

A: *I'm in the bathtub.*

D: How old are you?

A: *I'm seventeen years old.*

D: What are you experiencing?

A: *I'm looking at the razorblade, and I am pregnant. My boyfriend just told me to take quinine tablets and drink turpentine. And I want to die. Oh, boy . . . I don't like this period at all.*

[The following period happens as I move forward several years to a time after I had become aware of Dr. Peebles.]

A: *There's a light that came into my bedroom.*

D: A light?

A: *A light, and it entered into me. It's Dr. Peebles, and he's trying to help me feel a sense of joy in my life. He has always been around me in this lifetime helping me. He has been working with me, and he just told me that he intervened and told me that I could confront all these issues. There is so much going on.*

[Again I move forward in time.]

D: Where are you now?

A: *I was having thoughts about my mother and wishing she was dead. She hasn't died yet. I would feel so much relief.*

[More time passes.]

A: *Now she is dead, and I'm glad. I am glad because she is out of my life. She betrayed me so much, and I am glad she hurts.*

[The year is now 1989 and contact with extraterrestrials has begun on a regular basis.]

A: *Oh, they come almost every night, and I see them. People would think I am nuts, but they're real. I like them. I like them a lot.*

D: Like who?

A: *Aliens. I like them, and they know that, and they tell me things.*

D: Like what?

A: *They tell me things about the Earth, and they show me different planets, and they say that they communicate with thousands of people and that they communicate with the government and the government knows about them. They know that I like them because I am fascinated with them. There is one who wants to speak through me, and I know this one—and I have known him. There is so much love and wisdom that he wants to share with people about creation and fertilization. Someday I will do that, and they are letting me know that there are a lot of people that will be vehicles like I am for other consciousnesses to speak through us to help humankind in understanding their own awareness, and I find that exciting.*

D: In a minute we will have to come back to the present.

A: *That's fine.*

D: I'm going to count up from one to five, and when I get to five, I would like you to open your eyes to be back in the present, to have a sense of well being, and to feel fresh and alert. One, two, three, four, five. Feel fresh and alert and feel a sense of well-being.

44

Men Of The Golden Robes

Curiosity is lying in wait for every secret.
—Ralph Waldo Emerson

I dreamt it was night, and I was standing by the corner of a large building, hidden from view, peering through the branches of a tree. Although it was dark, there was a soft light enveloping the walls of the structure, which created a glow, enabling me to see.

I watched as a man in a golden robe stepped through the wall, materializing before me from the etheric realm into the physical plane. Both hands were clasped firmly below the center of the three-foot white cross he held six inches in front of his body. As his left foot came into contact with the ground, he pivoted sharply to his right and with military precision walked down the side of the building, his gait in a tempo of perfect rhythm.

Two men, one after the other, followed his lead, taking form from the invisible to the visible, each carrying a similar luminous white cross. Their druid-like appearance, draping hoods, and long golden robes told me they were of some ancient religious order. There was something highly secretive about them. I watched in fascination as they proceeded down the corridor, their golden robes swaying in perfect unison from left to right with the motion of their stride. They disappeared into the night.

Whatever they were guarding now opened before me. I was being allowed to witness something sacred that they had been protecting. I stood at the entrance of the large cement-like vault. Hundreds of open caskets without lids were lined up in perfect rows. I surveyed the vastness of the room. Each container housed a body that lay beneath a foot of dry ice. I could make out the forms; however, I was unable to discern if they were male or female. I felt as if I were viewing bodies preserved beneath the surface of a frozen lake bed.

I knew I was being shown my past lives.

45
Time Travel

Every journey has a secret destination
of which the traveler is unaware.
—Martin Buber

The session in which I experienced my life in review
caught me completely off guard. It was like one of those
experiences that hits you out of left field— even though
I figured there must have been a reason. Dr. Slavin and
I had scheduled another appointment, and for the next
few weeks I let the experience just settle. I reflected back
to something Dr. Peebles had told me some ten years
prior. He said that I was tying up loose ends in this lifetime. From my perspective, it seemed as if I was being
given an overview of my life.

Two weeks passed, and in our following session something from another dimension bled through the walls of
this reality and opened a portal to another time.

March 13, 1996

Dr. Slavin: I'd like you to take some really deep breaths,
getting calm . . . getting into that other special place . . .
feeling yourself layering . . . relaxing, progressing, further
and further down . . . In a moment, I'm going to count
from ten to zero and with each number back, I'd like you

to feel more and more relaxed, calm, and effortless, and, when we get to zero, I'd like you to be totally relaxed in a deep trance, and go to where you would like to start, whether it be where we left off or to a new place—it's not important. Ten . . . nine . . . eight . . . seven . . . six . . . five . . . four . . . three . . . two . . . one . . . zero . . . I'd like you to be in a full trance now. Whenever you are ready, tell me what is coming through for you, where you are, how you are feeling, what you see and feel.

Athena: *I'm not in this time.*

D: What time are you in?

A: *Two thousand years ago.*

D: What do you see?

A: *Christ.*

D: Where are you?

A: *I'm . . . I'm Roman, and I'm a man. . . . There are accusations being made about this one who calls himself a king, . . . and I have a lot of power at that time. . . . There are several that are under my command. . . . I'm not well liked, but I'm powerful.*

D: And?

A: *I don't understand this one that they call "king."*

D: Why?

A: *Because people flock to him . . . and he has all of these powers that I don't have, and . . . he seems not to be afraid at all . . . although he should be, because there are those that believe, as I do, that he is turning people away from our law, and they must obey our law or they will be killed—and I see to it that they are.*

D: That they are killed?

A: *Yes. I'm a tribunal judge, and those that disobey our laws are put to death and punished severely.*

D: Are you scared for this man or are you angry at him?

A: *I'm not scared for this man. I don't understand him, but I'm not scared for him. He is different, and I don't*

*understand what kind of power he has—yet I see it. I
don't understand it. Yet . . . he has far greater power
than I, and they do not fear him like they fear me.*

D: Is it confusing?

A: *It is confusing, but I don't let people see that.*

D: Do you like people fearing you?

A: *Yes, very much!*

D: Why?

A: *Because if they fear me, then they are under my
control, and they will do as I say.*

D: And that power feels good?

A: *Yes! For I am powerful, and people fear me, and
I make sure that they follow the laws of my land, for I
have been appointed, and I take great pride in my ability.
I enjoy seeing the fear in their eyes. I feel not bad nor do
I feel shame when they are put to death under my com-
mand, and I put to death many.*

D: What's going on?

A: *My body is getting very cold, and I am getting ready
to die.*

D: Are you scared?

A: *Yes.*

D: What are you scared of?

A: *There is that man . . . the one they call "king."*

D: Are you scared of him?

A: *I fear that I should have stopped that, but in
great ignorance, I did not know that he was truly the
one that they called the Son of God, for he was not in
his tomb.*

D: So are you scared of him now? [long pause] Where
are you now?

A: *I'm in spirit now. I am no longer in the physical body,
and there is the sense of great freedom and awareness
that I feel, and there are those that have come to me in
my confusion, and there are teachers here.*

D: There are what?

A: *Teachers that are helping me to understand what I created through my ignorance while upon the Earth. I feel great shame and sadness, but they are showing me that there will be opportunities for me to once again create situations in which I may be able to balance what I have caused to be out of balance where God's law is concerned . . . and those that I put to death still live, and some do not hold great judgment against me, . . . and that one who is known as the "king" has come to me, but I feel such shame that I have great difficulty looking upon him.*

D: Does he judge you?

A: *No, he does not at all—but it is I who judge myself, and I do so harshly.*

D: Where are you now? What do you see and feel?

[I left that time period and traveled back to this time-space reality to the time again when I had just moved to Los Angeles after my breakup with Ed. This was just prior to seeing Hildegard, the gestalt therapist.]

A: *I, ahhh . . . I, oh, I feel so tired. . . . I'm here in Los Angeles. . . . I just moved, and I just broke up with my boyfriend, and I feel so sad and hopeless, and life just seems so pointless, and I feel like I just want to be back in spirit so bad, and oh, God, . . . there's those . . .*

D: Those what?

A: *There are all those voices again.*

D: What are they saying?

A: *They're telling me to kill myself, and oh, God, . . . no matter how hard I try to shut them out—and I try so hard—it's just that they . . . they keep getting louder, and she . . . wants me to go down some stairs, and I don't want to do it. Oh, God . . .*

D: Who wants you to go down some stairs?

A: *Hildegard. She's a therapist. And I won't do it—I confuse her, but I won't do it. I think there is . . . oh . . . it makes me sick . . . I think . . . I think part of me is there, but I'm just going to have to be strong and not do that now . . . I don't want to do it now—not now.*

D: Why?

A: *Why? Because I'm not going down now. I'm just not going to do it. I don't think I can get back up again.*

D: Yes, you can. But you don't want to go down now?

A: *Not now—not with Hildegard. It's not the right time. It's not the right time yet.*

D: Then don't go down there.

A: *I can't. I can't. I've locked that door.*

46
Mining The Motherlode

The virtues we acquire, which develop slowly within
us, are the invisible links that bind each one of our
existences to the others—existences which the spirit
alone remembers, for Matter has no memory
for spiritual things.
—Honoré de Balzac

What lies buried within our consciousness is fascinating, and I found myself reflecting back to a session that I had with Dr. Peebles through his medium Thomas Jacobson ten years prior. There were certain feelings that I silently harbored where Christ was concerned that I never understood. I could barely think the thoughts to myself silently let alone utter the words out loud for another to hear. Seeing a Roman helmet sent shivers through my body and I might add, not in a good way. I remember the Doc telling me once that what I wanted to shove down, I needed to let come up. Wouldn't you know, another delightful opportunity for growth was about to surface. I had a session with Dr. Peebles in 1996 in which I had asked about the feeling I had around Christ and that of the Roman Empire.

Athena: *Dr. Peebles, I've always felt a sense of*

jealousy and resentment where Christ is concerned, and I have great difficulty looking at a picture of him, looking at his eyes. If I'm watching a movie about the crucifixion, I will get up and leave the room . . . . I've never understood it, and I feel guilty for feeling this way. I have a feeling I was a Roman and I wasn't very nice.

Dr. Peebles: Oh, yah! You've had lots of lives when you weren't very nice. One wizard to another, you know.

A: Pardon me?

Dr. Peebles: One wizard to another. You had two lives around Christ. One, you were a great clairvoyant and seer, and people would come to you from miles around for your visions, but you never had the vision of the coming of the Christ child, so you took your life through herbs and willed yourself back in the body immediately as a man, because you knew men had the power at that time. You were an up-and-coming tribunal judge. You were seen as quite arrogant by many. You never judged Christ personally; however, he looked into your eyes and that energy has stayed with you ever since.

Here was a man who wielded far greater power than you, and it was done through gentleness and love, not domination and control. Christ knew that he was no different. He knew that each man, woman, and child was the son or daughter of God. He never saw himself as special. His message was misinterpreted, but that was simply because of where mankind's consciousness was at during that period of time.

So here you were, going around trying to "clean up" those he was trying to save, and you felt no guilt about it whatsoever. It was simply part of the "school" called Earth. Incidentally, you imprisoned many along the way. Christ is a spirit who is aware of you and is around you periodically on the spirit side. We would invite you to find a picture of him, look into his eyes, and ask him to come look into your eyes on the spirit side tonight as you sleep.

That night I found a picture of Christ and forced myself to look into his eyes. I prayed that he would come to me that night and look into my eyes on the spirit side while I slept. I felt anxious and uneasy. I had a very lucid dream that a man was walking towards me, enveloped in a misty white light. All the while, I was transfixed on his eyes. They were beautiful beyond description. When we were three feet from each other, the resistance on my part became tremendous, and I tried to get away. But I was unable to break the connection of our eyes, although I tried. I was aware only of his eyes. There was a burst of white light, and the two of us became one.

I thought after that experience that I let that lifetime go. I contacted a friend to transcribe my recent session from tape with Dr. Slavin and we spoke very briefly about my time travel experience to my life around Christ. She chuckled as if the timing of all that transpired was perfect, as if she knew something I didn't. "Have you ever read the book *Jesus and the Essennes*?" she asked.

"No I haven't." "I have a copy I can loan you" she replied.

"Thanks, but not now. I still feel as if there is more to be unearthed and I don't want to read anything that would influence me in any way."

I knew intuitively there was more to surface, and I also knew that the perfect person to do the actual regression was Torah, the non-physical entity channeled by Shawn Randall. To facilitate a past-life regression takes a particular skill and knowledge of how to guide the individual through whatever lifetime their soul is seeking to heal. As skilled and competent as Dr. Slavin was, this was unfamiliar terrain for him. Because I went under so deeply with Dr. Slavin my intuition told me that if both agreed to participate in this session, I could get to the heart of this lifetime and the healing could begin.

Shawn and Dr. Slavin both agreed, and I scheduled the next session. It wasn't that I relished the idea of doing this, as I could tell by my feelings and the heavy sighs that rose from my toes that there was still a lot buried. And speaking of toes, it was strange that around that time I began having difficulty in walking: My feet really started to hurt—and in particular my left foot.

47
The King And I

So as through a glass and darkly, the age-long strife
I see where I fought in many guises,
many names, but always me.
—General George S. Patton

Torah: All right, we say greetings, greetings indeed then to the two of you. As always a pleasure and a delight to serve the growth momentum, the growth orientation, and the growth intention here today. We greet you with much love. Dear Athena, we say to you, oh, absolutely you are ready, ready, ready; with a capital R you are ready repeated three times! Dear Dan, is there anything you wish to say, anything at this time?

Dr. Slavin: It's nice to be here, and I'm glad that the two of you are going to do some work, and I'm looking forward to it.

Torah: All right. Athena, we will turn it over to you for your choreography and conducting skills. . . . How would you like to begin?

Athena: Thank you, Torah. I don't know if you are getting a hit on what it is that I am wishing to bring to a level of greater understanding with resolve and forgiveness for myself. Years ago, Dr. Peebles told me about a lifetime that I had around Christ. I had a feeling I was a Roman and he did confirm a lifetime that I had as a Roman tribunal judge. In my current life, as a child and into adulthood, I felt resentment and jealousy towards Christ, although I have never understood the origins of these feelings. I felt great shame and guilt for feeling that way. I have always had difficulty looking at a picture of Christ.

Recently I was doing some work with Dr. Slavin, and I went back to that life as a Roman tribunal judge spontaneously. I thought I had let go of that lifetime.

I'm in a place in own growth now where I want to open up to receiving more love. This has just come to the surface, so I feel that it's appropriate timing. What I would like to do, Torah, is to have Dr. Slavin put me under and then have you step right in and do the regression. I'll turn this back to you for any comment that you have, and I'm certainly open to anything else.

Torah: Have you done any releasing of the emotional pockets of this past life that are in your unconscious yet?

Athena: Yes, when he was not found in the tomb.

Torah: May we throw something in here?

Athena: Sure.

Torah: Hmm . . . let's see. . . . Maybe not. . . . All right. What we want to say, dear Athena, is that it is very possible that you will be experiencing what you have already stated about guilt. As we look at the situation here, definitely we see a man who feels one way and yet votes another because of the politics of the time and the state of the Roman Empire—and in that way, very torn between his heart and his mind. So just leave it at that for now.

Athena: Okay.

Torah: All right, . . . we'll depart for a moment.

Dr. Slavin: I want you to get as comfortable as you

possibly can. . . . Take some really deep cleansing breaths. . . . Feel the air coming up through the center of your body through the top of your head, . . . turning back down around, passing through the center again. I'd like you to think of a coal in your center that people often identify in their stomach. . . . As you breathe in, the coal is fanned white; . . . as you breathe out, the coal is fanned red, . . . bringing strength, energy and warmth to your body. . . . In a moment I'm going to count down from ten to zero, and when I get to zero, I'd like you to be in full trance, . . . to feel totally comfortable and relaxed. Ten . . . nine . . . eight . . . seven . . . six . . . five . . . four . . . three . . . two . . . one . . . zero. Where are you?

Athena: I'm . . . I'm in that time 2,000 years ago and I am watching a group of people. In this gathering, there are whispers, and they are aware that there are others such as I that watch for their activities. There is one—not only one—there is more than one who they follow, and they follow a certain belief, they follow certain teachings . . . and so we watch them carefully, the others as I, to see that these activities are controlled.

Dr. Slavin: I am going to turn this over to Torah now.

Torah: Moving forward, . . . tell us about your career . . . your career.

Athena: I'm a tribunal judge, and I am very powerful, very powerful—and I enjoy that power. It feels good to me to know that I have the ability to control people. I have been appointed by what is known as a Senate, and there are others that look to me for my guidance as to the obeying of the law.

In this law, I have the ability to put to death many, and I put to death many people, for there is one that they seem to follow. In this following, they say that he is the son of God. He is referred to as the "King"—the

"King. Who is this "King"?

Torah: Did you ever see this man when you were in your younger surveillance years watching the crowds? Did you ever see him in the earlier part of your career? It's all right to remember.

Athena: I stand back and I watch him. . . . He cannot see me but I observe him. I am hiding behind a stone fixture.

Torah: How old are you now?

Athena: I'm fourteen. It's very confusing to watch him, for there is one who cannot walk, who is very ill, that is brought to him. . . . They bring him to this man, who places his hand upon him. There is a feeling that comes forward from him, and this man is able to find strength again in what would be broken limbs, and he stands. . . . I do not understand this, and . . . [Torah interrupts]

Torah: How do you feel about this?

Athena: It frightens me.

Torah: Right.

Athena: I don't understand this. He frightens me because I have never seen something like this before, and it is contrary to what we are taught and what we believe. And so I turn away from him and I go in my own silence into the darkness of the night, and I ponder this. . . . I think about this, but yet again, I do not understand it. It has a great effect in my body; it makes me feel as if I am in some state of a shock, because I do not believe what it is that I have just witnessed. It is contrary to all law as I have been taught.

Torah: Is that what is happening to your body right now . . . the shaking? Is that the fear?

Athena: Yes, . . . it feels as if my whole body has been affected by what would be radiation or feeling, and it frightens me, it frightens me, and I do not know how to make this stop. . . . I do not know how to make this stop.

Torah: What do you do?

Athena: I find a stone and I begin to pound on my flesh; if I can hurt myself enough, . . . if I can cause enough pain, then it will make me feel a certain reality of the place that I am in at this time, and so I cause great pain to my physical body.

Torah: Where in your body?

Athena: On my foot, . . . on my foot. It is my left foot, and I cause great pain to that. I have trouble walking, I always have trouble walking for I have broken some bones.

Torah: Thank you for bringing that forward. Later as the tribunal judge, do you remember this or not?

Athena: I do remember this; however, it would be great weakness upon my part to convey this information to anyone, for they would see it as weakness. I have stated to my parents as that young boy of 14, that I was helping to load some stones into a cart and one simply fell upon my foot and crushed my foot. I do remember; however, I can make that memory go dim, and I do so skillfully.

Torah: When does it come back? Does it ever come back while you are the judge? Does it come back that memory, and when, if so?

Athena: There is that man that one they call "King!" He is looking in my eyes as he passes me. I stand with others and I watch him as he carries his cross upon his back.

Torah: Do his eyes trigger this memory?

Athena: Yes. . . .and there is that feeling inside of my body again, and . . .

Torah: What feeling? Let it come out. . . . Let it come out.

Athena: Shock, shock—it's shock.

Torah: Let it come out if you want.

Athena: There is something about this man that I don't understand. It is so confusing to me. I don't understand what kind of power he has. Here he has been condemned to death and yet he looks fearless. There is a calm about him. He looks fearless, and that make me wonder in silence. I wonder, and then I think back. . . . I think back. . . . I think back. . . . . I think back.[I become very emotional.]

Torah: Let it come out. . . . That's right, let it come out.

Athena: I think back to that time when he was . . . when he was healing those broken limbs, and I think about that now and he . . . he . . . he . . . is going to die, and I fear that if he dies that I will become diseased and weak. I will be thought a fraud. My strength will be seen as great weakness, but in my heart, I know. I know that he is . . . he is . . . he is . . . the son of God, and I cannot stop that and I feel too weak to stop that, for people look to me with great fear and they would think it was fear upon my part, and I don't know what to do.

Torah: Your foot holds all of it, doesn't it? Your foot tells the story, doesn't it?

Athena: [sobbing] It hurts, . . . it hurts. . . . It feels great pain and it hurts.

Torah: Would it be all right if we touched your foot? It would help release all of that guilt.

Athena: Yes.

Torah: Stay with us. . . . Stay with it. . . . Stay with it. . . . You don't have to back away from the fear. You don't have to back away from the fear this time.

Athena: But it's how I punish myself for not stopping what I could have stopped.

Torah: That's how you punish yourself. . . . That's how you punish yourself . . . .from other lifetimes. . . . It's all right. This energy can all be released now . . . the pain, guilt, but most of all the self-punishment.

Athena: I feel so much shame, for there is news that he is no longer in his tomb and I fear for my own life.

Torah: The only one that's really hurting your life is

you, with the shame and self-punishment. . . . Don't disappear, . . . don't hide it again. . . . Let the next wave come, and as it comes, remember that he forgave you. When Christ looked at you, he had forgiveness that was a giving.

Athena: [long pause] There is one that comes to me and is not afraid of me, for I am curious about what this religion is that they call Christianity. . . . Christians. And in secret, he begins to teach me.

Torah: Yes . . . yes.

Athena: And I am afraid that I will be found out, but I feel such emotion in my heart. I feel as if much of what I did was beginning to melt, and I don't know how to do this where I can still maintain a position with respect as a judge, and I do not want to put people to death . . . and so I begin to waiver in my decision to put people to death, and they are beginning to look upon me as weak and brand me as a traitor.

Torah: And it's going to be safe to remember what happens; as you remember and release it, it can go away.

Athena: I am stripped of my power. However, I am spared great punishment, but I am ostracized from being part of this community . . . and so I . . .

Torah: Which community are you ostracized from? Which community?

Athena: From the Roman community . . . I am ostracized from the Roman community, but it is all right because I am getting ready to die. I am so afraid of seeing that one that is known as the "King." There is one who has still remained my friend, who comes to me in secret and tells me that I have been forgiven.

Torah: Can you let that forgiveness go to the foot? Can you let it come in here where it gets held? Let's take it out, . . . take out the shame, take out the pain, . . . let the energy come out the bottom of the foot—out of the heel. It's time for it to come out of Athena; it's time for the shame to come out of Athena. Let it go a little more consciously. . . . Make a choice. . . . Do you want to make a choice? You don't have to hold it anymore. You know this foot does not prove anything anymore. It once proved that you felt guilt; it once proved that you believed the loving man they called the "King." . . . But you don't have to prove it anymore. . . .You don't have to hold on to it anymore. Let it go. There it goes, there it goes. All of the helpers helping you now to receive the true love, . . . the unconditional love, . . . to receive the deserved unconditional love. . . . You deserve this love. You deserve all the love that you choose to receive. You deserve it, and this foot deserves it.

Athena: I see him now, . . . and it is the "King" who has helped my foot and has washed my foot, and it has been his love towards me that has helped to heal.

Torah: If you choose, you can receive that love free from the pain, free from the guilt, free from the shame.

Athena: I was enveloped in a brilliant white light.

Torah: Let that light take the shame and the pain, . . . let it take the pain and the shame from your soul, from you altogether. See . . . that light sees your light, the light of Athena.

Athena: I . . . I . . . I . . . see my mother. . . . I see my mother, . . . and she is with him, and they both come to me [sobbing]—and my father, ...my father is with them, too. . . . There is so much love from all of them because we are one. . . . We are one consciousness!

Torah: That's right! It can come in an unlimited way. That's right, breathe. . . . Breathe. . . . Know all of the pain can be gone. Know all of the pain can be gone.

Athena: There is feeling coming into my pelvis, . . . and I can feel my legs. . . . I don't have to hang on to this anymore. . . . It can go. I don't have to hang on to this anymore. I am choosing to let it go, let it go.

Torah: Let the light and the love take it all away. . . . What you give up the light takes away. . . .

Dr. Slavin: This might be a good point in time to stop. Athena, take some really deep breaths, . . . deep cleansing breaths. . . . I would like you to be able to maintain whatever connection from the work that you have just done—whatever you would like to bring back into your consciousness. . . . Whatever you would like to leave, you can leave to visit at another time.

I'm going to slowly count from one to five, and when we get to five I'd like you to be able to open your eyes and to have a sense of well-being and to feel refreshed and alert . . . one . . . two . . . three . . . four . . . five.

Torah: All right, . . . thank you both for this loving co-creative cooperative healing. Much love to all, and thank you, Dan, for allowing us this very big space of allowance for her. Much love.

Athena: Thank you, Torah.

Dr. Slavin: Good work.

48
Portals Of Immortality

Intuition will tell the thinking mind where to look next.
—Jonas Salk

Dr. Peebles had told me something a long time ago that I found of interest. He said if there was a phrase that you use so frequently it becomes a belief, spirit will take you back to its origin or cause. *Here we go again,* I thought. My mantra has always been "it hurts too much to love." With Dr. Slavin setting the stage, Torah channeled by Shawn once again skillfully guided me to the lifetimes that explained the feelings of discomfort and fear.

Dr. Slavin: Get as comfortable as you can, and take some deep cleansing breaths. . . . As before, as you breathe in, the air is passing over a coal in your center, and it fans the air white, . . . and as you exhale, it fans the coal red. . . . Breathing easily and comfortably. In a moment, I am going to count down from ten to zero. As I count down, you will feel yourself becoming more and more relaxed. . . . When we get to zero, you will be fully in a trance. . . . You will repeat a sentence over and over again. Hear it and say it, in your own voice in your trance state. . . . Breathing easily and comfortably,. . . ten . . .

nine . . . eight . . . seven . . . six . . . five . . . four . . . three
. . . two . . . one . . . zero. . . . Fully and comfortably in
trance, . . . and the sentence is, . . . "It hurts too much
to love." After you do your work, at the end of the work,
we will count back up and come out of the trance. But
at this point, I'd like you to repeat . . . two times, at your
own pace, "It hurts too much to love."

Athena: *It hurts too much to love. . . . It hurts too much
to love.*

Dr. Slavin: A little louder.

Athena: *It hurts too much to love. . . . It hurts too much
to love.*

Dr. Slavin: I am now going to let go and leave you in
a trance until we finish, and I will count you back out.

Torah: Feel free to repeat the phrase and let it take
you to the appropriate time . . .

Athena: *It hurts too much to love . . . it hurts too much
to love . . .*

Torah: That's right, allow that emotion, . . . that emotional pocket to come, trusting in your higher self, . . .
allowing only as much as you are ready to heal today,
allowing only as much as you are very ready to heal
today.

Athena: *[beginning to cry] It hurts to much to love.*

Torah: What do you see? What are you feeling? You
are able to witness and experience at the same time as
you know to do.

Athena: *I am in Athens, and there is a plot, and I
am made aware of this plot. My husband is wonderful;
he is such a beautiful and powerful spirit because he is
so concerned with the good of the people. He is part of
a large group that is creating democracy, and he is one
that people admire, and they look up to him. He is very
kind, and he is very compassionate.*

*He has a wonderful relationship with the Gods and
he prays not only to the Gods but he prays to God. These*

spirits are very aware of him and they help to guide him in his decision-making for the good of the people, for he has been placed in that position. There is a group of men and they want to overthrow him; they want to revolt against him, for they seek to control the masses of people. They want to assassinate him and to kill him. There is one who is a very good friend of mine, who is aware. She is someone who places herself, at times, in great danger, because she is aware—someone has told her, somewhat in a state where he was full of spirits or of the wine—that they are plotting to kill my husband. I do not want him to be aware of this, and so I go to them when he is preoccupied, for he works with a group of founding fathers to create these laws for the people.

I am somewhat afraid, but I feel that the Gods will protect me. I go at night and I travel alone, and I go to this group, and they have been drinking. There are five of them, and they start to rip at my clothes, and they rape me, and they beat me, and one takes a knife and he stabs me and he stabs me. They leave me in the center of Athens as a message that others will see . . . but I am not dead yet. . . . I am not dead yet, but I know that I am going to die. He comes to me, and he is sobbing so hard, because he doesn't want me to die, and they try to heal me, but it doesn't work. My body becomes filled with poison, and I live for a period of time—some seventy-eight hours or so— and I can feel the life ebbing from me. He is so sad. . . . He doesn't want me to die. He is starting to feel great anger at these men, and I tell him that it is okay, that I would die for him over and over again—I love him, and it is okay, and I will always be in his heart. . . . I will always be with him.

Torah: Can you move to the moment of your death? To your last interaction with him? What you thought? Can you tell me what you felt?

Athena: *There is so much pain. . . . I don't want to*

leave him. I see such pain in his eyes, and he feels as if I am deserting him, and I'm not. . . . I'm not. He feels so sad. . . . I want to be with him, and I have to go. He is so sad, and I feel sad when I look in his eyes. I feel the pain in his heart, and it hurts so bad, . . . it hurts so bad.

Torah: What's the promise that you make to him and to yourself when you go?

Athena: *I will find him again.*

Torah: That's right.

Athena: *I will find him again, I'll find him again. . . . We'll be together again; I'll find him again.*

Torah: Yes. That's right. These walls of experience, of deep love . . . You learned so much in that life about loyalty and dedication, and the kind of love you had never felt before, . . . and it's alright to really let that lifetime go, for how beautifully it served you in deepening your capacity to love with loyalty and dedication.

Athena: *He is afraid. I see him from spirit and I observe him, and he is filled with such anger, and he makes a different choice. He makes a choice . . . he thinks about this and he is so angry at the Gods for taking me.*

Torah: What is his choice?

Athena: *His choice is not to love through loyalty because that hurts too much.*

Torah: He chooses not to love through loyalty, because that hurts too much . . . and that will affect him in this current life as David.

Athena: *And it affects him now. . . . It affects him now.*

Torah: Whatever his process—his soul's path, the journey for the moment—in your own journey, it's important for you to decide that love and loyalty, depth and integrity, *do* fit together. You lived for it, and you died for it then. It's real, the beauty of love that does have loyalty and dedication. As we invite you to look at that, we would like you to separate it, cut it out from the pain—much like putting facets on a raw diamond, chipping away at the stone, chipping away the pain to see that in that stone is a diamond that sparkles and shines—a diamond of love with depth, integrity and loyalty. Just hold that image for a moment, . . . for we want to go on to another lifetime, to hold that image that within that rough rock can be a diamond of love and loyalty and dedication that does not have to have life-and-death pain, . . . pain that poisons, . . . pain that hurts so bad. How does this sit with you before we move on?

Athena: *I need to place this in my stomach where I was stabbed.*

Torah: Thank you. Please place it in your stomach where you were stabbed. A beautiful diamond with the intolerable pain cut away. If you like, you can touch the place with your hand just to let the cells of your body know that this is healed, . . . this is healed, . . . filled with a beautiful diamond of possibilities of love with loyalty, integrity, and depth—placed now. We would say that there were other lifetimes before that one in which you did not know love with integrity and loyalty. You have that diamond within you; it is an infinite possibility for all your lifetimes now. It is valued as a standard, and it can be separate from intolerable pain. Intolerable pain, chipped away. . . . It does not have to be touched. What else do you need to do before you leave this lifetime?

Athena: *I feel complete.*

Torah: We invite you to take a deep breath and surrender to the guidance of your higher self and unconscious to take you to another lifetime, another place, another time, where you can witness and experience. Take your time.

Athena: *I'm in Egypt, and I am female and a priestess, and there is this man that I am very attracted to, for we communicate without words, and this is a man that*

I have known before, . . . and he has wonderful powers of alchemy, and he is seen by many as a magician. With his alchemy and symbols, he is able to create so many things that people think are mysterious, but it is because he understands the laws of physics and the laws of God, the law of Ra. And once again, there is communication with various Gods. He spends much time in silence. He is sought by those of royal position for his wisdom. I am not of equal position. He finds me quite beautiful in form, and we begin to see each other in secret. He is not in a position to pursue, for that would be looked upon unfavorably for his position within the royal compound.

Torah: Let yourself move forward now to the next significant event.

Athena: *I am being punished. Punished, for I am not seen as one and equal, and there are those that feel that I have weakened his power.*

Torah: Ahh . . . you've been found out.

Athena: *And so they make a mockery out of me, and I am flogged, and I am cut severely on my back by whips.*

Torah: What does he do?

Athena: *He does not stop it. . . . But he is in great inner turmoil, for he feels that he has to maintain a position for the greater whole of the people. In his turmoil he seeks to remove himself from feeling, . . . and when I look at him, he looks away. I do not die, but I am completely scarred and full of shame and I feel as if I am unworthy of any man, for I am looked upon with disgust.*

Torah: This issue of worthiness is healed in Athena's lifetime. She has made her stand with this man for her worth, and has stood strong upon her principals and her worth. It was very important because of you that she do this. The scars and the shame, the scars and the shame can be healed. Love does not have to contain the scars and the shame. You may have more to reveal to Athena, and we invite you to reveal more . . . perhaps at the time of her death?

Athena: *Several years pass and I see him once again. There is an illness that is in my body, and I am in a village with other people. There is great disease, the water is plagued and it causes great pain in my body, and he comes to me and confesses his shame. I am cold to him, for I have made myself turn to stone. I welcome death, and I drink more poison. I welcome death, for I do not want to live in death, I want to die to live . . . . and I want to do that alone. I am very cold, and I am very lonely, and I am very angry.*

Torah: What have you learned in this lifetime?

Athena: *I have learned that you cannot trust your heart, . . . and if your heart begins to feel, you must turn it to ice.*

Torah: Do you want to stay with that? Is Athena ready to release that?

Athena: [crying] *I don't want to feel like that. I have felt like that . . . I have felt like that in this life, and I don't want to feel like that anymore, because I have felt like that so much in my life. I have hurt so many people because I have felt like that, and I have hurt many men to make them feel what I have felt, and I have tried to release that in this life.*

Torah: Now that you know where it comes from, it's going to be easier to release it even more deeply. What we want you to do, because we know that you are in present as well, Athena, and we want to have you in your wisdom, the part of you that has your spirituality and wisdom. . . . We want you to look down upon her, see her on her death bed, see her energy, see her coldness, see her ice, . . . see that it didn't work.

Athena: *I see that same ice come over me as a young girl in this life. . . . I see that when I am six years old, I feel it come through my soul.*

Torah: It's ready to melt. It's ready to melt. Now, and

in order for it to melt, you still need the reassurance that love can be pleasurable and safe. For the moment, let's drop in on your higher self for that truth. Let your higher self give you a taste of that truth—to dissolve, to melt the ice, the remnants of the ice . . . for you're done with it. Your higher self can bring you, perhaps, a wonderful ball of light—however you see your higher self bringing it, . . . a vision of a transcendent love that can be safe.

Athena: *I am not going to punish myself in this lifetime anymore.*

Torah: And keeping the ice is also a form of self- punishment. It is ultimately the frozen one who loses. The ones that you punish with the ice, they recover, they move on. The one who turns to ice for the defense and for the safety is the one who gets hurt the most and you are ready to let it fully melt.

Athena: *I judged myself. He was afraid, but I judged myself for not being equal.*

Torah: So he did see you as equal.

Athena: *He did; others did not.*

Torah: Right.

Athena: *I judged myself for not being equal, for I thought they must know truth, they must see what I did not see.*

Torah: It's okay for you to trust yourself now, . . . in this present life. We have a very educated woman here, a very intelligent woman who has earned self-trust, educated herself, knows discernment, makes choices and decisions consciously.

You know you did consciously choose to love this man. You knew the potential consequences, and you consciously chose, and you trusted that choice. It became a growth choice.

Athena: *We knew this in spirit, David and I both know this, we knew this. We created certain dynamics and potentials and probabilities.*

Torah: It was a love and growth choice—dissolving the ice and opening to more possibilities and really healing those past two lifetimes, letting love have new experiences.

A short time after that session I discovered something quite mystical but completely normal for me. I had been drawn to a picture of an Egyptian priestess which I purchased a few months prior to this regression. I never noticed until after the regression that an Egyptian High Priest with dark skin was standing behind a pillar in the shadows. I never knew this lifetime was even in my subconscious. But it did explain why I have never had any desire to explore Egypt and my fear of public ridicule. Even more important, I understood the connection now of the event in the basement that I always described as "feeling as if someone poured ice through my soul." It was at that exact moment that I felt a literal wall encase me in steel. My muscles became taut, and I knew I had to be strong. Even now, writing this I am having an epiphany. That must have been the moment the Protector or the General took control. What would a kid do with all of that ice anyway?

49
Surrender Dorothy

Re-examine all that you have been told . . .
dismiss that which insults your soul.
—Walt Whitman

Growing up, I had tapes in my head from my mother's beliefs around sex. I remember Mom sitting on the edge of my bed when I was around eleven, telling me about, as she put it, "the facts of life": "You have to do it because it is your wifely duty. Sex is an animalistic streak in men." I listened and watched the disgusted, matter-of-fact look on her face. "So there you have it! Now you know about the birds and the bees!" She looked uncomfortably relieved, like she had accomplished some dreaded deed, and quickly scurried out of the bedroom.

I lay there confused and bewildered. I decided that I would marry some "old geezer" who was three days older than dirt so I wouldn't have to do it.

Newspaper articles were left around for us to read, especially Ann Landers articles about girls "who went all the way." Mother was full of aphorisms: "Why buy the cow when the milk comes free?" or "No man wants a worn-out shoe." My all-time favorite was "Let your upstairs control your downstairs." We were to be virgins when we married.

My father came home for one of his short, sporadic visits when I was around twelve. He had been lucky in Las Vegas, and I remember he kept placing one hundred dollar bills in our hands to give mother. Usually he showed up broke and "down on his luck," as Mom put it. She was thrilled! "Keep 'em coming!" We were so happy to be the recipients of that which placed such an ecstatic look of joy on her face. Later that night, I got up to use the bathroom. I stopped and listened outside their bedroom door in disgust, as I could hear them in a romantic interlude. I just heard him grunting. I woke my sister from a sound sleep.

"Connie, they're in there doing it!"

"What?"

"Mom and Dad—they're doing it!"

"Well, Jesus! They're married."

"I don't care, they shouldn't be doing it!"

"Leave 'em alone and go back to bed, you freak."

Who can think about their parents having sex? There is just something weird about it. I remember Mom telling me once that Dad didn't have a clue as to what he was doing in the bedroom. "Once, right in the middle of having intercourse, your father stopped and asked me, 'Did the man with the chicken fryer come yet?' 'Hell no, and neither did I!' I shoved him off! That's when we had the Coney Island restaurant."

As I began to mature, however, I do remember saying to myself, "Wait a minute, Mother, this is how *you* felt about it. It doesn't have to be how *I* feel about it." Gee, thanks, Mom; that took some undoing. To allow myself to be vulnerable with a man was frightening because it felt as if I was giving up my control, and if I did, I could be killed. An irrational thought, but it was how I felt. To truly allow myself to surrender to anyone was another story. I had to work hard at separating my beliefs from my early childhood experiences and to allow myself to repattern where my own sexuality was concerned. I took to heart a statement Dr. Slavin said to me one day when we were talking about sex and my fear of surrender or of truly letting go: "If you allow yourself to jump off the cliff the next time you let yourself go, each time you take the leap it will become easier and easier." I also knew and know that eventually, through repetition, what feels foreign will become familiar. But the real healer is trusting in myself to know when someone is safe.

I know it does not have the impact on my life now that it did. I could never think about my fragmented memories prior to my work with Dr. Slavin without feeling my whole psyche shudder with repulsion from the inside out. That no longer exists. Thank God! I could never sleep on my back, as I felt too vulnerable, too open to attack, and now, it's the only way that I'm comfortable sleeping.

In my own discovery process I have become aware that it isn't *Can I trust that person?* but more, *Can I trust myself to make the right judgment call when it comes to the character of another?* Am I able to see the red flags? And more important, do I listen? I'm getting better. Growing up in a house where the tools of discernment were absent, it has been like learning to walk with my ankles tied together, stumbling over my own feet.

A relationship, I was told once, is my final challenge. Have I met that challenge yet? I don't think so.

A few of my friends belong to internet dating sites. I can't even imagine. What would my profile say? 61-year-old burned-out makeup artist who sees dead people, likes interior design, has been probed by aliens, channels a 19th century spiritualist but makes a mean pot of soup!" I cringe at what might respond. Yikes!

50

I'll Swing The Lantern For You

Faith is the bird that feels the light
when the dawn is still dark.
—Rabindranath Tagore

I was no longer seeing Dr. Slavin on a regular basis. The exploration and healing of my childhood trauma had come to completion. I could live with this now. We both knew it was time. Once in awhile, if I felt the nudge from spirit to explore something for greater clarity, I scheduled an appointment, as the door was always open for me to do so. I was so grateful that I had done the work and that God had placed this perfect therapist, this wonderful healer, in my path.

My mother had died and was now on the spirit side. The resolution I had hoped for never transpired before her death. I was left feeling nothing more than sadness and relief. Over the next few years, I just let things settle.

It was late afternoon and I was driving home after a day of filming, listening to a talk program on the radio. The show was hosted by a husband and wife team, both of whom were psychologists. A woman had called in who had been raped in front of her brother at knifepoint by a man who had broken into her house. She stuffed it somewhere, as we so often do for survival, and it was rearing its head some years later for healing. I knew exactly what was going on; the more it tried to come up, the more she shoved it down. The psychologists were encouraging her to begin therapy but to no avail.

She was married with two children and a husband who had no doubt reached a maximum level of frustration with her inability to cope. My heart went out to her. I could hear the anxiety in her voice. All of her emotions had settled in her throat, like a rubber band that was ready to snap.

I pulled the car over to the curb, reached for my cell phone, and dialed the number of the radio station while saying out loud, "Okay, God, if I am meant to talk to this woman, put me through!" To my surprise, the screener came on immediately, and after a brief conversation said, "I am so glad you called. Hang on, you're on next." I didn't give them my real name, for it is never easy to discuss this issue in a public venue.

"We are speaking to Susan. Welcome to the program, Susan. We understand you would like to speak to our last caller?"

"Hi. Yes, I would. Jennifer, if you are still listening, let me begin by saying I was extremely moved by your call. I share a similar experience of repeated childhood rapes at knifepoint. Hear me with your heart. Woman, it's time to get your power back! You are entitled to all of those feelings of rage and anger—every single one of them—but you need to be able to express them appropriately in an environment that is safe. And you need help being guided through the storm by someone who is qualified to do that kind of work. You would be crazy not to feel what you are feeling. I am validating that for you.

"The part of you that reached out and made the phone call today is the part of you that is strong and wants to heal. I will not tell you that you won't hurt in the process, because you will. I will not tell you that it won't hurt coming up, because it will. You will walk through some fire to heal. But can you imagine living the rest of your life with the kind of fear and anxiety you are dealing with now? I know you are afraid that if you give over to the emotions that they will be bigger than you and you won't be able to survive it—*but you will.* You'll cry, but a few days later, guess what? You will feel a little lighter. If it hurt going down, it will hurt coming up, but it won't last forever.

"Despite your best attempt, your children will absorb your fear and perceptions like osmosis, as if it's being poured into them through a sieve. Do this for yourself first because *you want more* out of life, and your children will benefit from your courage to confront and make peace with your own demons. I am here to tell you that you can regain your sexuality as a woman. ***Take your power back!*** Don't exclude your husband; it won't be an easy ride for him, but he needs to be part of this process. And anytime it feels too dark, remember this call and know there is another woman out here swinging the lantern for you in the night."

I hung up, hoping that she heard the call in more ways than one. "Boy, she sounds strong," the wife said to the husband. She then alluded to, in a roundabout way, having experienced something obviously of a similar nature. I remember what felt like such hesitation on her part to reveal more to her listening audience of her own personal experience. I can understand that, for it is a subject not easy to address publicly; and there is often, more times than not, a shame that seems to stain the soul.

I remember the first time I walked into Dr. Slavin's office. I thought I could get hypnotized, look at the experience, and it would be a done deal. Yeah, right. I thought I'd understand it, and it would be over, and I would feel better about being alive. It didn't work that way for me. I discovered in my own journey that there were so many facets that interfaced with one another, trust and betrayal knotted tightly together, and it isn't something that is healed overnight.

I believe with all my heart that specific issues rise to the top to be addressed when we are strong enough as spirits to deal with them. Does it ever fully go away? I don't think so. It is kind of like learning to walk with an emotional limp. I found that there was hardly an area of my life that wasn't colored by those experiences. But it doesn't have to be debilitating, and it isn't. Life is different now.

Years ago, one of my spirit guides gave a message to me through Dr. Peebles. At the time, I didn't understand it, as everything was in a state of chaos. It was such a dark time. Now it makes perfect sense. I share this with *you* the reader. It is to you I speak. When it is dark and you can't see your way out, put your name in place of mine in the following passage, and know that the light of God within you will carry you through. It did me.

"Athena, you are a light bearer, and as you step forward with your gift of light to the world, first you must know darkness and the shadows of your own, and in knowing the same you will discover the desire not only to honor and to kneel before those dark places but to see them as beautiful and divine because of your willingness to be transformed through that darkness into the light."

51

If You're Dead, Why Do I See You?

Death is simply a disguised deliverance, or, like the
budding rose, it climbs up the garden wall
to bloom on the other side.
—James Martin Peebles

Working with spirit in the manner in which I do, I am deeply humbled by experiences where I can be used as a conduit that promotes healing of some sort for another soul. My experiences have been vast in nature, but there are a few that touch me in a way that feels almost sacred. Maybe it's because I know all too well the feeling of being lost, and from that perspective I can identify with and feel great empathy for these spirits. At times I am called upon to be of service in such a way that helps them move into the light, and frees them from the confusion which keeps them earthbound. The following is such a story:

I was on a business trip, sitting in the car, somewhat bored, listening to the conversation of two men as they discussed a potential land investment. We were driving along the highway next to a graveyard when an electrical current passed through my body from head to toe. I turned my head and looked out the passenger window. I knew spirit was about to manifest, and I quickly located the source of the frequency.

There she was, dressed in a white Victorian gown, her anxious face framed by long brown hair. She circled her grave in a continuous motion. There was a desperation in her pacing that caused her dress to sway back and forth.

"What are you looking at?" The man in the back seat inquired.

"Oh, nothing," I replied as I turned around, facing the windshield. David, who was my friend as well as my business associate, glanced in my direction, for he knew I had seen a spirit.

As soon as we were alone, I told David that I wanted to channel Dr. Peebles. I wanted to help this woman, and silently felt in my heart that the business trip was "life's disguise." The real purpose, I couldn't help but feel, was to be of service here. I instructed my friend to give Dr. Peebles the information, location of the grave site, and a brief description of what I had seen, in the hopes that spirit could help her.

I was in trance and felt myself step aside as the contraction in my solar plexus signaled with full force the presence of Dr Peebles.

"God bless you! Dr. Peebles here."

"Dr. Peebles, it's David here, and I am speaking on Athena's behalf. Today we were driving by a graveyard in Montana, and Athena saw a woman walking around a headstone and felt perhaps she was stuck and that you might be able to help her."

"Ah, one moment, David. Let's see here." After a long pause, Dr. Peebles began to call her by name: "Lorraine . . . Lorraine . . . It's Dr. Peebles here. That's right, just follow my voice. It's Dr. Peebles. . . . Just follow my voice. I understand, my darling, that you want to go back and live your life backwards, but you *must* understand that this dimension no longer serves you. God has never judged you; you've only judged yourself. There are those waiting for you on spirit side, those of family. . . . Follow my voice. . . . That's right! That's Mama. . . . It's okay to cry, my darling; those are very healing tears. . . . You will feel such a sense of relief. . . . God has never judged you. . . . Alright, alright. . . . Go to Mama."

Dr. Peebles paused. "Alright, Lorraine is with family."

"Why was she trapped, Dr. Peebles?"

"Well, David, we can give you a little information without being invasive to the privacy of her soul. Lorraine was a very rigid woman in life, and upon her passing, she saw the effects that her rigidity and belief systems had on her children, so she wanted to go back and live her life backwards as an opportunity to make it up to them. Spirit never judged her; however, she judged herself so severely as to create her own self-condemned hell. You can feel very good for Lorraine, for she is with family."

This was one of those times, for whatever reason, that touched me more deeply than others. Upon my return to Los Angeles, the saga was about to continue. Dr. Peebles had told me some three months prior to my experience with Lorraine that my mother and sister Judy, who had recently passed over, were going to appear to me in dream state.

Both Judy and my mother, however, appeared to me in physical form soon after. I was in the kitchen doing dishes when I felt the familiar current pass quickly through my body. "Spirit's here!" I said to myself as I quickly turned around, curious as to who was in my house.

Standing by a black wrought-iron railing in my dining room was a man dressed in a turn-of-the century black suit with a black hat. There was a very gentle presence about him, and I noticed he had a tear rolling halfway down the left side of his cheek.

"Who are you?" I inquired out loud.

"My name is Stanley," he replied. "I am Lorraine's husband. I came to thank you for the service you performed. We tried and tried to get her attention but to no avail. She is with us now. Thank you."

"My pleasure, Stanley. You're welcome." I matched his tear with one of my own.

Gratitude is a wonderful thing. I never know when or under what circumstances "the doorbell will ring," as I call it, and when the electrical current quickly passes from head to toe, it always alerts me to an adjustment of the frequency. The challenge then is not to intrude but to seek permission to give the message.

I have seen Lorraine and Stanley together on more than one occasion, and she is radiantly beautiful, always smiling, holding Stanley's hand. Once my friend, a very talented spiritual intuitive, and I were having lunch. Suddenly my eyes shut and my muscles contracted between my brows. Spirit was about to manifest. Ann started to laugh. "What did you see?"

"Oh, my God!" I chuckled. "Lorraine is on one side of you and Stanley is on the other."

They both looked happy as pigs in mud, smiling at me. Ann shut her eyes as they began communicating with her. "They are going to act as 'gatekeepers' when there are those who need help in crossing over." I thought of Disneyland's Haunted House ride where the seats are shared with a couple of ghost-like hitchhikers.

Over the years I have come to understand, through personal experience, that life creates disguises and that, beyond a shadow of a doubt, there is real purpose for the coming together of people. There is no such thing as chance or accident. I have come to trust in spirit whether the setting is social or work related. Dr. Peebles once said that, from spirit's perspective, "Trying to get a human being's attention is like trying to move a rock with a feather."

It was early morning, and I had a seven a.m. crew call, as we were going to be filming at the Doheney Mansion in Beverly Hills. "What room do you want to do make-up in?" the second assistant director asked as I quickly surveyed the surroundings. I never expected anyone to help me lug in my supplies, but Richard always said, "Here, let me carry your school books."

"Good Lord!" I said, "No one can be this ugly for me to need to carry all of these makeup supplies. The light in this one looks pretty good." I walked into the room and placed my make-up kit on the table.

"What's this?" I looked at the cardboard that had been taped to the floor of the room. It wasn't the same cardboard that was commonly laid to protect the floor and carpet from cables and crew when commercials were being shot. There, against the light brown cardboard, was the outline of a body drawn on with a black marker, just like at a crime scene.

"This was the room where they found Ned Doheney's body. Supposedly he was having an affair with his chauffeur, and his wife found out and shot him. That's the rumor." Richard handed me the day's shooting schedule. "We will need the actor on the set in a half an hour."

Leave it to me to pick the room the murder was committed in, I thought to myself. I began to unpack my bags and set out my make-up supplies. This place was magnificent; the grounds were sprawling and lush, and I thought it unusual that I had never filmed here before.

It was some time after lunch when the grips and gaffers were busy in the next room rigging the camera and setting up the lighting for the next scene. I wandered out into the foyer and sat on a step of the massive descending staircase, taking in the beauty and the expansiveness of the space. No one was around, which was highly unusual. Normally, the guys were hustling about, carrying cables, shouting orders to one another. I felt the familiar current pass through my body, and I quickly turned my head to the left. At the end of the hallway, leaning halfway out of a door, looking directly at me, was a man wearing a black suit with blood on his shirt. "Please help me," he said.

I looked to see if any of the crew was around. I was alone. I turned back to the ghost at the end of the hallway. "Okay." I headed down the hallway towards the spirit that I knew obviously needed help crossing over to the other side.

He didn't move, and I felt a chill as I walked past him through the doorway. When I entered the room I knew instantly why he liked it here. It was obvious to me that, in his state of unease, this was the room where he sought comfort during his life. I stood a few feet in front of him and began to invoke those of the angelic realm and the Ascended Masters. I silently said my invocations, and he became surrounded in a cloud of luminous white light. He smiled at me and said "thank you" as he faded from my sight.

Recently, I was speaking to my friend the gifted author Linda Pendleton, who wrote a book about Dr. Peebles titled *Three Principles of Angelic Wisdom*. Linda had done a lot of research on the Doc and was quite good at it. We had been discussing spirit, and I shared my earlier experience at the Doheney Mansion with her. I was curious as to the physical appearance of Ned Doheney while he was alive.

"Describe him to me."

"This man looked like he was in his early thirties and he was wearing a black suit with a white shirt that had blood on it. His hair was black and the top was long and combed over to the left. It was short around the sides by his ears.

"Did he have a beard?" she inquired.

"No, I didn't see him with a beard—a mustache but no beard."

Later on that day she emailed me a picture of Ned Doheney. He was identical in appearance. But what really astounded me was that in this photograph, he was peering around the same doorframe from which he was calling to me for help. I don't say this for the purpose of sensationalism but simply because of the clarity of vision, which I have come to trust. In a recent conversation with someone who worked at the mansion when it was the American Film Institute, she told me that others had seen him there as well.

Sometimes if someone leaves in a violent manner, they feel trapped in a realm from which they don't know how to cross over to the other side. It doesn't serve any of them to hang around here.

Andrea came to see me concerned about her father, who was getting ready to pass over. She loved her father dearly, and Doctor Peebles had confirmed that which she was feeling—that he would be making his transition within the next few weeks. "The exact moment," he said, "is between your father and God. You can feel good for him, for he is surrounded by his spirit guides and his transition will be very easy." He did pass a few weeks later, and shortly after, Andrea brought her mother for a session with Dr. Peebles. My heart went out to her; I can't even imagine what that must be like to lose a partner after forty or fifty years of marriage. I explained the process to her of how it worked, mainly for her comfort, and then felt myself move into trance.

I saw a skinny man pick up a huge boulder and place it on his shoulders like Atlas. I heard loudly the words, "Rock of Gibraltar." After the session when I was fully present again, her mother was standing in front of the chair with a sense of excitement and tears in her eyes. She couldn't wait to hug me. "All of my life," she said, "my husband always told me he was my 'Rock of Gibraltar,' but he said through Dr. Peebles that in all reality, I had always been his." He also told his daughter Andrea to buy some chocolate for his wife. She left with a wonderful smile, because beyond the aching, for a brief moment, she knew his spirit was alive.

Several years passed, and Andrea contacted me in regards to doing another session for her mother. Her mother, now bedridden and in her eighties, was not able to travel to me, so I agreed to drive to her house in Beverly Hills. Two nights before our scheduled session, in the middle of the night, I felt his presence in the room. "Take her some chocolate! Please! Take her some chocolate!" The next day I made a point of buying some good chocolate at the store, so I would have it for our session the following afternoon.

I woke in the middle of the night, as I often do, craving something sweet, and scrounged through the kitchen but to no avail. Then I remembered the chocolate bar, and it was a struggle between good and evil—not something to do to a woman who is experiencing PMS and bloated by swinging hormones. *That's all I need*, I thought to myself, *is her husband "haunting my ass" for eating her chocolate.*

Andrea opened the door and greeted me with a big smile and a hug. I followed her into the bedroom where her mother was resting. There she was in her bed, wearing a pale pink bed jacket, fully made up. She was a beautiful woman, and I liked her very much. The situation was quite different years ago, when she had been distraught and anxious; now, she was looking forward with anticipation to her session with Dr. Peebles.

I put the recorder down on the table, took the candy out of my purse, and placed it in her hand. *"This chocolate bar,"* I said, "is from your husband. Incidentally, when I was craving something sweet I almost ate it." Her eyes lit up with excitement, and she propped herself up on her elbow and quickly unwrapped the gold foil. With the sparkle of a young teenager, she said with her thick, charming accent, "Oh, I love choc-o-late! My husband used to bring me choc-o-late all the time!"

I opened the door and welcomed Ryan into my home, directing him to sit on the couch. He was not a big man in frame, and there was something that felt slightly wounded about him. He was gentle, with big soulful eyes, and seemed a little apprehensive and unsure of himself.

Ryan wasn't new to channeling or the experience of Dr. Peebles, for he had several prior sessions through Thomas Jacobson. It was, however, his first session with me, and I knew he was curious as to what it would be like to hear the Doc channel through a woman. Although there are great similarities, there are differences as well, in particular as to what aspect of himself he can effectively bring through the framework of another channel. I liked Ryan, and I could sense there was a lack of confidence that he struggled with. As I sat on the couch, I felt the electrical current pass through my body.

"Ryan, can I share something with you?"

"Sure."

"There is a man standing next to you with a trumpet in his hand."

Ryan's eyes grew big, and he spoke slowly, as if he were trying to digest what I had just said. "That's my father," he said, somewhat stunned. "He was a trumpet player in a big band."

"Well, he wants you to know that he is going to help

you with your music. He wants you to find your own song."

Ryan's eyes filled with tears. "I'm a professional trumpet player, a studio musician myself, but I've never felt I could ever live up to my father's level of excellence."

I knew in Ryan's discovery of self, in understanding his own illusions of separation, that his fear was simply a doorway through which he would regain his greater power. I have a feeling one day Ryan will pick up his trumpet and play with a sense of passion rediscovered because of all he is allowing himself to explore. As the Doc once said, "Mozart could never have created the symphony if he would have excluded the low notes."

My friend Sharon and I drove down the two-lane street in a small southern town. I caught a glimpse in my peripheral vision of a small, corner-lot cemetery surrounded by a weathered picket fence. "Sharon, turn around quick." The electrical current passed through my body as we made a u-turn and parked the car next to the curb.

The confederate soldier stood erect in full uniform staring straight ahead at the asphalt highway and the passing cars. It was apparent to me that he was in a state of shock. Such a strange contrast to the modern conveniences that represented the time and space I was in. I wondered if he was aware of the road and cars, and I was certain that, if he was, they must have added to his confusion. The last thing he knew, he was in the middle of the Civil War. That's a bizarre thought. Sharon read the inscriptions on the neglected headstones, while I walked to where the soldier was standing, which was close to the sidewalk. I wondered about the family he had left behind, if he was married and had children. I did what I know how to do and watched as he was enveloped in the light. Directly behind the soldier, facing the opposite direction, was a headstone with the inscription of a soldier who had died as the result of a political assassination.

I never know where they will show up, and it isn't always my task to cross them over; it can be to simply give a loved one a message. I don't care where it is—a post office, a restaurant, or a drug store—I pay attention when they appear. They can be relentless in their desire to communicate to a loved one. In my experience, they just want them to know they are alive and okay. A few years ago, I was in a hospital for some lab work and I saw a man standing next to one of the nurses. He kept staring at me while insisting that I give her a message. I didn't. I really regretted not having followed through with his request and felt as if I let him down. A year later I was back in the hospital with my daughter, who was having blood work done for upcoming surgery. I felt the electrical current. It was the same man I saw the previous year standing next to the nurse. "Please tell her he is with me."

Tina recognized the look. "Who did you just see, Mom?"

"I was here a year ago and that same man was standing next to that nurse and wanted me to give her a message."

"Mom, go tell her." When I gave her the message, she began to cry and hugged me. "My grandson had died and I was praying that he was with my father. Thank you! Thank you!"

With regards to my own family, this experience was simply magical. It was Thanksgiving Day, and I was standing at the sink peeling potatoes when the song "The Wind Beneath My Wings" by Bette Midler came on the radio. That was my song for my sister Judy, and I played it at her memorial. I felt overwhelmed by love and loss as the tears rolled down my cheeks. I missed her. She *was* the wind beneath my wings. Just then the current flowed, and I spun around to see several family members now on the spirit side standing in my kitchen smiling at me. Just then, my sister Susie walked in with Judy's daughter, my niece Pam, following closely behind.

"What's wrong?" Susie said. Pam was rubbing her eyes and said she was asleep when something shook her awake and said, "Get up! Go into the kitchen now!"

"They're here." I said.

"Who's here?" Susie inquired.

"Mom, Judy, Ted, and Gary." Gary was Susie's husband, who died of cancer several years prior to this. Ted was Judy's husband.

We stood together, overwhelmed with emotion, all huddled together in a hug, crying. "The Wind Beneath My Wings" finished, and it was immediately followed by another Bette Midler song, "The Rose." "The Rose" was the song Susie played at Gary's funeral. Next followed mother's favorite (ironically), "Teach Your Children Well," by Crosby, Stills, Nash & Young. Those songs were played at their memorials and they played now *in succession* without a commercial interruption. How magical was that!

And speaking of family . . .

I had an uncle by marriage who was a dirty old man and always looked for any opportunity to "cop a cheap feel," not only from me but my other developing teenage sisters. Our complaints to mother fell on deaf ears.

"Uncle Maynard is a pervert, Mom."

"Shame on you girls! You're just getting innocent family affection mixed up with something else!"

Once a year, we would hear his old lime green shit

barge of a car spit, sputter, and die in our driveway. Reluctantly, at mother's insistence, Susie, Connie, and I lined up at the door to greet him.

"You go first,"

"No! You go first!"

"I'm not going first, you go first!"

"I don't want that bastard grabbing my tit. You go first!"

Like I said, the pervert was an uncle by marriage. Aunt Aggie had cut him off 25 years before. One night, Mom fell asleep on the couch and woke up to Uncle Maynard feeling her up.

"Get out of here, you damned fool! What the hell do you think you're doing?"

"No harm done, Ruthie, no harm done."

When Mom told us in the morning what he had done that night, we laughed our asses off. "Aw, come on, Mom! No harm done. . . . You're just getting innocent family affection mixed up with something else." Revenge was sweet. Why is it that there is always a pervert lurking somewhere in the family lineage?

After Uncle Maynard died, I had a very lucid dream in which I saw him in his "light body," and I was telling him, "LOOK! I didn't like you when you were alive, and I'm not going to pretend to like you now that you're dead!" So much for unconditional love.

52

And Then Along Comes Mary

If a man dies shall he live again?
And if he lives why may we not know it?
—James Martin Peebles

"Did I know you before?"

Dr. Peebles paused. "Ahhh . . . just one moment," he replied. I could feel his hesitation. I had the distinct feeling that he was conspiring with others on the spirit side as to the wisdom of revealing the answer to my question. After a long moment, he continued. "Well, . . . we knew this was going to come up sooner or later. I will tell you this: I knew you well. I knew you intimately; you were not in my peripheral vision. We worked on several projects together. I love you very much, and you are as a sister to me. Your name was Mary, and you were a medium through and through. That's all we are going to tell you. You will be exploring this down the road."

Interesting, I thought to myself. That answered a lot of questions. It seemed to me as if I had been born into this lifetime with feelings of great familiarity and fascinations that had no basis or reference point in this incarnation. It was almost like a psyche tug that said to me, "Something about this feels really familiar." It answered the electrical feeling I had the first time I heard his voice on the radio and it felt to me as if on some level I already knew him. I couldn't explain it further; it was simply a feeling.

I have always been drawn to the 19th century, and if there was an era in which I identify with the clothing, it would be the turn of the century. I love the slender dresses with their high necks, intricate lace, and cameo pins, their Gibson-girl hairdos, and the large feminine hats. They were elegant and beautiful. Who knows why we love what we do or relate to a specific period? We do because we do. I was unaware that a collective memory from a previous life lay hidden from my conscious mind. Fascinations and interests became more pronounced and sought expression as I entered my teenage years.

I remember the first time Dr. Peebles came through me in 1984 in Thomas Jacobson's class. Thomas asked Dr. Peebles if he (Thomas) could assist, to smooth the initial connection. "Oh no," Dr. Peebles replied. "There is great fear here of possession." When I began to explore channeling, I was terrified of obsession and possession. I know now it was simply a doorway that I had to walk through, leaving behind my own judgment and fear.

Several years passed after Dr. Peebles had confirmed our relationship, and I found myself, as a natural evolution of my mediumship, beginning to think about that lifetime. I was seeing spirits physically with great clarity and helping them cross over. And I found, with my inner vision opening up, that mystical events were transpiring in other areas of my life. It wasn't that I had this burning desire to extract all I could from that or any other previous life. I just felt as if I was being tugged by something to do so, and I will always pull on the thread if it feels right.

I contacted my friend and author Linda Pendleton. Linda had done in-depth research on Dr. Peebles when she and her husband Don co-authored the book *To Dance with Angels,* a book about Dr. Peebles. She was also aware of the information that Dr. Peebles had shared with me some years prior to this about knowing me and working with me as the medium Mary. Who knew—I was just exploring.

"Linda," I said, "I'm curious about 'Good Ol' Mare,' Mary the medium. I'd like to find out where she is buried and put some daisies on the old gal's grave." I could hear her laugh on the other end of the phone.

Linda called me later that day with a "check your email." There it was, from the San Francisco list of mediums: "Mary T. Longley Md. Cures obsession and possession, gives readings regarding business for $1.00." (I've raised my rates since then.) She lived on Olive Street in Los Angeles. I began to shake. What an emotional feeling washed over my body. It was completely spontaneous and organic. Linda also directed me to a website that had several of Mary's books, including a photograph and in-depth biography. I whipped out my credit card and ordered what books were available and had them sent ASAP.

Around that time, a script supervisor and fellow mystic said to me, "I have a turn-of-the-century antique dress, and I keep thinking you should have it." It fit me like a glove, and there was not a rip or stain upon the delicate material. That was icing on the cake.

The books arrived, and the excitement I felt was beyond description. To hold something that I supposedly wrote, and furthermore, to read her biography and see an actual photograph, was intriguing.

I carefully cut through the clear tape of the cardboard box. The last thing I wanted to do was to damage the contents. I removed the brown paper from a dark green book. There it was. *The Spirit World,* by Mrs. M. T. Longley, and as a bonus, Mary's picture. Good Lord, there she was, in her lace dress, with the funkiest looking Gibson-girl hairdo. Now I understood why I became a hairdresser. I was amazed at the thread of similarities of what I have come to acknowledge as a past-life echo.

MRS. M. T. LONGLEY

I have always been drawn to the New England states. *Mary T. Longley was born in Boston, Massachusetts in 1853.*

I am a trance channel and medium and saw my first spirit, my father, as a teenager. *Mary became a trance medium at the age of 14. Thousands of spirits gave messages through her.*

I entertained the idea of a career in the medical profession. *Mary was a physician.*

I enjoy public speaking. *Mary lectured publicly to up to a thousand people.*

I am currently writing a book. *Mary authored several books.*

I was terrified of obsession and possession. *Mary*

cured obsession and possession.

Mary gave psychic readings and so do I.

I have worked with Dr. Peebles as a trance channel for 25 years. *Dr. Peebles and Mary Longley worked together on several projects. They both worked at* The Banner Of Light, *he as Editor and she as Assistant Editor and medium. Both were very active in the National Spiritualist Association and Mary Longley held office as Secretary from 1898 to October of 1907.*

Mary Longley was married to composer Professor C.P. Longley. There are several testimonials promoting Professor Longley's collection of songs in the back of the book. I was shocked to find the following:

> The composer has been overwhelmed with testimonials to the value of his work, a few of which are hereby given. *Dr. J.M. Peebles writes, April 13th 1906: "A splendid bound book of nearly one hundred pages full of melody; songs and words adapted to Spiritual meetings and social home gatherings. These cheering, inspiring songs of Prof. Longley will live long after he has passed to the highlands of Immortality where motion is music and harmony is as abiding as the stars."*

I call her Shi (pronounced "shy"). It stands for she and I. Around the time I was learning all of this, a friend and a psychologist, Dr. Fred Bader, who also felt a connection to both Dr. Peebles and me, once asked another channel who lived back east if we all knew each other in the 1800s. The channel's reply was yes, indeed we did, and that I was a medium named Mary. This happened a few years prior to my knowledge of the incident, as the information was never shared with me at the time it occurred. I do know that from the first moment I met Dr. Bader, I felt an instant connection, like I had known him forever.

A day or two after having received the books by Mary Longley, I decided on the spur of the moment to drop into a Saturday afternoon channeling class. Torah happened to be speaking about prior incarnations and was going around the room giving us our names from a previous life. I had not said a word about this to Shawn, who was channeling Torah.

"And you, Athena, . . . your name was Mary Langley."

"Torah, do you mean Mary Longley?" I was stunned.

"Yes, Mary Longley."

I love the mystery and the intrigue of the fact that I could have stood at the port of Ellis Island as a sixty-year-old woman and watched my father, a young immigrant boy, disembark the boat that had brought him from Greece. I could have said to him face to face, "In this same century, young man, you will be my father." Now, that is a fascinating thought!

Why this information fell into my lap as it did I am not sure. On the other hand, I don't need to know why. I was told once, years ago, by Dr. Peebles that I was tying up loose ends in this life. There is a saying that the fruit doesn't fall far from the tree, and to me that statement explains the unexplainable.

53
The Crow That Liked Yogurt

To be admitted to Nature's hearth costs nothing.
None is excluded but excludes himself.
You have only to push aside the curtain.
—Henry David Thoreau

Once I saw a crow flying with a cherry Yoplait yogurt carton hanging out of his mouth. No matter how hard this little guy tried to stay in the pattern of the flock, it was of no use. His flight plan, erratic in comparison to the gliding formation of his feathered friends, was uniquely his own. I completely related to him.

"You are not your normal bear," my friend Sally said with a smile on her face.

"Yeah, I guess I'm not," I responded. I had another friend tell me not long ago, "You always have some weird shit going on in your life." I have given that a lot of thought lately. It's not as if I wake up every day and say to myself, "Alright, Athena, what kind of weird stuff can you experience today?" I get up and have my coffee like any other person, stand and look out my kitchen window, and watch the activity of the day begin. For instance, there's a man walking in front of his dog on purpose, lips puckered, whistling a tune, barely glancing over his shoulder at his mutt, so that if his dog craps on my lawn, he won't have to pick it up. He'll claim the fifth. I stare at the butt-ugly apartment building across the street that greed built and that still stands empty. I watch the Jewish father dressed in black, with his Torah tucked close to his side while his children trail closely behind like baby quail. This is something a normal person would do. Then there is the sign on my refrigerator door that says, "Normal people are jealous of me." I say to myself, "Surrender, Dorothy; it is what it is."

It has been a life jammed full of experience, and there are times I wonder what it would have been like not to have a focus so drawn to that which lies beyond the veil. On the other hand, that would be like trying to cram my big foot into a size six shoe. It is what it is, and "I yam what I yam," as Popeye would say.

'Weird,' by Webster's definition, is "of unearthly quality," so yes, I am weird, for that is what feeds my soul—the unearthly part, looking through windows into other worlds. Hand me the Windex; I want a better view.

It was a beautiful, sunny day, and a friend and I were having lunch in the backyard. I was watching a squirrel scrounging around the ground trying to find something to eat. I took a walnut out of my salad and tossed it on the grass, some six feet away. The squirrel returned, took a bite from the nut, and scampered off to bury it in the flowerbed. A blue jay, hot on its trail, dug up the nut and ate the buried treasure. Kathy and I laughed as we watched the comedy of errors. I tossed the nuts, the squirrel buried them, and the blue jay, on toothpick legs, immediately dug them up.

I tossed the nuts closer to me, the squirrel came

closer, and eventually I laid a walnut on the grass close to my foot. She inched closer, still guarded. "If you come everyday I will feed you," I vowed. She took the nut and scampered off. A few days later, I was in the backyard having lunch again. I looked down by my feet, and there she sat, looking up at me.

A week later, I was walking past my dining room window, which was at the opposite side of the house, when something caught my eye out of my peripheral view. There, standing on her haunches with her little squirrel paws on my window, looking inside my house, was my friend, "Fluffer Butt." On some level, she had understood, and she took me at my word. It became a daily ritual: She would stand on her haunches looking for me, and once she saw me head into the kitchen to get her food, she would run up to my front door and wait. I would sit on my porch and feed her pecans, walnuts, and peanuts out of my hand.

One day, while she was on tree branch in my courtyard and I was behind my screened window, we became completely focused on each other through eye contact. I kept sending her light, focused on the thought that there is only God, that her consciousness is God, my consciousness is God, and we are one. She jumped right from the tree onto the screen, trying to get to me. Once while I was deep in meditation, "Fluffer Butt" showed her face to me along with the thought, "Thank you for my food."

"Fluffer Butt"

One morning, I was rushing to get my makeup supplies loaded in the back of my car, as I had an early crew call of six a.m. I flashed on Fluffer Butt, unlocked the door, and ran back into the house to make sure she had her food. There she was, standing on the ledge looking for me through the dining room window. We always had this wonderful telepathic communication.

I am not sure when my love affair with the unearthly began; I think, like anything else, it has just been an evolution of becoming more aware of God's energy as consciousness and that all life is that consciousness manifest. In my meditations, I always focus a pillar of light in my home, and I believe that all of God's critters respond to light. One afternoon, I sat down and put my feet up on the ottoman and sat back in my big comfy chair to take a break. I looked up and there on my drapery rod sat a fat little bird puffed up like a tennis ball, preening himself. "Alright, Dozer, you are welcome here anytime you want; just don't crap on my drapes. I am going to keep the front door open and you can leave whenever your little heart desires."

Doctor Peebles once said that a good exercise was to increase one's appreciation of beauty by ten per cent daily; to see God everywhere. I began to incorporate that exercise as a ritual on my daily walks though the neighborhood, morning or night. I like walking at night. I like the peace that I feel and the hush that stills the craziness from the day. I have always loved street lamps, for they create an illumination that is almost magical. Couple that with the light from a full moon and it can be breathtaking at times. One night, while I was feeling a sense of inner peace, a doorway into another dimension began to open. I had become increasingly aware of the elemental kingdom in my studies. All energy we release through spoken word or feeling does affect all life, and that energy imprints itself on Mother Nature as well. I also found fascinating that Saint Germain taught that storms and cataclysmic events were Mother Nature's way of throwing that energy back on man, as a way to rebalance and to purify herself again. That makes perfect sense to me.

I began silently blessing trees and shrubs on my evening walks, for I was beginning to feel a deeper connection with all life around me. I reflected back to the fear I felt at night as a child at the thought of something evil reaching for me. It did, and it was evil. Now, in contrast, I was enjoying the peace and beauty of the night, and I could not have felt safer. I marvel at that. How sacred.

The magic began as I walked in deep contemplation of God. Things in my world internally felt right. I reached out and touched a magnificent tree in passing. As I touched its bark with my fingers, I silently said, "God bless you." I had been consciously touching trees and shrubs within arm's reach and blessing them for quite some time. Then one night, the strangest thing happened. I had touched the bark of a tree with my fingers. "God bless you." Instantly, a strong current of energy shot up my arm through the tips of my fingers. I knew well the signal. A vibration and frequency was changing. "Whoa! What was that?" I spun around, watching as the tree's aura expanded in recognition of the blessing. A shimmering translucent blue green with a center of pastel pink enveloped the tree in its sacred luminosity.

I thought back to something Saint Germain had so often said; if you begin to flood the powers of nature with light and love, the powers of nature will respond and bless you back. Now, I was experiencing it first-hand. It was as if my recognition and love opened up my inner vision to another dimension with still more to unfold.

Dr. Peebles once said that on the spirit side they look forward to the vibration of another and they engage it. On Earth human beings seek safety and sanctuary from fear of being penetrated by anything foreign. We fear what we don't understand; we fear those of other races and cultures whose beliefs differ from our own; we fear new settings or experiences. "Love the native or what is close or familiar, but be fascinated with what is foreign, for God lives there, too," Doctor Peebles has often said. "God is present everywhere, the fruits of the labor not fully translated yet on Earth, but God is present everywhere."

On another evening, I reached my hand out to bless a tree and again received the signal of a vibration change. Some twenty feet up the block, I witnessed a tree elemental step out of the trunk. It stood in the middle of the sidewalk looking directly at me. *Oh, my God, I see him!* I kept walking, and the distance between us shortened. Again I held the single focus that we are both of God, one in consciousness. I didn't hesitate; on the contrary, I was fascinated, and I thought of Dr. Peebles saying how they look forward to engaging different vibrations on the spirit side. There are billions of life forms that exist; just because you don't see them with your naked eye doesn't mean that they don't exist.

His circumference was that of a newly planted tree trunk of perhaps five or six inches, and he was approximately four feet tall. He resembled the tree, with the same characteristics of knots and uneven bark, and although he looked like part of the tree, he chose to separate himself for my viewing. I knew he was there to protect the tree, as a spirit guide of sorts, and to promote the tree's growth, as a guardian. "I am going to walk right through this little being! As I did, butterflies and pure joy completely exploded in my solar plexus and showered through my body. It was electrifying. It was like going over a huge speed bump in a car.

It was pure magic.

I made it a habit to stop every night upon my return home and sit beneath a tree in a small neighborhood park. I liked listening to the sound of the water that cascaded over colored lights in a large fountain. Streetlamps illuminated the flowers, trees, and grass with a soft glow. I always sat in the same spot beneath a large tree, and there I flooded the park with white light. I could feel myself spontaneously moving into an altered state of consciousness. I opened my eyes one night as a current flowed. The grass looked like a velvet green carpet that had been strung with white Christmas tree lights. I could sense and see a cohesive continuum of consciousness that connected this particular vibration and frequency of form, each blade to the other.

Another elemental stepped forth from a tree approximately fifteen feet from the bench where I sat. He was much shorter than the other tree elemental I had seen, and although similar in appearance, this one took on more of the individuality of this particular tree. "Ye see me" he said. Like the other, I sent him love and white light. I was aware of other consciousnesses such as this wonderful elemental; however, they were not the least bit interested in communicating with me. Although I was aware of them, it was as if they weren't aware of me or didn't want to be. Our mutual curiosity—the tree's and mine—must have bridged our consciousness to one another, or perhaps I had raised my vibration to the frequency in which he existed. Most of our telepathic communications transpired while I was in that altered state of consciousness, and a thought would occasionally float through my mind: *How could I record this?* I looked forward to my nightly visits, and as I continued to establish the pillar of light without fail, Curious George would step out of his tree.

One night, upon entering the park, I sat down and noticed a young couple sitting on a bench under George's tree. Bummer. Most nights I had the park to myself. I decided to close my eyes and stay there for a few minutes and enjoy the peace and the sound of the fountain. I knew George would remain hidden from view. I felt myself begin to move into a deep state of relaxation. A smell wafted in my direction. This was not night-blooming jasmine. I heard some sharp intakes of breath, a long pause, and then deep exhales. "Pssst . . . Pssst . . . Hey! Hey you! You want some?" I barely opened one eye and glanced in their direction. "No, thanks." *Trust me*, I thought to myself. *I'm higher than a kite.*

54
Upon The Heel That Crushes It

Forgiveness is the fragrance the lilac sheds
upon the heel that crushes it.
—Mark Twain

Around 1989, I was asked to share my personal story about sexual abuse and the healing of it, a request that was inspired by Doctor Peebles, in the book *To Dance with Angels*, by Don and Linda Pendleton. Actually, I have shared my insights in books by the Pendletons twice around that subject, since the healing reached deeper levels as the years passed. Some of this is taken from that book and some from Linda's most recent book about Doctor Peebles, *Three Principles of Angelic Wisdom:*

At times, the depth of rage, betrayal, and pain seemed all-consuming, and I never knew a body or heart could produce so many tears.

The illusion of separation veiled the experience from my understanding for a long time. What I wanted to understand was, *Why did I create this experience?* Dr. Peebles told me that I had made a decision to leave the body in an accident, but he and my teachers intervened, and I decided to stay in the body and confront the issue.

He said I chose the experience as a form of self-punishment and that I wanted to be bold about it and to experience it in very dynamic terms—that I didn't want to be shy about it or put it off. It stemmed, he told me, from a life as a prostitute, and in that life, I had judged myself severely.

He said, "Your society operates under a massive illusion of victimhood, and to most, the idea that soul would chose such an experience as sexual abuse is revolting, repugnant, and disgusting. What has been most difficult for you, Athena, is how you looked at it as a *child* rather than a *soul*, so think of it in terms of a soul *choosing to* accelerate their growth. The one who has chosen the experience is seeking to *increase* their communication concerning their sexuality. The perpetrator or abuser is operating from *decreased* communication concerning their sexuality. So you see, my dear, the two serve each other."

Now I understood why I felt such empathy toward prostitutes. Just a few weeks earlier, I had considered doing some volunteer work in that arena. Shortly after I completed my work with Dr. Slavin, I had an experience that still to this day leaves me shaking my head in complete amazement. A prostitute, dazed, defeated, and confused, walked directly up to me as I was coming out of a store in Marina Del Rey, California. I had thought it highly unusual, for she was completely out of her element. "Are you a spiritual woman?" she asked.

"Yes," I replied somewhat hesitantly. "What's the matter?"

In one fragile breath, she told me, "I'm a prostitute. I'm running away from my pimp, and I'm going to kill myself." I suggested a woman's shelter, and her reply was, "He knows where they are. He'll kill me." She then recounted for me the horrible ways that he had punished her physically. She mumbled, "I need to find a church. I need to go to

Texas, I have a friend there. A church, . . . maybe they can get me a ticket. Are you a spiritual woman?"

The shop owner stood listening wide-eyed and watched in disbelief as I put the woman in my car. I drove around looking for a church and listened as she began to describe crazy parallels between her childhood and mine. It seemed a different time and place, surreal, and I felt as if I were part of a Salvador Dali painting, some abstract symbol melting down the side of a mountain. *Ah, to hell with it,* I thought to myself as I pulled into a travel agency and whipped out my credit card. One hundred and seventy-eight dollars later I dropped this poor, decrepit creature off in front of United Airlines. I knew she was telling the truth. Whether or not she got on the plane I don't know, and it's not important. What was important was that something inside me had to respond. Dr. Peebles later confirmed that the act of kindness was an act of forgiveness to the prostitute of my past life, and this act had released the remaining karma associated with it. Magical.

At the sharing of my story in *To Dance With Angels* several years ago, I had self-righteously claimed I had forgiven my mother. The truth of the matter was I had felt a sense of relief at her passing. I felt as if a diseased portion of my life had been cut out and removed, and I was so damned angry because she wouldn't take any responsibility for her part in allowing the perpetrator of my sexual abuse into our lives. Even a little acknowledgment would have helped. I felt as if all of this was dumped in my lap to resolve however I could. That infuriated me. But beneath it all was a whole lot of hurt. I needed the space and the allowance after her death to simply let things settle and move into the next phase of healing naturally. Here I was experiencing first hand one of Dr. Peebles teachings: the principle of loving allowance for all things to be in their own time and place, starting with myself.

What I learned for myself was that I had to allow the thunder and the lightning, the sadness, loss, and grief of my emotions their equal time, their equal space, and to allow them to be exactly what they were—raw, passionate, and real. I couldn't bypass the anger at Point A and jump to forgiveness, Point Z, without *moving through* them. To do so was nothing more than an empty affirmation. *I forgive you. I forgive you. I forgive you with my head but not my heart.* I read once if you can't forgive, you can't forget, and if you can't forget, you can't forgive.

Shortly after my mother's death, I asked Dr. Peebles how she was doing. He said, "She is constantly wiping her brow with the back of her hand [as she did in life]. She wants to go back and live her life backwards. In other words, spirit is telling her that she lived her life exactly as she had to."

I'm not sure exactly when the shift began to happen, but I know that when I thought of Mom, my feelings felt softer somehow. I inquired of medium Ron Smith how my mother was doing. The reply was, "She weeps much in her slumber." I felt such a wave of sadness flood through my body. Those words broke my heart.

I found myself reflecting back to the time in which, under hypnosis, I spontaneously experienced my time in spirit prior to this incarnation. The feeling of awareness and clarity, of safety and love, expanded my vision of a grander overview and gave me the ability to see before me opportunities to be gained or missed. How great my mother's pain and disappointment in herself to see where she had detached herself out of fear and pain and to view the rejection response of her child, a soul to whom she had given birth. How great her pain. She weeps much in her slumber.

One of the greatest gifts my mother ever gave me came

in the form of contact through a very gifted medium and internationally recognized channeling teacher, Shawn Randall. Torah, a non-physical multi-dimensional consciousness channeled by Shawn, agreed to help set the stage for this communication to take place. I listened in anticipation as Torah began to make the connection and lovingly coaxed my mother forward, reassuring her that she was safe, that it was okay to enter this dimension, to feel the love present in the room, and that this could help to heal her as well. I watched in amazement as the medium began to hyperventilate and to grab at her heart just as my mother always did in life. I placed my hand upon her heart and spoke to my mother. I felt as if I was the mother and *she* was the child, unsure, scared, and vulnerable *yet willing,* despite her fears, to reenter a dimension that represented so much pain for her. She didn't deny me; she acknowledged me. That meant more to me that I can ever convey through paper or pen.

Later that evening, the medium told me that for a week prior to our meeting she kept repeating, "Who's Ruth? Who's Ruth?" Ruth is my mother.

To truly forgive my mother meant letting go of the illusion of victimhood. *That was scary.* What would I blame my own inadequacies on? I couldn't blame any failures on my childhood, or lack thereof. I couldn't blame my unwillingness to engage or embrace life on him, her, or circumstance. To be free is a choice in every moment.

I went to my mother's grave in February of 1998. There I sat on the grass and spoke to her of my discovery, insights gained, my healing, and about my new-found enthusiasm for life. I reflected upon her many beautiful qualities, her sacred reverence for nature, her love of poetry and gift of pen, her silent quest for God, and her ability to find humor in conditions that at times seemed utterly deplorable. I know now she did the best she could. Her denial was so great that her pain would have engulfed her. That she feared the most and I can understand that.

What I so deeply wanted to convey to her was for her to feel within her consciousness how much I desired for her to be free without self-judgment or condemnation. We both had suffered enough. It was time. I opened my heart and felt the love; I visualized the white light surrounding her, penetrating and healing her spirit. I read once that, Forgive actually means give for those incapable of giving. In giving for my mom, I gave for myself a new beginning.

Next to her picture, pressed between glass and paper, is a flower from her grave, an echo to my own soul, and an oracle of wisdom stated eloquently: "To be born again is to let the past go and look without condemnation upon the present." —*A Course in Miracles*

After her death, Dr. Peebles told me that mother's challenge in life was to bring her very private thoughts about God public through her writing. One afternoon, while rummaging through an old cardboard box, I discovered her words scribbled on a dog-eared envelope that had yellowed with age. I reflected back to something mother had said to me on more than one occasion.

"Maybe one day we can write a book together."

"Yeah, Mom, who knows? Maybe one day we will."

I guess in a strange way, we did. Mom, this is for you.

ALL DAY LONG

All day long dear God, I had
a hill too hard to climb,
all day long, the "reaching up"
and searching numbed my mind.
So I took me off to the countryside
where the air was clean,
and the space was wide.
And I dug my feet in the good clean earth—
and I thought of life—
and I thought of birth.
I thought of beginnings—and I thought of ends,
I thought of enemies,
and I thought of friends.
I thought of the "Lamb" & the
"Good Book's Creed,"
I thought of Vietnam, and the "Lion's Need"
and the restless people
all over the world—
yes, the restless people
all over the world.
Then my eyes took sight of a scene to behold
fields of purple, splashes of gold;
Flowers of elegance, flowers of pride,
with the lowly mustard side by side;
spreading their scent to same sweet air,
Praying their prayer to the same "great" prayer
Drawing their strength from the same good earth,
that had nurtured their seeds
and given them birth.
Oh why can't we learn a lesson from them—
And learn to live with our fellow men?
A lump of gold, a piece of clod—
All look the same in the eyes of God.
Ruth James, April 1966

55
Morning Has Broken

We shall not cease from exploration and the end of all our exploring will be to arrive where we started and to know the place for the first time.
—*T.S. Eliot*

And so I end where I began. The memory lingers of being on the spirit side, surrounded by the love of masters and teachers showing me the experiences that would shape my perception, build my character, and mold my reality. Their love stays with me still. They showed me how I could change in this life. Whether or not I would choose to do so was yet to be seen. My platform of choice, *Victim* or *Creator,* would define my perspective and impact every area of my life.

In spirit, I felt overwhelmed at the magnitude of what I was about to encounter as "soul lessons" for growth in my earthly sojourn. I knew there was much I wanted to accomplish as a spirit in this incarnation, if only I could stay present.

I left my in-between life stripped of my expansive state of awareness. Awaiting future discovery, my God self lay hidden behind the veil. I entered the schoolroom of Earth starkly different. I emerged a small and restricted consciousness. I went to sleep.

All I ever wanted as a child was to return home, beyond the veil, beyond the forgetting. The earth is hard, and some of my lessons were brutal. My exhaustion was my rebellion and my rebellion became my resistance. I have screamed and balked, thrown tantrums, and spewed my own venom at God. It made little difference. I was still loved anyway.

Rarely understood by onlookers, my experiences have been shaped and designed by my own creation—whether I own them or not. They are the threads woven from one incarnation to another with my soul's intent and principal purpose: to discover the divine within.

This is the dream, the illusion. Awakening was painful but beautiful in its brilliance. I discovered the law of cause and effect and that my sloppy thinking creates sloppy reflections, just like a warped mirror creates distorted images. Now I am too aware to be unaware, too conscious to be unconscious.

These insights have driven me inward in relentless pursuit to connect with the greater all. Some days I am more successful at staying connected. Other days I want to crawl off and create safety and sanctuary. It takes conscious, determined effort to redirect thoughts to focus on the divine principles. No one else can do it for me, although at times I wished they could.

I have learned that there is always a jewel buried in the scum of any experience no matter how humiliating, defacing, or hard to confront. Take a deep breath, feel the fear, and go for the discovery. Illumination will follow. Walking through fire burns away the illusion. Resurrection is holy.

I have held others captive by my unwillingness to forgive. In the end, I found I couldn't swim with cement blocks tied to my feet. I was stuck treading water in a stagnating pond. I have embraced the belief that if it hurts going down, it hurts coming up, but it doesn't last forever. It's a process. My sacred mantra: "This too shall pass." When I tell myself that, it helps me know I will come through the other side. There *is* light at the end of the tunnel, and every dark cloud *does* have a silver lining. Look in the sky—truly they do. Relationships can be rebuilt.

When the walls came tumbling down and I allowed others to witness me a complete blubbering mess, in that state of raw vulnerability I discovered it was then that I was loved the most. Magic happened. I touched them, and they touched me.

I have sought to find wholeness in relationships and I have not always loved wisely. At times I have put my own pleasure and indifference above the needs of another, ignoring the impact it had on their world. What I have searched for is within, and I know the real answer lies in my relationship with God. No person can fill that void.

My destructive patterns boomeranged back and swiftly tripped me at the ankles. I fell in the same hole, over and over again. The repeated issue became the stumbling block in the sidewalk. Different face, different scenario, same old tired energy.

My attention on other people's pain was a clever diversion that kept me from healing myself. If I could focus on them, I had little time to acknowledge my own inner turmoil. It never worked. Pain, I learned, is a grand teacher. What a lesson that was. I can't save another to feel better about myself. They have their own path, as I have mine. Let the master within them pick the fruit from the tree that they will.

Listening to the feedback of another is hard, especially if it is full of criticism. The times I have been able to stand present and not turn a deaf ear I have grown the most. All life wants to be heard.

But oh, those angels, the beacons of light who fan our flames with their love, care, and compassion. Let me strive to be like that, God. That's a dream worth dreaming.

EPILOGUE
Captain Of My Ship

O CAPTAIN! my Captain! our fearful trip is done;
The ship has weather'd every rack,
the prize we sought is won.
—Walt Whitman

Sometimes I am shown by Spirit crystal-clear dreams or visions, which I have learned to interpret as milestones or markers, direct reflections of my growth, or answers to my persistent demand for truth to be revealed. I honor these, and I am ever grateful to Spirit for giving me these signposts as confirmation. "You go this way. You're on the right track; don't give up. . . . This way to God."

These experiences, rich and vivid, are lucid and to me more "real" than everyday life. They temporarily strip away the illusion and struggle of the human self. I am able to experience the grandness of my soul with such clarity and in such a way that it fills my sails with another gust of wind when being present feels, at times, insurmountable.

Most of my life, I felt as if I were swimming in an ocean of fog, vulnerable to that which I couldn't see, treading water, listening for the sound of a distant fog-horn—anything to show me which direction to go. It's a horrible feeling to be lost, but when the fog begins to lift, how different the perspective. The challenge then is how to sustain and nourish that seedling of light and awareness, that it may take root and grow.

The following, given to me by spirit, was such a dream, a lucid vision:

I am captain of my ship, alone at the helm, calm and relaxed, my right hand bent at the wrist, resting on the crest of the steering wheel, my left arm comfortably positioned on the edge of the boat. The night is hauntingly beautiful, illuminated by moonlight; the vastness of the turbulent ocean lies before me. The heavens, an indigo backdrop with purple-grey shadows of moving clouds gives me the distinct feeling that either a storm is clearing or I am about to encounter another. Whatever. It makes little difference, for I am at the helm, filled with a sense of peace and tranquility as I navigate my ship through the rolling waves.

The waters are choppy, the swells high, and as the boat rocks almost vertically to one side, I steer the ship deeper into the hollow of the curling wave. There is no fear of the boat capsizing, for I instinctively know somehow it will right itself. I feel my elbow touch the water's edge, as the spray of the saltwater moistens my arm. The ship finds its equilibrium once again, and I am filled with a knowing that it is *not the goal in life* that matters but rather *the journey*. As I pull the boat upon a stretch of sand, all becomes small and earthbound once again, but I carry with me the distinct understanding and feeling that I will always be all right. I will always regain my balance, because God is on this journey with me.

To those in life who were my most bitter pill to
swallow, I thank you,
for you became my grandest teachers.

"IT'S A WRAP!"

About The Author

Athena Demetrios has maintained a 30-year career in the film industry while providing service to clients worldwide as a professional trance channel for Dr. J. M. Peebles. She continues her metaphysical studies with the Ascended Masters, and travels the country facilitating workshops in higher consciousness. Athena makes her home in Northern California. She has a beautiful daughter, two wonderful grandchildren, and a mutt named Milo, also known as the Professor and "lovingly described" as a "walking ottoman." Her web address is www.IAMwithin.com.

CPSIA information can be obtained at www.ICGtesting.com
Printed in the USA
BVOW020843280313

316705BV00001B/3/P